GREEK MYTHOLOGY

World Mythology in Theory and Everyday Life

Series Editors: Tok Thompson and Robert W. Guyker Jr.

This series presents an innovative and accessible overview of the world's mythological traditions. The inaugural volume provides a theoretical introduction to the study of myth, while the individual case studies from throughout time and around the world help guide the reader through the wondrous complexity and diversity of myths, and their widespread influences in human cultures, societies, and everyday lives.

The Truth of Myth: World Mythology in Theory and Everyday Life
Tok Thompson and Gregory Schrempp

Old Norse Mythology
John Lindlow

Greek Mythology: From Creation to First Humans
Carolina López-Ruiz

GREEK MYTHOLOGY

From Creation to First Humans

Carolina López-Ruiz

Oxford University Press is a department of the University of Oxford.
It furthers the University's objective of excellence in research, scholarship,
and education by publishing worldwide. Oxford is a registered trade mark of
Oxford University Press in the UK and in certain other countries.

Published in the United States of America by Oxford University Press
198 Madison Avenue, New York, NY 10016, United States of America.

© Oxford University Press 2025

All rights reserved. No part of this publication may be reproduced, stored in a retrieval system,
transmitted, used for text and data mining, or used for training artificial intelligence, in any form or
by any means, without the prior permission in writing of Oxford University Press, or as expressly
permitted by law, by license or under terms agreed with the appropriate reprographics rights
organization. Inquiries concerning reproduction outside the scope of the above should be sent
to the Rights Department, Oxford University Press, at the address above.

You must not circulate this work in any other form
and you must impose this same condition on any acquirer

CIP data is on file at the Library of Congress.

ISBN 9780190944797 (hbk.)
ISBN 9780190944803 (pbk.)

DOI: 10.1093/oso/9780190944797.001.0001

CONTENTS

List of Figures and Maps | vii

Introduction | 1

1. From Chaos to Olympos | 22

2. First Humans and Their Gods | 71

3. Facing East | 112

4. Resilient Myths | 162

Conclusion: The Many Lives of Creation Stories | 213

A NOTE ON FURTHER READING AND RESOURCES | 217
BIBLIOGRAPHY | 219
INDEX | 231

LIST OF FIGURES AND MAPS

Figures

I.1 *A Reading from Homer*, by Lawrence Alma-Tadema (1836–1912). Philadelphia Museum of Art. 18

1.1 "Venus in the Shell," fresco on the garden wall of the "House of Venus" in Pompeii, Italy, first century CE. 39

1.2 *Saturn Devouring His Son*, by Francisco de Goya (1746–1828), one of the "dark paintings" on the walls of his house. Prado Museum, Madrid. 41

1.3 A carved rock or betyl at the Sanctuary of Apollo at Delphi, Greece, one of several representing the navel of the world and the stone swallowed and vomited by Kronos instead of baby Zeus. 43

1.4 Zeus fights the hybrid monster Typhon, here in supplicating position. Relief engraved on an Archaic bronze shield from Olympia. 45

1.5 Black-figure painting on the so-called "Pyxis of Painter C," representing the birth of Athena from the head of an enthroned Zeus, mid sixth century BCE. Louvre Museum, Paris. 47

1.6 (top). "Bacchic-Orphic" Gold Tablet with Greek text, mid-fourth century BCE (note small proportions: $2.2 \times 3.7 \times 0.1$ cm. or $7/8 \times 1\ 7/16 \times 1/16$ in.).
(bottom). Orpheus plays the lyre to wild animals; Roman-period floor mosaic from Tarsus, Turkey. Hatay Archeology Museum in Antakya. 68

viii *List of Figures and Maps*

2.1 Painted wood panel (*pinax*) representing a sacrificial offering of a lamb and other products, accompanied by flute and lyre playing, sixth century BCE; from Pitsa, near Corinth, Greece. National Archaeological Museum of Athens. 75

2.2 Clay figure of a women baking bread along the walls of an oven, from Cyprus, ca. 600–480 BCE. 78

2.3 Woman on a threshing sledge in the countryside of Corinth, Greece, with the Acrocorinth and Temple of Apollo in the distance. 84

2.4 Temple known as the Erechtheion, west side (finished in 406 BCE). 95

2.5 "The Victory of Dinysos" in a Roman-era mosaic, with the god carried by panthers and accompanied by winged Nike ("Victory") and a Maenad (Bakche). Zeugma Mosaic Museum, Gaziantep, Turkey. 100

2.6 Vase-painting representation of a bride preparing for her wedding and receiving a container of cosmetics or jewelry; attributed to the Eretria Painter, ca. 440 BCE–415 BCE; from Attica, Greece. 106

3.1 The Mesopotamian god Ea sitting on his throne over the waters of Apsu, receiving another god. Impression of engraved cylinder seal from Ur (Akkadian period, ca. 2350–2150 BCE). 118

3.2 Cosmological scene from the *Egyptian Book of the Dead*, representing the gods Nut (Sky) and Geb (Earth), with Shu (Air) standing in between them. Greenfield papyrus from Deir el-Bahari, Thebes, Egypt, eleventh-century BCE. 121

3.3 Photo of Jebel al-'Aqra', the Mt. Saphon of Ugaritic texts (the "Olympus of the East"), at the border between Turkey and Syria, seen from the north, with 1,717 m./5,633 ft. of altitude. 135

3.4 (left): Basalt stele with relief representing the Hittite Storm god Teshub/Tarhun, ninth century BCE; from Babylon, Iraq. Archaeological Museum of Istanbul.
(right): Storm god Baal ("Baal with Thunderbolt") carved on a limestone stela from Ugarit, Syria, fifteenth–thirteenth centuries BCE. Louvre Museum, Paris. 136

3.5 Clay model of a nude couple making love on a bed, from Mesopotamia, ca. 1800. 141

3.6 Alabaster vase, known as the "Warka Vase" (three ft./1 m. tall), from ancient Uruk, southern Iraq, ca. 3000 BCE. National Museum of Iraq. 154

4.1	Zeus- or Yahweh-like figure in glass, at door of the Rockefeller Center General Electric building, New York.	163
4.2	Adam and Eve are expelled from the Garden of Eden, in a scene from the Sistine Chapel ceiling paintings by Michelangelo (1508–12).	197
4.3	Kronos fights with Zeus (small figure at the top, hurling his thunderbolt), from George O'Connor's graphic novel *Olympians, Book 1, Zeus: King of the Gods.*	201
4.4	John Roddam Spencer Stanhope, *Orpheus and Eurydice on the Banks of the Styx,* 1878.	203
4.5	Flooding in Bangladesh, May 2018.	206
4.6	Perseus leaves Zeus behind (Sam Worthington and Liam Neeson, respectively), in movie *Clash of the Titans* (2010).	209

Maps

| 1 | The Aegean and the Near East in the Late Bronze Age. | 9 |
| 2 | Greece and the Aegean in the Archaic-Classical periods. | 98 |

Introduction

For all its material advantages, the sedentary life has left us edgy, unfulfilled. Even after four hundred generations in villages and cities, we haven't forgotten; the open road still softly calls, like a nearly forgotten song of childhood.
—Carl Sagan, in *Wanderers*, a short film by Erik Wernquist

Why Creation Myths?

We can imagine our sedentary ancestors thousands of years ago feeling thirsty for answers, as they sat in front of the fire or peered into the starry sky from a mountain peak or in the middle of the sea. How far does our universe reach? How did it begin, and when or how will it end? And what is our place in this vast continuum? This curiosity is wired into our human brains.

Ancient Greek and Near Eastern texts open the first window into these inquiries in the Western world. Creation narratives hold the key to their entire mythological worldview, and they are the foundations of many mythical narratives that came afterward. Cosmogonies capture the human effort to answer the ultimate, universally poignant questions: How did it all begin? What did the gods have to do with it? Where do we human beings come from, and what is our place in the universe? There are other ways of thinking about those questions coming from cosmology, theology, philosophy, biology, and astrophysics, among other disciplines. Like other premodern cultures, however, the Greeks formed their answers first in the form

1

of poetry and song, of stories in which natural and supernatural forces were one and the same, and where the lineages and quarrels of the gods explained the order—and disorder—of things.

In cosmogony, therefore, lies the true "mythical" narrative of any culture, set in a time outside historical time and inseparable from religious beliefs or narratives. The entire Greek mythological system rests on theories of beginnings, which provide a backdrop for the Olympian gods; their rivals; their heroic, semi-divine offspring; and their early interventions in the world of mortals. On this scaffolding are built other myths we are familiar with, those about Theseus, Herakles, the Argonauts, Oedipus, the Trojan War, Odysseus, Aeneas, and many others. These are properly the matter of legend, in the sense that their narratives are tied to the historical timelines of specific communities. As we will see, in the Greek worldview, the time of creation (what *we* may call strictly mythical), the "heroic" time (more hazily connected to a prehistorical timeline), and the historical time in which our authors were writing were not seen as ontologically different, as dimensions separated by degrees of reality. They were situated along a reconstructed past that was relevant to the present; these stories informed and explained the world around real people—not only the natural world but also the social order and religious-ritual life they were familiar with.

Outside of cosmogony, it is difficult to separate the study of "myths" from that of legends, on the one hand, and from folk tales and even other types of traditional narratives, on the other. The Trojan War offers a perfect example of the blurry line between "myth" and "reality" for the ancient Greeks, as both laypeople and historians thought of it as a historical event at the dawn of Greek history, roughly corresponding to the end of the Late Bronze Age (around 1200 BCE). This is clear even from the fact that historians later attempted to rationalize or historicize it by peeling the mythological layer off the poetic elaboration and refocusing on the geo-strategic reasons behind the famous war (Herodotus 2.112–120;

Thucydides 1.9). Their anchoring in a time and place sets what we conventionally call "myths" apart from folk tales. Other characteristics of our myths are that they draw connections with other stories and characters in the same universe and timeline, and that they involve gods and heroes, as well as other supernatural creatures like hybrids and monsters.

As such, mythology is inextricably tied to religion and often gives or receives meaning from ritual customs and gestures, even if that is not necessarily its raison d'être, as generations of scholars proposed in the early twentieth century (Johnston 2018: 34–64). Modern takes on Classical myth have both contributed to and been shaped by the study of world mythologies by anthropologists, sociologists, folklorists, and psychoanalysts, all contributing their own "keys" to help the modern Western mind "decode" what they used to call "primitive" societies and mentalities encoded through centuries in these stories (Thompson and Schrempp 2020: 37–98). Notwithstanding deeper, universally shared symbolisms and meanings, even those hidden in the cultural and even biological makeup of their human audiences, we draw closer to the ancient experience of myths if we think of them as deeply connected to Greek culture and bound up with multiple levels of the social experience, including (foremost) those of religion, education, group identity, and entertainment.

In short, we can think of Greek mythology and world mythologies in general as a society's transmitted body of traditional narratives of collective importance, usually involving gods and heroes and other supernatural creatures and events. In other words, mythologies are culture-specific and have been transmitted for generations because of their value for a particular society (Burkert 1979: 23; Graf 1993: 1–8; Johnston 2018: 8–9). Or, as Tok Thompson and Gregory Schrempp (2020: 7) worded it in the first volume of this series, *The Truth of Myth,* "myths are narratives of profound cultural and individual importance that in some way help establish our symbolic sense of the ultimate shape and meaning of existence."

What Is Classical Mythology, and How Did It Reach Us?

The term "classical" is subjective. It expresses a built consensus of the timeless value of a style or a piece of art or other human creation, be it music, cars, movies, or something else. A "classic" is esteemed to represent the refinement of popular or previous traditions, perhaps establishing a canon or setting a model for generations afterward. A "classic" item is perceived to possess a quality and beauty that does not age. In the Western world, Classical myth and literature refers to the Greek and Latin texts preserved since antiquity and deemed foundational for Western education as well as intellectual and artistic life.

Stories about gods and heroes did not circulate only in texts, and perhaps not even primarily in texts. Most people would experience and learn them more often in oral versions and in artistic representations (examples collected in *LIMC*; Gantz 1993). Wherever the average person went, they would come across scenes on stone reliefs, vase paintings, and other media that alluded to mythical narratives. These images are sometimes difficult to interpret when the myths they refer to are not preserved in texts, as the literary corpus we do have is but a fraction of what circulated in antiquity. Besides those lost oral traditions, the Classical myths we study were often the matter of epic poems—that is, long narrative poems. This is the first literary genre attested in ancient Greece, represented by Homer's *Iliad* and *Odyssey* and Hesiod's *Theogony* and *Works and Days*. If there were other such long poems composed around that time or in the following generations, they did not make it to the "canon" of Classical works. For instance, we know the titles and topics of other early poems about the Trojan War that formed part of the Epic Cycle, though these were composed a bit later than the *Iliad* and *Odyssey*, by different poets, as was an epic about the Theban Cycle known as the *Thebaid* or *Thebais*. Later poets emulated Homer by composing long epics such as the *Argonautika* by

Apollonius of Rhodes, written in Hellenistic times, which retold the entire adventure of Jason and the Argonauts, but this was a rare feat (a rare example, much later, is Nonnus of Panopolis's epic in Greek about Dionysos, the *Dionysiaca*). In turn, Roman authors started rehearsing the genre in Latin in the third century BCE, with a fixation on their recent political history, especially the wars against their archenemies the Carthaginians, which were raised to epic narrative in Naevius's *Bellum Punicum* and Silius Italicus's *Punica*. These epics narrate the First and Second Punic Wars, respectively. In his *Aeneid*, Virgil (70–19 BCE) picked up this thread for the service of his patron, Augustus: through Aeneas's journey from Troy to Carthage to Italy, the poet threaded together the Trojan Cycle, the Carthaginian conflict, and the rule of Augustus, who claimed descent from Aeneas's line.

But Greek myth was conveyed in other types of works too. From the seventh century onward, we have poems that praised particular gods, known as the *Homeric Hymns*. These *Hymns* were composed in epic verse, dactylic hexameters, and in Homeric style, although they are not as long and artful and are not believed to be by the same author as the *Iliad* and *Odyssey*. These hymns are great sources for the "personal stories" and mythical personalities of the gods and their internal relations, especially the longer hymns to Apollo, Aphrodite, Demeter, and Hermes. The genre was revived by the scholar-poet Callimachus in the third century BCE. He composed hymns to the main gods and created fresh poetic versions of their myths in the context of Hellenistic-period scholarship of Alexandria (Egypt). Mythical stories were also evoked in poetry of various other kinds, be it lyric, choral, or epinician (i.e., in honor of athletic victors), by great poets like Pindar, Sappho, and others. Myths surface in these poems through playful references directed at learned audiences, rather than offering complete or self-contained stories. Mythical allusions sometimes reveal different variants of well-known stories and sometimes even completely unknown myths, and hence their intent can be difficult to understand or appreciate—a reminder

6 GREEK MYTHOLOGY

of how little of the entire mythical universe we have in comparison with that of the ancient audience.

A selection of Greek tragedies and comedies from Classical Athens has reached us, authored by Aeschylus, Sophocles, Euripides, and the comedians Aristophanes and Menander. The tragedies especially stand as an enormous mythological resource. We still face the challenge that the authors were, again, playing with clever allusions and ad hoc modifications of traditional myths, for which we do not always have a point of comparison, and thus we can miss their intended effect. In turn, prose works began to proliferate also since the fifth century BCE. Ancient historians, such as Herodotus, Thucydides, and Xenophon, transmitted mythological traditions, even when they did so in order to explain them away or contradict them as they put them through the test of their historical enquiry about the past. Myths feature in the philosophical tradition too. Particularly influential was the way in which Plato transformed popular and traditional elements in order to create his own myths, deploying them as exemplary tales that could puzzle and educate his audience (see chapter 4).

In Roman times, we see elaborate and original revivals of Greek myths, not only adapted to Latin poetics, but also to new aesthetic preferences and philosophical preoccupations; such are the extraordinary *Metamorphoses* by Ovid (43 BCE–17 CE), a younger poet contemporary of Virgil, who most artfully and movingly strung together Greek mythical stories; or the tragedies written by the statesman and philosopher Seneca (4 BCE–65 CE), also of Greek theme (*Medea, Phaedra, Thyestes*, etc.); as well as the stories conveyed in various essays by the Greek author Plutarch (46–119 CE), especially the *Isis and Osiris* and *Parallel Lives*. We also owe to the Roman reception of Greek myths the existence of collections or "digests" in plain, encyclopedic-style prose; these relied on previous mythographic works and poetic traditions and are an essential resource for our study of Greek myths: Hyginus's *Fabulae*, written in Latin in the first century BCE–first century CE, and Apollodoros's (also called Pseudo-Apollodoros)

Library (*Bibliotheke*), of unknown date, written in Greek for an educated Roman-period audience. More rarely, an author elaborated an entire mythical narrative that stood alone, but that is just the case of the story of Cupid and Psyche in Apuleius's *Golden Ass* or *Metamorphoses* (second century CE). The Roman author from Madauros in North Africa was well educated in Greek literature and philosophy, and yet he wrote a novel in Latin (an innovation in and of itself) and drew on folk traditions for his wonderful mythical and philosophical digression about Love and the Soul (Cupid and Psyche). A movement of renewed fervor for all things Greek among Roman elites ensued in the second century CE, also known as the "Second Sophistic." This trend fostered many works that may not have focused on myths but recovered for us mythical traditions along the way, for instance interwoven in Pausanias's (110–180 CE) account of his journey around mainland Greece and the Peloponnese (*Description of Greece*).

*

The transmission of Classical works is in itself an extraordinary story, one of survival and resilience. From hand to hand for centuries until they could be printed, these texts were copied, edited, illustrated, translated, and taught, through all of antiquity until medieval times (Vallejo 2022). The renewed interest in the Greco-Roman tradition and the recovering of further texts and artifacts during the Renaissance and the expansion of Classical education during the Enlightenment cemented the place of Greco-Roman literature in Western culture. We do not have nearly a fraction of what was written in those centuries, but the texts we have survived against incredible odds: Hesiod's *Theogony*, Homer's *Odyssey*, Virgil's *Aeneid*, and other Classical works are part of a larger body of ancient literature curated and transmitted through uninterrupted manuscript tradition, first through hand-copying, then in print. Together with the other exception, the Hebrew Bible, these texts survived over the centuries thanks to particular historical circumstances that made them into important artifacts for a collective, and also pillars of their cultural identity (and in the case of the Hebrew Bible, religious identity as well). In other words, it is not only that Greek and Roman texts are classical just because they have survived very long and hence form part of our tradition, but also that they have survived and become part of our tradition because every step of the way someone decided they were worth reading and passing down to the next generation. In the case of Greek myths, they were embedded in literary creations that were cherished because of their artistic and humanistic quality and/or the value of the knowledge and instruction they contained, be it philosophical, historiographical, geographical, scientific, or some other sphere of knowledge. These texts were valued by Romans as part of their own "classical" tradition, of which Greek culture was the cornerstone; and this merged Greco-Roman corpus in turn (if increasingly eroded) had just the intellectual and literary value that allowed it to survive the change of religion into Christianity and Islam, and to become the core of European education, arts, and sciences.

At the same time, Greco-Roman literature is not an inanimate corpse, despite the fragmented state in which it has reached us. In some ways, it is alive and growing. First, because new inscriptions and papyri continue to be found (and also, though much more rarely, manuscripts), enriching the gamut of ancient texts containing mythical allusions. Second, in the sense that we need not limit our idea of the ancient "classics" to Greek and Roman literature anymore. Greek culture thrived in cultural milieu that included the Near East (See Map 1). An astonishing wealth of texts have been discovered through excavations since the nineteenth century, and the decipherment of Akkadian, Egyptian, Hittite, Ugaritic, and other languages opened the gates for the mythologies of ancient cultures that surrounded the Greek world since the Bronze Age. Even if these sources have come too late into the picture of Western culture to be part of the Classical canon, we have slowly seen them incorporated in the study of Classics and Classical mythology not only at the scholarly level (e.g., West 1966, 1997; Burkert 1979, 1992; Morris 1992) but

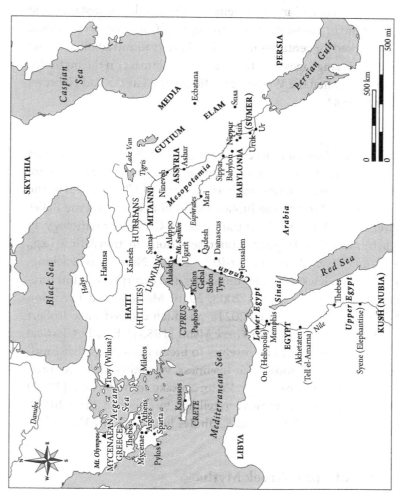

MAP 1 The Aegean and the Near East in the Late Bronze Age. Source/Credit: Map by Alliance USA.

also at the pedagogical level (e.g., López-Ruiz 2018; Trzaskoma et al. 2016; Powell 2002). These literatures have a great deal to offer not only in terms of comparative material, but also because some of them were "classics" in every sense of the word. For instance, the Mesopotamian Flood story and the *Epic of Gilgamesh* were copied and preserved for centuries in the Near East, read and adapted across cultures and languages, and they had a deep impact on the mythologies that informed the Western tradition of the Greeks and Hebrews (see chapter 4).

*

Finally, how does one access these stories? For those who can read them and study them in the original language, these texts are collected in various series, such as the Oxford Classical Texts, the Loeb Classical Library, the Bibliotheca Teubneriana, and the Belles Lettres collections, while anthologies of Classical mythology in English and other languages offer selections in translation (e.g., Trzaskoma et al. 2016; López-Ruiz 2018). Numerous teaching-oriented overviews combine summaries and excerpts with interpretation (Gantz 1993; Martin 2003, 2016; Morford and Lenardon 2007; Hansen 2020; Powell 2021a, all much evolved since Robert Graves's landmark study *The Greek Myths* [1955]). Finally, Classical myths continue to lend themselves to literary retellings that captivate the reader and show their liveliness, versatility, and relevance, from Edith Hamilton's rather Victorian take in *Mythology* (1942) to the vibrant recent creative retellings by Stephen Fry (2018), Charlotte Higgins (2021), and Sarah Iles Johnston (2023).

How to Interpret Greek Myths

Myths have been searched for universal meaning, from many angles, as conveyors of behavioral, social, and psychological patterns. This was a favorite tool for cultural-social anthropologists, sociologists, and psychoanalysts who dissected not only Greco-Roman myths but also those from more distant cultures that became available as the colonial world expanded. It is still challenging to access what these stories meant to *their audiences* and what they codify about the values, concerns, and deep cultural history of particular societies—or (going one step further) of the human species.

The reader can find excellent overviews of the trends of interpretation of Classical and world mythologies (Segal 2004; Thompson and Schrempp 2020; for Greek myths, Graf 1993; Morales 2007; Edmunds 2014; Martin 2016). Perhaps the most influential trend in the study of ancient myths has been the "ritualist approach," or "myth-ritual approach," which for much of the twentieth century permeated studies of ancient and modern myths not only by classicists, but also by Semitists, folklorists, anthropologists, and sociologists, of the stature of William Robertson Smith, James Frazer, Jane Harrison, Lord Raglan, and Bronislaw Malinowski. In all its variants, scholars sought in myths explanations of ritual actions, which had obscure meanings and origins even for their own performers. They proposed different types of relationships between the narratives and the rituals, whether the myths preceded the rituals, were created to explain the obscure customs, or the myths and rituals emerged and developed together. In general, this approach focused on the relationship between myth and ritual as complementary and holding the key to understanding each other (Versnel 2014; Johnston 2018: 34–64).

For scholars interested in ancient religions, this framework of interpretation is still useful, with various nuances, while the search for the deeper meaning of myths has veered toward other areas of culture. Following foundational psychoanalysts such as Sigmund Freud (1856–1939) and his pupil Carl Jung (1875–1961), scholars have theorized myth as a vehicle for the unconscious articulation of the human psyche's deepest wounds and concerns. Leaning on the methods of linguistics and anthropology, another school, spearheaded by Claude Lévi-Strauss (1908–2009), looked for the main themes ("mythemes") that formed the structure of mythical narratives, and for what essential values and dichotomies they articulated, such as "nature and culture" or "justice and injustice." These, in turn, were often related to larger social categories, such as the often-invoked tripartite division between kings, warriors, and husbandmen in Indo-European societies. The underlying idea is that language and narratives (and their structures) are connected to the entire sociocultural system, which is itself a superstructure (Thompson and Schrempp 2020: 77–80).

Both psychoanalytical and structuralist modes of analysis informed the way scholars such as Lord Raglan, Otto Rank, and Vladimir Propp looked at narrative patterns. The search for an underlying "monomyth" underpinning Greek and other mythologies was especially popularized through the books of Joseph Campbell (1904–87), whose postulation of a "hero pattern" or basic narrative surrounding the journey of the hero has deeply influenced movie scripts and popular culture (Thompson and Schrempp 2020: 82). In turn, the ritualist, psychoanalytical, and structuralist approaches had an enormous impact on the study of Classical myth, intersecting in various ways with the study of Greek religion and society (e.g., Eliade 2005 [1954]; Burkert 1979, 1983; Vernant 1980; Detienne and Vernant 1989; Vidal-Naquet 1986). Structuralism also informed a line of comparative mythology that searched for the ideological principles of Indo-European societies, as best exemplified by the work of Georges Dumézil (1898–1986), which was not without political and even racial overtones, as long since noted (Lincoln 1999; Nagy 2014).

What all these approaches have in common is that they look at the stories from a universalist and transcendentalist viewpoint (Johnston 2018: 55; Thompson and Schrempp 2020: 83). They go beyond the surface of a story to seek what it may reveal about individual or social beliefs, behaviors, or assumptions. Generally, this does not require engaging deeply with the myths' cultural context, as their sought meaning transcends their particular form and time.

By detaching the bare bones of the plots and characters from their literary vehicles and artistic expressions and discarding details or elements that are not relevant for the particular pattern under consideration, this scholarship conducts a sort of archaeology or surgery of the ancient texts, mining them for universal meanings or information that may or may not be evident or accessible on the surface to the narrators or their ancient or modern audience.

Universalist approaches were propelled by the trend of linguistic and cultural comparativism in the nineteenth century, whether centered on Indo-European languages and cultures or working with the more universal scale of anthropology. Without disregarding the findings of Indo-European studies, in the mid-twentieth century attention shifted toward the eastern Mediterranean context of Greek culture, and as a result interest grew on the influences from Mesopotamian, Egyptian, Anatolian, and Syro-Palestinian cultures (see chapter 3). Sometimes scholars deploy the tools of Indo-European-based structuralism and Near Eastern comparativism in the same works (e.g., Kirk 1970; Burkert 1979).

*

Regarding the first question of how we can know what these stories meant to *their audiences*, there is no simple answer either. Myths were part of everyday life and permeated every aspect of culture. Attempts to gauge whether (or to what degree) the Greeks "believed" in their myths are necessarily inconclusive (Veyne 1983), just as such generalizations do not work even in our own times, when we can interview live subjects and access theoretically quantifiable data. Perhaps the most important factor to bear in mind is that, for the ancient Greeks and Romans (and for other religions outside the Abrahamic traditions), there was no "sacred text" or dogma to guide or restrain depictions of the gods. Thus, stories involving the supernatural ranged from overtly entertaining to those more closely tied with the sacred. Many stories or details within a story served as *aitia* (explanations) for a particular ritual action or festival. For instance, the *Homeric Hymn to Apollo* narrated the god's birth and journey to find his rightful worship place at Delphi, where his most famous oracle lay. A similar shortened hymn to the god containing parts of the story was also inscribed on the walls of the Athenian treasury (small building) at Delphi, raising that version of the story to a different sacred plane than the bedtime rendition of the god's fight with the monstrous serpent Pytho who inhabited the place before he arrived there. The depiction of Theseus's fight with the Minotaur on the metopes of the same small Athenian building was not only entertaining (visitors could point to it, recall the story, and talk about it) but it provided a shortcut for Athenian civic pride, identity, and representation at the Panhellenic sanctuary.

As recent scholars have emphasized, our experience of religious holidays is also colored by an array of characters and scenes (real and fantastic) forged through the centuries or sometimes in very particular versions (Coca~Cola's Santa Claus, the Easter Bunny, animals flocking to Noah's Ark, and DaVinci's *Last Supper*), and depictions of religious scenes in picture books, movies, serial shows, and commercials shape how we imagine the gods and heroes of Greek myths and our own traditional characters and stories. At a fundamental level, myths helped create and sustain belief (Johnston 2018: 17–21), independently of where each individual stood in the spectrum of that belief. We should not underestimate the human capacity to form relationships with "invisible others," whether they are real, said to be real, or explicitly fabricated for entertainment, and still sometimes attaining near real ontological status (think of Sherlock Holmes or Don Quixote) (Johnston 2018: 17–22; cf. Calame 2009, 2015; Luhrmann 2020). In the end, it is more useful to consider that a more abstract belief *in* (in the gods, their powers, the afterlife) need not be coterminous with belief *that* (that Zeus committed adultery, Appollo killed Pytho, or any other story). And still beliefs would have been informed and modulated to different degrees by the colorful representations of the gods in the myriad narratives an individual was exposed to during a lifetime, whether conveyed in literature or in mouth-to-mouth storytelling. Not only myths, but encounters with statues or paintings, not to mention deep impressions caused by ritual actions and invocations, also shaped the individual and collective experience of the divine and heroic world.

Here is another seeming paradox. It is clear that the search for nondivine explanations of the world spurred natural philosophy and science. These two different worldviews, however, the "mythical" and the scientific, never displaced one another. To our day, scientific and mythological discourses continue to provide alternative and sometimes complementary ways to grapple with the complexity of the human experience and all the "unknowns" that surround us. Science is absorbed more easily by the layperson when it is conveyed in the form of a narrative, such as in a popularizing book or a visual documentary, and ancient poets, historians, and philosophers knew that a story well told had the best chance to convey the desired information and make an impact in the intended audience. We are as likely to weep or laugh at a fictional story, joke, or anecdote as at an accurate report of a real event. This may well be what Hesiod was getting at when his Muses said that "we know how to tell many fantasies that seem real, and we know, if we want, how to sing of real things" (*Theogony* 27–28). In less cryptic words, the power of poetry and fiction is to be both real and unreal, escaping the dichotomy between truth and falsehood (Heiden 2007).

In the end, no general theory of myth can unlock every dimension of ancient mythologies and their effect on their audiences. These stories are timeless precisely because they contain multiple layers that speak to their audiences at different times, even when revisited by the same person. Engaging with a good story is somewhat like delving into Heraclitus's proverbial river, but the reverse: the text might be static, but we may experience it differently every time we go into it, since our mindset and our questions have changed. To offer one example, Hesiod's *Theogony* and *Works and Days* contain stories that can and have been read in any number of keys through all methodologies listed here, each helping us access different aspects of the society that produced them, and perhaps also universal concerns. The figure of Prometheus, for example, can be discussed comparatively alongside trickster gods and culture heroes from Native American to Norse and other mythologies, while the myth of origins of sacrifice is right on the purview of the ritualist approach. Likewise, the first woman, Pandora, conveys gender stereotypes reflected in the Adam and Eve story of Genesis and other traditions, while the myth of the Five Races has been analyzed from a structuralist stance as reflecting social, cultural, and psychological categories (see chapter 2). In turn, the cosmic fight between Zeus and Typhon in the *Theogony* has been seen as a reflection of geomythical traditions, capturing experiences with volcanos, typhoons, and other catastrophic events (Barber and Barber 2004; Thompson and Schrempp 2020: 154–58). In addition, through comparison of the *Theogony* with myths from the Near East, we can appreciate the close entanglements between all these cultures in the first millennium BCE, as well as the originality of the Greek mythical tradition itself (see chapter 3). Finally, the prominence of the Prometheus figure in North American imagery of the early twentieth century shows how the Greek figure could be used to embody America's technological leadership and daring attitude vis-à-vis European Western powers (Morales 2007; see chapter 4).

About This Book

This volume focuses on creation myths. This may seem a narrow topic, but its ramifications cannot be broader. Just as in the *Iliad* the wrath of Achilles opens a window into the entire Trojan War and the world of its heroes, stories about the beginnings of the world and human beings set the stage for the Greek myth-world and, by extension, Classical mythology. Moreover, Greek myth became a cornerstone of Roman mythology, and Western philosophy emerged in dialogue with it. A closer look at these stories, therefore, provides a privileged springboard into the long tradition of Western engagement with Classical culture. The narratives discussed here formed part of a busy and interconnected "story world" and were interwoven with other important mythical threads about heroes and famous wars through genealogies and interactions between characters (Perseus and Herakles, the Trojan War, the Argonauts, etc.; see Johnston 2018: 121–46).

The poems by Hesiod, the *Theogony* and the *Works and Days*, are the center of gravity of the next chapters. A self-fashioned shepherd from Boiotia, Hesiod might be less glamorous than the bard called Homer, but his poetry is as old and as crucial to understanding the Greek gods. The stories of Hesiod's poems are in fact as familiar to us as those of the Trojan War and Odysseus, even if we do not realize it: The separation of Earth and Sky, how Kronos devoured his children (all but Zeus), Zeus's rise to power as king of the Olympians, his fights with the Titans and with Typhoeus, Prometheus stealing fire and giving it back to people, and the creation of Pandora, the first woman, whose curiosity brought troubles to the world, among many other episodes, have been rewritten and reimagined by Greeks, Romans, and scholars and artists throughout the centuries.

The poems of Hesiod and Homer are the earliest preserved in the Greek language and in Europe. Both can be safely placed sometime in the late eighth or early seventh century BCE. Not long before, around 750 BCE, Greek speakers adopted the Phoenician alphabet, after long centuries of illiterate life. These authors used the hexametric verses typical of oral poetry and strung them in long narrative compositions, now made longer thanks to writing. These are what we call *epic poems*. Because they lie at the dawn of written tradition, we know next to nothing about the poets as individuals, and since we lack older texts to compare, it is equally difficult to gauge the extent of Hesiod or Homer's originality. The poetic craftsmanship and internal coherence of the poems, however, suggest a deliberate

FIGURE I.1 *A Reading from Homer*, by Lawrence Alma-Tadema (1836–1912). Philadelphia Museum of Art. Source/Credit: Wikimedia Commons.

authorial hand that masterfully wove together traditional tales and put new spins on them, which must account in part for their success and fame among ancient Greek and later audiences (see Figure I.1, capturing both the oral and written dimensions of Homeric poetry) (Montanari et al. 2009; West 2011).

The way in which Hesiod immortalized stories of origins became a point of reference, a "classic" of enormous influence within ancient Greek culture. This does not mean there were no other versions of the gods' origin stories. We catch glimpses of them in the *Homeric Hymns* and in allusions from later literary and ritual texts. As we will see in the following chapters, some cosmogonic traditions seem to have been completely independent, while for others the reference frame to follow or challenge circled back to Hesiod. By contrast, while myths of creation appear in the earliest Greek literature, this type of story did not seem to be part of Roman lore. When the Roman poets resorted to them, they were creatively adapting Greek mythology.

The trajectory of Greek creation myths also explains the structure of this book: we will focus first and foremost on the foundational Greek texts, first on the cosmic and divine beginnings (chapter 1) and then on the stories that pertain to the first human generations and their dealings with the gods (chapter 2). In these chapters I discuss Hesiod but also "alternative" cosmogonies and theogonies in the Greek tradition, such as the nonmainstream verses from the Orphic poems. Then we will explore the Near Eastern parallels to themes of cosmogony and creation and destruction of humans, which open up for us a broader view of the ancient Mediterranean mythological repertoire (chapter 3). Last, I explore the intellectual journey of these myths among later Greek and Roman writers and philosophers and offer some insights on the place of these stories in our own modern culture (chapter 4).

People interacted with these stories and their characters in many unrecorded ways, some nonretrievable (songs, fireplace stories, jokes), others still producing wonder in standing temple pediments, recovered statues, and painted vases. But we cannot escape the fact that ancient myths have reached us mostly through particular texts. Therefore, I will often lean on my own translations of sections from these texts, especially Hesiod's poems. Each chapter will provide main clues for interpretation and discuss sociocultural aspects of the myths, from their literary form and performative contexts to their social and religious relevance. Their reception, both in later antiquity and in modern times, will be the focus of the chapter 4.

The figure of Zeus/Jove (or Jupiter) provides a thematic and interpretive thread through the chapters. I follow the "character development" of the highest god within Greek and Roman tradition, including comparison with the mirroring Sky and Storm gods of the Near East. His role and transformations in mythology and art shed light on the evolving trends of mythological and philosophical speculation. Goddesses will also feature prominently, especially those most connected with generative powers, such as Gaia and Aphrodite, alongside others. But the towering figure of Zeus was, after all, the topic of Hesiod's *Theogony,* and "the will of Zeus" drove the plots of countless epic stories, as we can read in the opening of Homer's *Iliad.* But he was also the regenerative Sky god of Orphic cosmogony and was all but replaced by an all-encompassing, nameless divinity by Greek and Roman thinkers. Thus, Zeus provided a degree of reconciliation between traditional stories about the gods and abstract philosophical ideas.

*

Some of the most famous and impactful myths in literature were not popular topics of artistic representation in antiquity, if they were represented at all (for instance, we find no scenes of Prometheus preparing the sacrificial meal, or of the castration of the Sky by Kronos, or of the Flood story). My selection of images to accompany the chapters is idiosyncratic and hopes to showcase some prolific forms of art where myths were frequently represented (vase painting, sculpture, mosaics), as well more rarely preserved ones (such as wood, wall painting, papyrus preserved in Egypt), but they also reflect the relationship of myths with landscapes and cultic landmarks that were part of the audiences' daily lives, while in some way featuring "mundane" activities and social actors (women, children) who are underrepresented in the Classical texts. They were, nonetheless, inspiration for creation and other stories and are inseparable from them.

Regarding proper names, I have preferred the Greek forms (Olympos, Kronos, Dionysos) to the Latinized ones (Olympus, Cronus, Dionysus). Even if this may seem dissonant to readers used to the Latin versions, these forms bring us closer to the original languages and traditions, and defamiliarize us in a fresh way with these key characters in Western literature.

As is conventional, capitals are used for name such as "Earth" or Sky" and other divinized elements when the word most clearly refers to the god, while I leave the lower case when the context seems to indicate a more general meaning. However, this is an English-language distinction, as the ancient Greek had no capitalized names and the ambiguity of what these elements-made-gods represented is also baked into the underlying theology and the narrative.

Translations are my own if not noted otherwise.

Acknowledgements

I want to thank Stefan Vranka, editor at Oxford University Press, and the editors of the series, Tok Thomson and Robert Guyker, for entrusting this monograph to me and allowing me to tailor it to my vision of the book, and for their crucial feedback. I thank also the project editor, Zara Cannon-Mohammed, for her help with the editorial process, and everyone involved in the careful production of the book. Over the years in which I have intermittently worked on this project, colleagues have helped me with specific sections and questions related to the book. I especially thank Tom Hawkins, Sarah Iles Johnston, Anthony Kaldellis, Fumi Karahashi, Katie Rask, Jack Sasson, and Marcus Ziemann, as well as Ben John for his input and editing in the first version of the manuscript. I also thank Raquel Martín Hernández and Esther Rodríguez González for their help with images, and graphic novelist George O'Connor for sharing an adjusted file of his art for the book. Finally, this work has been shaped especially by my teaching of myth to college and graduate students. Whether in large lectures or small seminar classes, at The Ohio State University and more recently at the University of Chicago, the students' curiosity and surprising associations nurtured my own interest in mythology and helped me become a better student of it. I dedicate it collectively to them, wherever their life paths have taken them. Thank you for keeping mythology vibrantly alive!

1

From Chaos to Olympos

Cosmic Beginnings in Hesiod's *Theogony*

Hesiod was not the first to ask the perennial questions, but he is the first Greek poet whose verses about them are recorded. While doing so, a great deal of innovation seems to have gone into the *Theogony*, making it into the point of reference of a new genre in Greek poetry. The *Theogony* seems to have built on both oral epic tradition and hymnic poetry in order to create an extraordinarily expanded poem about the ascent of Zeus. We can see shorter versions of such hymns from the Archaic period in the so-called *Homeric Hymns*, all composed later than Hesiod and Homer. Like Hesiod's poems, and written in the same Homeric style, these focused on a particular Greek god, honoring the chosen deity by recalling their stories and praising their powers. But Hesiod (or some tradition he was drawing on) turned a hymn to Zeus into a full cosmogony, hence the innovation, probably inspired by earlier Near Eastern creation epics. The *Theogony* not only narrated the god's birth and accomplishments but also peered into the very beginning of everything, building an appropriate backdrop for the greatest god's new order. Why now? First, Hesiod and Homer took advantage of the aid of writing, a newly acquired technology, to go beyond the limits of oral poetry and its technique based on memory and improvisation (West 2011; Montanari et al. 2012). Second, they took important cues from the older Near Eastern literatures.[1]

---

[1] We have no other information about Hesiod than the poems' internal references to him as author (something we lack for Homer) and the ascription of these poems to him since the

From Chaos to Olympos 23

The first poems we have preserved in Greek, those of Homer and Hesiod, date back to precisely to the time when the Greeks adopted the alphabet (ca. 750 BCE), after centuries without writing, during which stories circulated only orally (a palace-administration writing system known as Linear B was used until around 1200, then completely abandoned together with the Mycenaean palaces). At about the same time when they adopted the alphabet from their Levantine neighbors the Phoenicians, in the eighth century BCE, Greek communities were expanding their horizons by trading and settling around the Mediterranean, a process that triggered a quick cultural transformation involving not only the adoption of the alphabet but also an infusion of new ideas and technologies reflected in artistic motifs and experimentation. This phase is known as the Orientalizing period (ca. 750–600) or even "Orientalizing revolution" (Burkert 1992). But it was not visual themes and artistic models only that influenced Greek art. The older and famous long poems composed in the Near East, such as the *Epic of Gilgamesh* and the creation stories of Mesopotamia, were just as important as models for the now-literate culture west of Asia. Just as the Babylonian *Enuma elish* framed the rise and establishment of their Weather god Marduk within a creation epic that started at the very beginning (see chapter 3), Hesiod sewed together a song about Zeus and a creation narrative, preceded by an expanded invocation to the Muses, as fitting for Greek epic tradition. With the aid of writing, therefore, Hesiod produced a poetic tale that takes us from the empty beginning to the world ruled by Zeus and populated by heroes. Whether he was the first one to do so, or the first to do it with a particular skill and in a way that spoke to Greeks from many communities, his poetry

earliest traditions preserved. Modern scholarship has long preferred to treat Homer's and Hesiod's poems as lacking individual authors, or to use "Hesiodic/Homeric poetry" to indicate the lack of historical clarity regarding who these authors were. It has become increasingly preferred to think of them as creative poets working with orally transmitted stories and poetic techniques, and there is no reason not to use the received names, Hesiod and Homer, to refer to those authors, just as the ancient Greeks did.

24   GREEK MYTHOLOGY

became a point of reference for generations to come and for the Greek and Roman literary canon to our current day.

How did Hesiod present these myths? (a meta-poetic frame)

Speaking about the world's beginning is not easy. There are too many factors, too many questions; the possibilities are endless. The farther back you go in time, the more removed you are from stories tied to places and local lore, and the more you delve into the realm of speculation, whether dressed as theology, philosophy, natural science, or revelation. Detached from idiosyncratic stories about heroes and local kings, the cosmogonic poet offers a universal explanation of the world. There is more room for outright invention, and hence more need for validation. The poet becomes either a philosopher or a prophet. As Martin West (1966: 166) put it, "the ability to see into the distant past is no less marvelous than the ability to see in the future," especially in societies with no written records, as Hesiod's was.

And indeed, in the first section of the *Theogony* (literally "Birth of the Gods"), Hesiod claims to sing about "what exists: what will be and already was" (*Th.* 38, cf. 32). The same expression is used for the prophetic knowledge of the seer Calchas in Homer's *Iliad* (*Il.* 1.70). Is Hesiod's work prophetic, and is he referring to "the present, the future, and the past," as this line has traditionally been read? It is often noted that Hesiod never addressed the future in his *Theogony*. Therefore, other readings are necessary. Perhaps he is drawing a contrast between mortal and immortal things, what "there is" or exists but is fleeting in comparison with entities whose existence span past and future—that is, the gods (Clay 2003: 64–65). Mortal beings, however, barely feature in his *Theogony*, while the Muses instruct the poet to celebrate "the race of the always-existing gods" (*Th.* 21, 33). In my translation of the line, "what exists: what will be and already was," I signal that Hesiod's *Theogony* is foremost a poem about the eternal gods, who hover over everything that "exists" but will continue existing after we are long gone.

Hesiod is thinking in cosmic terms, inviting us to turn our gaze into the past, and by doing so presenting us the future as well, perhaps following an intuition that, at that scale, time is not linear, that the universe is one single thing in motion. And he would be right, since the matter that forms the universe is one, though it transforms itself into the complexity that surrounds us. In other words, the two ends of the cosmos, beginning and end, are part of one entangled fabric, expanding in a way *we* perceive as linear, and subject to the entropy that underlies what is often referred to as the arrow of time (Rovelli 2018: 19–36). But the *Theogony* is about the gods, who live outside time and are oblivious to its ravages. Greek epic language stresses this contrast with mortal people (*thanatoi*) with epithets such as immortal (*athanatoi*), "always existing" (*aien eontes*), and "imperishable" (*aphthitoi*), while the *Theogony* does not even include a deity of Time. In turn, in his other preserved poem, the *Works and Days*, Hesiod delves into the "daily works" of common men and women and their time-cycles, providing a foil to the *Theogony*'s universe (Clay 2003). In the *Works and Days*, Hesiod turns inward into human nature and its toils, into the life of the villager, who can't help but gaze into the sky in wonder, as Carl Sagan evoked. But that is another story (see chapter 2).

With that frame in mind, let's see how Hesiod opens his cosmogony, which is not with the awaited "in the beginning" line, like the book of Genesis. Instead, Hesiod begins by invoking the Muses:

> Let us begin to sing of the Helikonian Muses,
> who hold high and sacred Helikon...
> They are the ones who once taught Hesiod beautiful song
> as he was tending his sheep at the foot of sacred Helikon. (*Th.* 1–2, 22–23)

Like a Greek Moses on his mountain, Hesiod portrays himself as a simple shepherd from landlocked Boiotia visited by the Muses, at

26 GREEK MYTHOLOGY

night, while tending his flock. His knowledge is, thus, quasi-prophetic. The Muses signal this by handing to him a laurel branch or staff, laurel being the plant that symbolizes Apollo's prophetic power. Hesiod received "divine voice" from the Muses, who taught him a song about "how at first the gods and the earth came into being, and the rivers and the infinite sea," and much more (*Th.* 108–109). Every Greek poet needed the Muses by their side. They were the daughters of Mnemosyne—that is, Memory. As such, they granted not only artistic "inspiration" (as we usually picture them) but the poetic craft itself, and the knowledge transmitted through poetry, which was passed down orally from generation to generation, and eventually also through writing. In exchange, they demand that Hesiod praise and celebrate them alongside the Olympian gods, and to do so always "first and last." This is why epic poets invoked the "Muse" or "Goddess" as allies in their compositions: The *Iliad* opens with "Sing, Goddess, of the rage of Achilles son of Peleus...," the *Odyssey* with "Tell me Muse of the man...," and Hesiod's *Theogony* with "Let us begin to sing of the Helikonian Muses,..." (*Th.* 1–2).

Hesiod's first hundred lines serve as a preamble to the creation story (also called *proem* or *proemium*). This "introduction" provides a meta-poetic framework and also works as a hymn to the Muses in their own right: it recalls their birth, their functions, and how they interact with Zeus. Hesiod's song to the Muses is, in other words, a mini-theogony of these daughters of Zeus and Memory. In turn, the Muses provide a model for the mortal poets, since they serve the same functions as the poets of the gods in Olympos. Hesiod makes this clear in his second invocation to the Muses:

> *Sending forth their immortal voice,*
> *they first praise in their song the revered race of gods,*
> *(45) from the beginning, those whom Earth and broad Sky begat,*
> *and those who were born from them, gods, providers of goods.*
> *Then in turn they celebrate Zeus, father of gods and men,*
> *as they, goddesses, start and end their song:*

From Chaos to Olympos

how much he excels among gods and is the greatest in power.
(50) And then, singing of the race of human beings and mighty Giants,
they please the mind of Zeus inside Olympos.

When the Muses do their singing and dancing, Zeus rejoices, perhaps even laughs out loud, his heart lightened by their entertainment. The Muses are "the Hesiods" of the gods, and perhaps therefore poets are like Muses among mortals. All of them sing cosmogonies and praise Zeus, and all of them invoke how things were (and will be?) far passed our short time. Secondary to these lofty concerns, almost an afterthought, is the world of human beings. Only one episode in the *Theogony* deals with the human sphere, that of Prometheus's help to people and the creation of the first woman. In this vignette, mortals are merely pawns in a quarrel among gods. This approach contrasts with the rest of Greek epic, which focuses on heroes. Hesiod is not oblivious of this tradition, however. In passing, the *Theogony* mentions various heroes, such as Oedipus, Perseus, and Herakles, even if they are marginal and only mentioned because they killed primeval monsters and hence helped settle Zeus's order. However, the end of the *Theogony* ties the genealogies of the gods to those of demigods and mortals, as it offers an account of goddesses who bore heroes to mortal men. In turn, instead of a clear ending, the text of the *Theogony* as we have received it moves seamlessly into another poem, known as the *Catalogue of Women* (*Ehoiai*), which lists mortal women who bore heroes to both gods and mortal partners (West 1985). Finally, the *Works and Days* contains a tale of human beginnings, the so-called "Five Races" or "Five Ages" of humankind (see chapter 2).

But the question lingers: Who is Hesiod to transmit such knowledge? The poet himself projects some modesty (whether sincere or as a posture) as he makes three "false starts" before his cosmogony is unveiled, humbling himself in front of his audience as the Muses insult his kind as "rustic shepherds, lowly and disgraceful, nothing but stomachs!" (*Th.* 26) (This sort of humiliation seems to be part of what gods do when they appear to mortals and establish their authority, as it happens also in the *Homeric Hymns*.) But perhaps these circles are a way to increase interest and suspense as well, even as a revelation of such matters through a "rustic shepherd" seems the more unlikely and, hence, awe-inspiring. The awkwardness of these lines is augmented by the obscure proverb of line 35: "But what do I care about these things of tree and stone?" (*Th.* 35). While the immediate context makes us understand the phrase as a mere "let's not get distracted with arcane or irrelevant things," expressions that pair "tree and stone" appear in Near Eastern literatures associated with divine messages, origins, and access to obscure knowledge (López-Ruiz 2010: 56–73).

Through these meta-reflections, Hesiod presents himself both as an ordinary person and as one who is chosen as a channel of the Muses, whose craft can convey both fictions and truths with equally convincing effect. The opening in the *Theogony* thus emphasizes the inspiration that the Muses give to human beings, especially poets and kings, and their privileged role in establishing authoritative views on humanity's place vis-à-vis the divine order.

From first elements to a complex world

Then, and only then, does Hesiod dare to take us to the very beginning:

(116) *Truly at first Chaos came into being, and then*
Earth of wide bosom, as an eternal sitting-place for all
the immortals who hold the peak of snowy Olympos,
and then steamy Tartaros, in the cavity of the earth of wide paths,
(120) *and Love, the most noble among the immortal gods,*
the looser of limbs: in the chest of every god and human being,
he dominates their sense and their thoughtful decision-making.

Four elements appear first: Chaos, Earth (Gaia), the Underworld (Tartaros), and Love (Eros). They were not born or created. They came into existence by unknown mechanisms in an undefined time and space. This is the opening or void Hesiod called "Chaos." It is difficult to know what exactly he meant by Chaos, however. In English we simply reproduce the Greek word (*chaos*) and leave it open for interpretation. This is the very first time the word is attested, and all subsequent uses seem to derive from this famous instance. It seems that a neologism was needed to propose a solution to the impossible question of what there is/was *beyond* the boundaries of our finite universe. Hesiod (or a previous source) found a name for that space where all things came to be, using the same Greek root for "chasm" and "to open" (*chasma, chaino/chanein*) that is also used for a gaping mouth that yawns or utters a sound. In modern English and other languages, even in antiquity, "chaos" evolved into a synonym of disorder or messy confusion, but this is not how Hesiod and his early interpreters understood it. Aristotle and other Greek thinkers and poets were already somewhat removed from Hesiod's time, but they understood this first state of the cosmos as an unlimited empty space, a chasm or an abyss.[2] Nothing existed to be disordered yet.

It is from this void that the trajectory toward complexity began: The Earth and its foil, the Underworld (Tartaros) appeared, as the necessary seat and repository of everything in an Earth-centered view of the cosmos. And then, Love or Desire (Eros). Without it, nothing else happens. Love represents the dynamics of attraction, the force that drives some elements toward others, and the sexual union and reproduction needed for the continued existence of living creatures, who in the Greek worldview included the gods. The creation narrative then follows a logical path departing from a state of initial simplicity, even emptiness or nothingness, from which cosmic complexity grows. The poet attempts to order this knowledge by naming and categorizing the elements by groups and drawing relationships between them through genealogies.

---

[2] For etymology and meaning range, see Beekes 2010, s.v. χάος ("chaos").

The idea of Chaos and what followed deserves a further explanation. It is often said that ancient Mediterranean creation stories move away from the lack of definition and order, and toward order and organization. This is the case in the very symmetrical and orderly account of Genesis, for instance (see chapter 3). But the picture in Hesiod is rather more in line with the principle of entropy, whereby the cosmos "moved" from a state of fewer interactions (lower entropy) to one of higher complexity and multiplicity. It is *we*, moderns, that, contrary to Hesiod, call that later state "chaos." What we see is the effort to grapple with the exponential agglomeration of aspects of reality that resulted in "our world." Language and narrative are our tools to "capture," mentally arrange, and explain this complexity, composed of both tangible and intangible things, real and imaginary, including the gods.

Greek myth has a strong tendency to turn physical and socially constructed concepts into abstract divine entities, foreshadowing the development of natural and moral philosophy. Thus, even Earth, Tartaros, and Love in these first lines sound more like realms and forces than like anthropomorphic gods with bodies and agency who participate in the plots of Greek myths. The line is in fact blurry between the two concepts, and it is up to the audience to read the names as cosmic elements or personified entities, or both. Other primeval elements emerge, either generated by one entity without "mating" (what we call parthenogenesis) or through the combination and coupling of the first primeval entities. From Chaos alone emerge Darkness (Erebos) and "black Night," and from this couple of darkness emerges their opposites, Aither or "ether" (the clear "Upper Sky") and Day. Earth by herself generates her foil, the Sky (Ouranos), "equal to herself, to cover her from all sides," and mountains, and the Sea (Pontos). The Sky is not as much a basic separate realm of the cosmos as an extension and supplement to Earth (Tartaros can be interpreted this way too). Once this set-up is established, from Chaos to those first primeval elements, the narrative follows a more anthropomorphic plot, a family drama structured around the fight

From Chaos to Olympos   31

for power between generations, culminating in Zeus's enthrone-
ment as king of gods and mortal people. In other words, Hesiod's
poem moves from a cosmogony (the birth of the universe) to a
theogony proper (the birth of the gods), and into a narrative about
the main gods' struggles, which I overview in the next section.

This storyline does not accommodate a full account of the rest of
the universe in all its facets. How does Hesiod offer a more complete
worldview? Interspersed within the next sections of the *Theogony*,
we find numerous digressions that show where the legion of divine
beings (often physical and moral concepts) came from. These are
organized by family lines that follow a certain logic driven by semantic or functional relations. For instance, Night's set of children and
grandchildren include Doom, Death, and Sleep, but also gods associated with aspects of human interactions with these dark realms,
such as Dreams, Blame, Pain, the Moirai ("Destinies"), traditionally
portrayed as those who spin, apportion, and cut the thread of life,
and the "painful avenging Fates," who punish human and divine
transgressions (*Th.* 217–20). The Hesperides are also among Night's
offspring. These nymphs are "daughters of evening," who lived in the
far West, where the sun sets, and are keepers of the famous golden
apples (which unleashed a famous discord that led to the Trojan
War). Night also generated Revenge (Nemesis) and Deceit, as well
as Intimacy and Old Age. She also gave birth to Strife, who is the
proliferous mother of Night's grandchildren: Toil and Forgetfulness;
Famine and Sorrow; Fights and Battles; Murders, Manslaughters,
and Quarrels; Lies and Stories; Polemics; Lawlessness and Ruin;
and Oath, "who troubles earthly men the most, when someone
deliberately swears a false oath" (*Th.* 231–32).

Other genealogies take care of entire realms of the cosmos,
such as the family of Pontos, the primeval Sea god created by Earth
(*Th.* 233–336). Pontos engendered a series of sea creatures, such as
the "Old Man" Nereus, father of the sea-nymphs or Nereids. Down
the line, Pontos's family produces famous monsters, which Hesiod
catalogues too: the three Graias and the three Gorgons (including

32 GREEK MYTHOLOGY

Medousa, the only mortal one), whom Perseus killed, and the snaky monster Echidna. Like many monsters, Echidna combines both beauty and horror, and is described as

> divine and strong-hearted, half a nymph of vivacious eyes and beautiful cheeks, but half a monstrous serpent, terrible, huge, specked, bloodthirsty, under the hidden places of the blessed Earth. (*Th.* 298–300)

Echidna mated with Typhon to bear monstrous children, many of whom became famous monsters fought or killed by later heroes: the canine guardians Orthos (guardian of Geryon's cattle) and Cerberos (guardian of the gates of Hades); the Hydra of Lerna and the lion of Nemea, both eliminated by Herakles; but she also bore hybrid monsters, specifically the Chimaera, killed by Bellerophon, and the Sphinx, destroyed by Oedipus (perhaps she bore some of them with Typhon and others with Orthos; the text is ambiguous). This family line offers Hesiod an opening to allude to stories of human heroes, among them Perseus and Herakles, who were sons of Zeus, lest we forget that they too had a role in establishing Zeus's order down on Earth. Earth, for her part, with her son Sky, bore the Titans, who produced their own set of descendants. Among them, the children of Iapetos (Prometheus, Epimetheus, Atlas, and Menoitios) are quite famous, but it is the children of Kronos and Rhea, Zeus and his siblings (often called "Kronids"), who attained a special place on Olympos.

Zeus was the youngest of Kronos's children. His dealing with his enemies and allies is the central topic of the *Theogony*. But first, Hesiod's digression on the Titans focuses on the lineage produced by *other* Titans (*Th.* 337–82). Most important perhaps are the host of rivers and spring nymphs born from the Titan Ocean, known as "Oceanids," who protect the youth, and only a minimal portion of whom Hesiod's mortal voice can account for. These nymphs are attached to the nooks and crannies of local landscapes, but "each of those who live around one of them knows them." Another group of deities comes from the Titan named Theia, a goddess of "sight" (her name can be read as "Divine" but is connected with the Greek verb *theaomai,* which also lies behind the word for "theater"). With Hyperion, the primeval Sun god, she gives birth to other celestial gods, such as Helios (the more common sun god), the Moon (Selene), and Dawn (Eos). And from Dawn and Astraios (an astral entity descended from the Pontos/Sea and Earth), come the three main winds, blowing from the north, the west, and the south: Boreas, Zephyros, and Notos, to whom later tradition added the southeast/ east wind Euros.

Without the time of advanced astronomical observation, from Hesiod's viewpoint, the Earth is our permanent and fixed "seat" at the center of the cosmos. She is the mother in whose bosom all life abides (there is no separate "Nature" goddess). Indeed, way before human beings walked on Earth, she arranged the universe around her, birthing the Sky and the Sea and everything in them. In Hesiod's scenario, the celestial luminaries are part of the firmament that roofs Earth, and the streams and winds, like everything else, either come out of her directly or from the sea and sky whom she created and who embrace her. In turn, from the Titan Ocean comes another "stream" that haunts the human and divine races: the Underworld river Styx, who bore Rivalry and Victory, Power and Force. These children of Styx sit near Zeus for eternity (*Th.* 402) as he dispenses justice among gods and mortals. Styx is the oldest daughter of Ocean, and she is both respected and "hateful to the immortals" (*Th.* 775), connecting her name to the adjective *stygere,* "hateful, loathsome." Upon her deep waters the gods swear their oaths; only because of her can they be held accountable and punished with a nine-year exile from the community of gods (*Th.* 775–806). In other words, just as human beings swear by the gods (especially by Zeus), the gods need to fear a higher authority and some kind of consequence if they break their oaths, which is imagined here, perhaps most appropriately (since they are immortal), in the form of disenfranchisement (and the loss of power it brings) and sheer loneliness.

The primeval element Tartaros has his own description in Hesiod's *Theogony*. When Zeus defeats the Titans in the epic battles known as "Titanomachy," and sends them to Tartaros, Hesiod does not miss the chance to describe how deep "under the earth of wide paths" this realm is, and he does so in quite specific terms: it is not just very, very far, but exactly as far below the earth's surface as the sky above is from the ground. One may ask, just how far is *that*? How can we even measure it? Hesiod ventures a specific image: "a bronze anvil, falling from the sky for nine nights and days, would reach the earth on the tenth," and that much distance there is to the Underworld (*Th.* 720–723). By a modern rough calculation, an anvil might in that time fall through our planet's core and come out the other side. Despite the overstated guess, it is remarkable that Hesiod provided a spatial, potentially measurable image for what was an unfathomable, unmeasurable distance. What is more, he articulated this idea through the concepts of speed (a free-falling anvil) and time (nine nights and days), which are indeed the vectors we also use to measure distance (think of our concept of "light years").

In the midst of his cosmogonic narrative, through side genealogies and descriptions, Hesiod has offered us a view of physical and nonphysical elements that constitute our universe, and even some good nuggets of rudimentary physics.[3] In turn, a few passages connect the *Theogony* to the human world of villages: in Tartaros Hesiod describes the fate of human souls according to the traditional view of the afterlife, the same one represented in the *Works and Days* and Homer's epics: all souls descend to a gloomy realm of no escape, governed by Hades, where they are but shades of their earthly existence and where punishments are exacted in some cases, with few

---

[3] For an interactive and expandable Chart of the Greek gods and their genealogies, see the Theoi Project (https://www.theoi.com/Tree0.html). In other online charts, Chaos is often set as the progenitor of the other first three gods (Gaia, Tartaros, Eros), as well as of those mentioned as his children, Erebos and Nyx (Darkness and Night), but the Greek text does not indicate this type of generative relationship between Chaos and the first three gods.

From Chaos to Olympos   35

rewards except for the especial place reserved for the heroes (called Isles of the Blessed or Elysian Fields, e.g., *WD* 171, *Od.* 4.563). Hesiod also introduces the cosmic role of monster-slaying heroes, who further Zeus's new order, and he dedicates some time to the powers of the goddess Hecate, who favors human leaders (when she wants to). The central story of Prometheus and the first sacrifice also connects Olympian and human realms and leads to the creation of the first woman and, with her, a new era of troubled existence for mortals (see chapter 2).

A family affair

Where does the lineage of the Olympians begin, and how was the divine order established? Zeus and his siblings descended from Gaia and Ouranos, the Earth and the Sky, through the Titans, a group of old gods born from them. These first Olympians and their children all coexisted with the other descendants of Gaia (such as Pontos and his offspring) and with the Titans themselves and their other children, including giants, nymphs, and other eternal beings. As we shall soon see, human beings ultimately also stem from the Titans, whether (as Hesiod had it) because they descend from Epimetheus and Prometheus (sons of Iapetos), or, according to others, because they were formed from Titans' or Giants' matter. And many "tribes" of mortal people claimed descent from Zeus and other gods through heroes born from the mating between gods and mortals.

Most readers are familiar with the three-act plot of the *Theogony*, what has come to be called "the succession myth." In a nutshell, the divine rule over gods and people passed from Ouranos (Sky) to his son Kronos, and from Kronos to his son Zeus. The youngest sons displaced their father in each of these phases. In the end, Zeus secured the throne forever and was acclaimed by the other Olympians, as his rivals were either overpowered or turned into allies. In a sort of aftermath, however, Zeus faced new challenges, and only after defeating Typhon and performing some actions to preempt his own succession did he become a firmly established ruler, while his efforts show he was well aware of being potentially vulnerable to challenges just as his predecessors were.

The first divine couple, Earth and Sky (Gaia and Ouranos), had created the generation of the Titans, alongside two groups of giants: the ones called Cyclopes, because they had one eye (in the *Odyssey* the Cyclops Polyphemos is the son of Poseidon), and the so-called Hundred-Handers, whose names were Kottos, Briareos (or Obriareos), and Gyges (*Th.* 147–53, other mentions in *Th.* 50 and 185). The first conflict had to do with male sexual dominance and reproduction. Earth's son and partner, the Sky, covered his mother/partner completely, oppressed her, and prevented the birth of her children. He pushed them back inside the "tremendous Earth" as she groaned in pain. Sky's wickedness is shown by the fact that he abhorred his own children "from the start" and that he "took pleasure in this evil deed" (*Th.* 155–58). Thus, Earth formed a plot to rid herself and her children from the oppression, and recruited their help: the last one conceived, Kronos, courageously took the lead, and volunteered to castrate his father with a sickle when he came over their mother Earth at night, just as he did every night:

(176) *And great Sky came, bringing night along, and extended himself up against*
and around Earth, with desire for lovemaking, and stretched out in every direction;
but his son reached out from his hiding place with his left hand,
while he grasped in his right one the tremendous sickle,
(180) *long and sharp-toothed, and with vehemence he reaped the genitals*
away from his own father, and threw them back to be dispersed
behind him. (*Th.* 176–82)

The castration act confirms the sexual nature of the Sky's oppression over Earth. In turn, the savage attack on the Sky is highly productive,

From Chaos to Olympos   37

showing that "energy in cosmogonic myth is never wasted" (Martin 2016: 47): the blood from Kronos's castrated genitals fell on Earth and generated powerful entities, such as the Erinyes (Furies, or spirits who avenge blood crimes), another group of Giants armed to their teeth, and the Melian or Ash-Tree Nymphs, from whom, according to some traditions, human beings came (*Th.* 185–87; cf. 563, *Works and Days* 145).

The weapon used for the act, a sickle, provides another interesting detail, as it connects with other myths: a sickle is the primeval weapon used in the cosmic struggles of Hurro-Hittite myths (see chapter 3), and also the tool used by Perseus to behead Medousa. Here the artifact is made of adamant, an imaginary unbreakable material (whence our "diamond"). The use of a sickle brings agricultural connotations to the episode and reinforces views that Kronos was at some point a god connected to agricultural cycles. His festivals in the ancient world, the Greek Kronia and Roman Saturnalia, were celebrated in mid-December around the winter solstice and were connected to abundance, merrymaking, and temporary breaking of social rules, including temporary freedom of slaves. As for Kronos's apparent association, even conflation with "time" (*chronos*, not *Kronos*), the two are not originally the same. But Kronos's ties to rituals of seasonal change, his use of the sickle in the story, and the rough similarity of the names reinforced their associations (these are already evident in Orphic literature and magical spells; López-Ruiz 2010: 151–67).

Even more interesting is Hesiod's account of the birth of Aphrodite: she sprang from the foam generated by Kronos's castrated genitals as they splashed into the sea. Aphrodite's genealogy, therefore, makes her a celestial being, while it bounds her with genitals and sexuality. The cultic resonances of the myth are also clear. The story sets her birth at sea, which points to her role as protector of sailors and harbors. By making her go first to the islands of Cyprus and Kythera after her birth, Hesiod's narrative explains her names Cypris and Kythereia, and honors her old and famous cult on

Cyprus. Aphrodite's cult on Cyprus, especially strong at Paphos, overlaid the prehistoric cult of the island's fertility goddess and in some places that of Phoenician Ashtart (Budin 2003; West 1997: 56–57; López-Ruiz 2015: 378–80). While her worship on the island of Kythera south of the Peloponnese was not nearly as old and important, Hesiod (and others after him) believed the island's name lay behind her "nickname" Kythereia. This otherwise obscure title, however, may have a completely different origin tied to the god Kothar, who was the Semitic equivalent of Hephaistos. This would also explain the mythical tradition used by Homer whereby the lame blacksmith is Aphrodite's husband (López-Ruiz 2023).

Thus, not only does Hesiod's narrative address the goddess's domains and cultic life, but he adds skillful word-games, using the adjective *philommeides* to hint at her love of both flirtatious smiles and genitals (*medea*), and providing a popular explanation of her opaque name, as if it derived from "foam" (Greek *aphros*), even if that may not have been the original etymology of Aphrodite (West 2000). The scene of Aphrodite's birth was frequently evoked in art, where she appears as the epitome of beauty and desire, and a force that dominates nature (as appropriate choice for a villa's garden, where nature meets culture, see Figure 1.1, where she is shown sailing on a shell, naked but adorned with coifed hair and gold jewelry, catching the wind with a cloth and accompanied by winged cupids).

In the *Iliad* and *Odyssey*, as well as in the *Homeric Hymns*, Aphrodite is assumed to be the daughter of Zeus, which makes her a mainstream Olympian, instead of the primeval deity we see in Hesiod, born from Ouranos like the Titans. Even as Zeus's daughter, however, Aphrodite (and Venus) is tied to the Sky, as she is called Ourania (in Latin, Caelestis, or "Celestial"), and she is symbolically associated with the crescent moon and the "evening-morning" star (Venus). These are all astral symbols of fertility and renewal and (in the case of the star) an orientation for sailors, whom she guided as well. The goddess absolutely dominated the love life of gods and mortals alike, even of Zeus, with the only, but notable, exception of the virgin goddesses Athena, Artemis, and Hestia (*Hom. Hymn to*

FIGURE 1.1 "Venus in the Shell," fresco on the garden wall of the "House of Venus" in Pompeii, Italy, first century CE. Source/Credit: 123RF.

Aphrodite, Hymn 5, 1–44). In turn, only Zeus could, on rare occasions, make the Love goddess fall in the trap of passionate love, as when she fell for Anchises and begat Aeneas near Troy. In that story, preserved in the *Homeric Hymn to Aphrodite,* she was also portrayed as a "Mistress of Animals," who induced sexual arousal in wild creatures around her (wolves, lions, bears, leopards) as she walked down Mount Ida looking for her mortal lover. This is an aspect of her lifefostering nature, which she shared with her Near Eastern counterparts, mainly Isis, Hathor, Ishtar, and Ashtart, who are often represented as lions or holding lions or other wild animals. The double nature of Aphrodite must have inspired the idea that there are two sides to Aphrodite, the "celestial" one and the "popular" or "down-to-earth" one (Ourania vs. Pandemos), which capture different dimensions of love and attraction, the spiritual one and the physical and reproductive one (Plato, *Symposium* 180d).

With the liberation of Earth and her children, the Titans rise to power. Foremost among them are Kronos and Rhea, who will be the parents of the Olympian gods and have active mythological roles.

Rhea is another earth goddess, duplicating the role of Gaia. Kronos, as we saw, resists classification, but was probably connected to agriculture. The other Titans, also called "the earlier gods" (*Th.* 486), are prominent mostly for their descendants. Starting with the less famous ones, there is Kreios, who will produce some offspring with the maritime entity Eurybia (daughter of Gaia and Pontos); the Titan Sun-god Hyperion (less frequently invoked than Helios, his son); then Iapetos, who is mostly known as the father of Prometheus and Epimetheus, but also of Atlas and Menoitios; Themis, who represents "Divine law/order"; and Theia ("Divine"), mother of the Sun (Helios), Moon (Selene), and Dawn (Eos) with Hyperion; Mnemosyne ("Memory"), mother of the Muses; Koios and Phoebe ("Shining"), who beget Leto and Asteria (Starry One), and through Leto lend their astral quality to their grandchildren Apollo and Artemis (associated with the Sun and the Moon respectively); and, finally, Tethys and Ocean, who form a primeval watery couple in Homer's cosmogonic tradition.

Hesiod does not dwell on the qualities of Kronos's reign. He merely depicts him as a "crooked-minded" tyrannical figure who turns on his own offspring, just as his father had done. Fearing his ousting, he devoured his children as they were born, causing great sorrow to Rhea, their mother (*Th.* 459–67). The terrifying image was the focus of much distress and disgust by later philosophers and interpreters (see chapter 4). This is not the sort of episode we find in Attic vase paintings or classical sculpture. But Kronos (Roman Saturn) became a metaphor for family violence, even the horrors of civil strife, and of all-devouring Time (see Figure 1.2, where Goya expressed the horrors of the civil conflict and religious prosecution he had witnessed in his contemporary Spain).

Kronos had been warned by Earth and Sky that he would be overthrown "by the plans of great Zeus." These children would become the Olympians, also called "Kronidai" after their father:

Hestia, Demeter, and Hera of the golden sandals, and powerful Hades, who inhabits his residence under the earth and has a ruthless heart, and

FIGURE 1.2 *Saturn Devouring His Son,* by Francisco de Goya (1746–1828), one of the "dark paintings" on the walls of his house. Prado Museum, Madrid. Source/Credit: Wikimedia Commons.

> *the resounding earth-shaker (Poseidon), and wise Zeus, father of gods and men, due to whose thunder the wide earth trembles.* (*Th.* 453–58)

Like her abused mother Earth, and also advised by Earth and Sky, Rhea managed to trick her overbearing partner. She reached the island of Crete, where she safely gave birth to Zeus. As a great accomplice, grandmother Earth hid Rhea and baby Zeus, and swapped the newborn with a great rock that she handed over to Kronos, swaddled in baby clothes. Only a year later, seemingly persuaded by Earth, did Kronos "return" the children, specifically by vomiting them, with the rock coming out first (*Th*. 497). There is a deep similarity between the actions of Ouranos/Sky and Kronos, the one oppressing Earth before her children are born, the other devouring his children at birth: both male gods attempt to revert the pregnancy of an Earth mother-goddess. In the case of Kronos he all but impregnates himself with them as he shoves them down his belly. By co-opting the reproductive process, they aimed to prevent their replacement by the unwanted children.

All the while, Zeus's "strength and splendid limbs" grew in what seems the snap of a finger, for time is not relevant for the gods. Hesiod does not bother to detail exactly how he defeated Kronos, the "king of the early gods," only that he did so thanks to his tricks and force. But the results speak for themselves, as we know Zeus ruled next. We also learn that Zeus planted the vomited rock that Kronos had swallowed at Delphi (called Pytho, *Th*. 499), on Mount Parnassos. Delphi was home to the oracle of Pythian Apollo, and was thought to mark the "navel of the world." A carved rock of betyl (or several of them through the centuries) was shown at the site and was a cult object (Figure 1.3). With this move, Hesiod pegs this cosmic myth onto a cultic site and even an object that Greeks could see and touch (Bassi 2005).

We only learn later (*Th*. 851) that Kronos is locked up down in Tartaros, where he will remain in the company of the other Titans, after Zeus fights them next. As far as Hesiod's account goes, the succession this time involved no father-son violence, no castration by the youngest son. Zeus, we already notice, is a different kind of god and a different kind of king, wise and not "crooked-minded." He is powerful but strategic in his use of violence.

The Olympians were not the only ones that Zeus saved from the grip of a tyrant-god, as the new king also liberated the Cyclopes, who had been chained by their sibling Kronos. With this first

FIGURE 1.3 A carved rock or betyl at the Sanctuary of Apollo at Delphi, Greece, one of several representing the navel of the world and the stone swallowed and vomited by Kronos instead of baby Zeus. Source/Credit: eFesenko/ Alamy Stock Photo.

"diplomatic" act, Zeus secured his key weapons, thunderbolt and lightning. These had previously been concealed under the Earth and were now delivered by the Cyclopes to Zeus in gratitude. Hesiod tells us here of some other sorts of troubles coming from the line of the Titans: down on earth Zeus also needs to demonstrate his absolute power, which Prometheus undermines, as he is prompted to help human beings. But these are petty earthly troubles (see chapter 2). From Sky to Kronos to Zeus, a new order has begun. Will the father-to-son succession cycle stop here? How does Zeus manage to remain king of the gods?

Titanic rebellions and political consolidation

After his preliminary success, Zeus still has to confront two violent revolts against his rule, first against his uncles/aunts, the rebellious

44 GREEK MYTHOLOGY

Titan gods, and then against a new cosmic enemy, Typhon, who had been created by Tartaros and Earth. Zeus now flexes his political muscles, forging alliances and distributing powers to others—learning to delegate, in other words. He understands his stability depends on the trust and loyalty of other gods, and that this is the only way of breaking the seemingly unstoppable inertia of generational challenge to the ruling god.

The Titanomachy, or "battle of the Titans," lumps these older gods together in a non-individualized way, so we assume most of them, and possibly some of their children, confronted Zeus, all except the already defeated Kronos and presumably not Zeus's mother, Rhea, who was a Titan too. On the other camp, Zeus and the Olympians had the alliance of the liberated Cyclopes (non-Titan children of Ouranos), from whom he had obtained his thunderbolt and lightning. The mighty clash goes on for ten years, we are told, without a clear winner—that is, until Zeus expands his forces by liberating the three Hundred-Handers. Thanks to Zeus's political savviness, these potential enemies now join his army despite being giants born from Ouranos and Rhea, and thus naturally aligned with the Titans and the Cyclopes (cf. genealogical chart referenced in note 3). And so the battle finally tilts in Zeus's favor, as each giant adds to the Olympian forces their hundred arms per capita and multiplied the missiles these could throw. The final battle is described with language that evokes extreme noise and heat, as the earth and the waters boil, struck by Zeus's electrical and fiery weapons:

And all around the life-giving earth roared as it burned,
and all around the immense woods crackled loudly.
(695) The whole earth boiled, and the streams of Ocean
and the barren sea; and a hot breath surrounded
the earthly Titans, and an unspeakable flame reached
the divine aether,...
(700) and an astonishing heat invaded the chasm,...
just like when Earth and broad Sky from above approached. (Th. 692–703)

Zeus, now victorious and with a host of allies by his side, sends the Titans under the earth, to the Underworld (*Th*. 716–718), where they join their brother Kronos. But Zeus needs to confront one more cosmic challenge, against the hybrid monster Typhon (or Typhoeus), a frightful and powerful creature described as being both fiery and watery, sea-bound and volcanic, a chaotic hybrid mixture traditionally encapsulated in a snaky shape (Figure 1.4). It remains a mystery why it was Gaia, the Earth mother, who created this last enemy, mating with Tartaros in her own depths. Was she

FIGURE 1.4 Zeus fights the hybrid monster Typhon, here in supplicating position. Relief engraved on an Archaic bronze shield from Olympia. Source/Credit: Drawing by Esther Rodríguez Gonzáalez.

46 GREEK MYTHOLOGY

upset that Zeus had defeated Kronos and the Titans? They were her children, after all, and the youngest of them, Kronos, had freed her from her mate the Sky god Ouranos. Perhaps she was upset at the constant overturn in the order of things she had fostered, and took offense at the newcomer Zeus? At a more basic level, these are fitting origins for Typhon, since monsters are often associated in Greek mythology with the dark depths of Earth and the Underworld, such as Chimaera, Cerberos, Echidna, and others, all descended from Pontos, the deep sea begotten by Earth.

Whatever the case, Zeus also defeats Typhon with his thunderbolt and with the help of allies, in a battle that produces earthquakes and tsunamis, and which makes even Hades himself tremble (*Th.* 850). Zeus finally hurls Typhon into Tartaros, which had by now turned into the permanent prison of defeated, yet immortal, rebellious enemies.

At last Zeus has established his rule, underpinned by his wise politics and by the advice of Earth/Gaia (yes, the same goddess who had begotten his enemy Typhon). Only now Zeus can form the first counsel of gods, and distribute powers adequately, for which he is now acclaimed as a fair king of the gods:

> *Then indeed they encouraged Zeus, the far-seeing Olympian,*
> *by the advice of Earth, to be king and rule over the immortals;*
> *and he made a fair distribution of prerogatives for them.* (*Th.* 883–85)

Finally, Zeus can sit assured on his throne. Or can he? Is the cycle of succession really over? Or must Zeus await the same fate as his father and grandfather? Zeus knows he needs to take further, preemptive action to secure an eternal rule. That is why, first of all, he marries an appropriate wife, Metis, a daughter of the Titans Tethys and Ocean. She is the goddess of wisdom (her name means "mind, counsel"), an essential quality in any long-lasting rule. As it happens, Zeus was already warned by Earth and Sky that children "of superior mind" would be born from her, who could take away his royal prerogatives

(Earth and Sky had also issued the same, correct prophecy to Kronos). They foresee that Athena will be born first, who will possess "strength equal to her father and also intelligent counsel," an appropriate attribute for Metis's daughter (*Th.* 896), but then a son will be born, "a king of gods and men" (*Th.* 897). So, following inherited tendencies, when Metis is pregnant with Athena, Zeus swallows her, preventing the birth of her future children (*Th.* 886–900). One can say that Zeus falls into Kronos-style behavior, but the move increases Zeus's wisdom too: by gulping down Metis, Zeus acquires good counsel forever. Another difference is that, somehow, Zeus manages to give birth to his first child, "bright-eyed" Athena, from his head, which is fitting given her intellectual qualities. As in the many representations of this momentous birth, where she is born in full armor, in Hesiod's account she is from birth not a challenger but an ally of Zeus, one who is "bellicose, army-leader, indefatigable" (*Th.* 924–26; see Figure 1.5).

FIGURE 1.5 Black-figure painting on the so-called "Pyxis of Painter C," representing the birth of Athena from the head of an enthroned Zeus, mid sixth century BCE. Louvre Museum, Paris. Source/Credit: RMN-Grand Palais/Art Resource, NY.

48 GREEK MYTHOLOGY

In this worldview, by virtue of being a female god, Athena was not a viable rival to Zeus. Nonetheless, perhaps because of her special link to Zeus and her birth from his head, in many stories she appears to act as his second in command, almost a surrogate, endowed with intellectual and military prowess, just like the city she oversees, Athens. Her birth was represented in the east pediment of the Parthenon, the one receiving the rising sun's light, while her victory over Poseidon for the patronage of Athens decorated the west side. This was Zeus's way to stop the succession cycle, even if episodes in Greek myths suggest the threat is never out of sight (López-Ruiz 2014a). Zeus averts the birth of his successor son, while his daughters are less likely to generate legitimate successors, some of them being virgins (Athena, Artemis), others married to unfitting partners, such as Aphrodite and Hephaistos in Homer's account (Graziosi 2014: 26). In a sense, Zeus simply resorted to the old trick of repressing, reverting, and appropriating the birth of potential successors that had failed his predecessors; but, unlike Ouranos and Kronos, his success lay in introducing order and political wisdom, thus establishing a more universally acceptable and stable order.

After this first marriage to Metis, which completes Zeus's ascension, Hesiod tells us about the other goddesses with whom Zeus mated: his offspring with Themis ("Divine Order/Law") were entities related to justice and fate; he also mated with the beautiful Oceanid called Eurynome, and with his sister Demeter, with whom he begets Persephone; with Mnemosyne (Memory) he fathers the Muses; with Leto, Apollo and Artemis; and, last but not least, Zeus took as wife his Olympian sister, Hera, goddess of marriage and family. Upset at Athena's birth from Zeus alone (jealousy seems to be her constant), however, Hera also produced her own child, the blacksmith and craftsman god Hephaistos, who "excels among all in Olympos with his skills" (*Th.* 927–29).

At this point the *Theogony* drifts into the theme of genealogies that link the world of the gods to that of mortals. It is difficult to know how the *Theogony* ends, since the preserved verses do not

From Chaos to Olympos   49

signal a closing. The transmitted text adds a list of other mythical procreations, first among gods begetting other gods or divinized heroes (Herakles, Ariadne), then of goddesses mingling with mortal man and begetting heroes, and finally sliding into what is considered another poem altogether, known as the *Catalogue of Women* (or *Ehoiai*). Only fragments of this "sequel" of unknown author (probably not Hesiod) have been passed down, but it narrated the coupling of gods and mortal women and the offspring they produced, including not a few children by Zeus. In contrast, it is puzzling that Zeus begets so few children with Hera, his "lawful wife." It is perhaps the fear of succession again that drove this restrain, and indeed none of Zeus's legitimate children were suitable rivals for the succession: Eileithyia (goddess of childbirth) and Hebe (Youth) were minor goddesses, and the god of war, Ares, is represented in myth as hateful and not a god of cult. Hera, in turn, attempts to produce rivals on her own, who also seem unfit to rule (Hephaistos) or are monstrous (Typhon) and hence doomed to be defeated, even if they still show that Zeus's order can be potentially challenged (López-Ruiz 2014a).

The slightly later *Homeric Hymns* articulate some of the same themes: most strikingly, the newly born Apollo (son of Zeus with goddess Leto) appears as a potential threat, and he makes the gods tremble when they first see him (*HH Apollo* 2) but is quickly appeased by his parents. In another section of the same poem, Hera acts as another Gaia when she is said to beget Typhon to challenge Zeus (*HH Apollo* 350–52), just as Apollo's fight with the snaky Pytho mirrors on a smaller scale that of his father and Typhon in the *Theogony*. Appropriately for Apollo, the Sun's rays put an end to the serpent's corpse (*HH Apollo* 371–74) just as Zeus's thunderbolts did with Typhon. This is only one example of how the *Homeric Hymns* complement the grand narrative of Hesiod by exploring the hierarchies and prerogatives of the gods, which, it seems, were somewhat in motion even as Zeus had become victor (Clay 1989).

As for the Muses' charge to Hesiod, of celebrating Zeus, the *Theogony* certainly does so and shows how Zeus secured his place

50 GREEK MYTHOLOGY

not only as a god of the bright sky and thunder but as a wise and durable ruler as well, who changed the rules of the game and established a new order.

Other Theogonies: Night, Time, and the "Brilliant God"

Greek speakers across the ancient Mediterranean seemed to agree that Hesiod's *Theogony* captured a view of the beginnings and of the divine order they could share, so they transmitted it and it became a "classic." Indeed, some have called the *Theogony* the "Bible" of the Greeks, as a figure of speech, but Greek religion functioned without sacred scripture. Mythological representations in poetry and art supplemented and enriched the individual and collective religious experience, and traditional knowledge about the gods was passed down without the constraints of dogmas or religious "commandments" (Burkert 1985; Parker 2011). In this scenario, it is the more expected that there would be variants and versions of the stories that differed from Hesiod's. Sometimes we encounter them in scenes represented in art, which we cannot explain with the extant literature. Such is the case of the reliefs on a large Archaic vase from Tinos (a Cycladic island), which shows an armed winged creature emerging from the head of another (of ambiguous gender), who is seated in a throne-line position and guarded by other seemingly divine creatures.[4] The scene may or may not be related to the theme of Athena's birth from the head of Zeus, and the acompanying winged genies suggest we could be dealing with another story altogether (Morris 1992, 91–92). In this section I offer a brief overview of some of the other cosmogonic ideas that are preserved outside the *Theogony*, from Homer to the Orphic poems, which represent only a fraction of the

---

[4] Image of the Tinos pithos (early seventh century BCE) can be found online; see, e.g., https://commons.wikimedia.org/wiki/File:Pithos_090754.jpg.

From Chaos to Olympos 51

range of traditions that must have circulated at the dawn of written culture in Greece.

The Homeric universe

Although cosmogony is not the concern of Homer's epic poems, a few ideas about origins come to the surface in his verses, and they reveal important differences in the cosmogonic traditions Homer was leaning on. The first one appears when Hera alludes to "Ocean, origin of the gods, and mother Tethys" (*Il.* 14.201, 302). The concept of these watery Titans, Ocean and Tethys, as the primordial couple is absent in Hesiod's tradition. This repeated line led Martin West to postulate a lost "Cyclic theogony" associated with the Epic Cycle—that is, the mythology about the Trojan War. More generally, the concept of Ocean as a great river that encircled the world appears not only in myth but as a frame for the known world in early geography, as we know from Hekataios of Miletus. In Greek myth, all water streams were born from Ocean (Okeanos) (e.g., *Il.* 14, 246) and Odysseus had to go to Ocean's western end and cross it to access the Underworld (*Od.* 11.12–13). This cosmogony is strikingly similar to that in the Babylonian epic of creation, *Atrahasis*, in which the sweet and salty waters, represented by the male god Apsu and the female goddess Tiamat, initiated the generations of gods. The name of Tethys may even be a version Tiamat's, perhaps distantly connected with Ugaritic and Hebrew *tehum* ("deep sea, abyss") and the *tohu-wa-bohu* of Genesis (West 1997: 143–47; Burkert 1992: 91–92). More generally, the idea that water lies at the beginning of everything was shared by the Mesopotamians, Egyptians, Phoenicians, and Hebrews, and appears in the thinking of the so-called pre-Socratic philosophers or natural philosophers, most famously in Thales of Miletus's formulation of water as the first principle (Burkert 1992: 92).

But the *Iliad* reveals another idea of divine order that differs from the Hesiodic scheme of things: the universe was divided into three realms, the Sky, the Sea, and the Underworld, allotted in equal parts to the three Olympian brothers Zeus, Poseidon, and Hades. We learn this from Poseidon: bullied by Zeus, the Sea god reminds his brother of this original arrangement, in order to command respect (*Il.* 15.187–93). This horizontal "triple division" is also alluded to in the *Hymn to Demeter* (85–87) and differs from the vertical linear succession by which Zeus rose to power in the *Theogony*. This sort of "triumvirate" of gods resembles the structure of the Canaanite pantheon, as we see in the Ugaritic *Baal Cycle*: in that epic Baal (the Storm god) becomes king only by slightly rising above his rivals Sea and Death (Yam and Mot), with the definitive assistance of his sister Anat, who shares her warrior quality with Athena (López-Ruiz 2014a: 4; see chapter 3).

While Homer's Olympians are often called Kronids or Kronidae ("children of Kronos"), and their lineage and that of other gods may otherwise not have deviated much from that in Hesiod's poems, we can only imagine that this tripartite distribution would require much more political maneuvering and compromise from Zeus, and this is certainly how he plays his cards in the *Iliad*. Still, as in the *Theogony*, in Homer's worldview it is the "will of Zeus" that prevails (*Il.* 1.5).

Orpheus and alternative theogonies

As Socrates faced his sentence and reflected upon what might await after death (if anything at all), he mused over the traditional idea of the afterlife: "[H]ow much would any of us pay to converse with Orpheus, and with Musaeus, Hesiod, and Homer? I would like to die many times, if this is true" (Plato, *Apology* 41a.6–8). Of these four, most readers are familiar only with Homer and Hesiod, since we have long full texts attributed to them. Orpheus and Musaeus, mentioned first, however, belonged in a more legendary plane, as personas invested with great mythological clout, as we will see. Orpheus and Musaeus were especially revered as authorities in divine matters, and their names were associated with the transmission of cosmogonic, philosophical, and prophetic wisdom, even if we have only allusions and fragments of texts attributed to them.

Musaeus's name is inseparable from the Muses, the goddesses that inspire epic poetry, and he may just be an abstraction of their art. Nonetheless, many fancied him a true legendary Athenian figure and pupil or son of Orpheus. Orpheus, in turn, was a most productive mythological character. He appeared in famous sagas, interacting with epic heroes (e.g., the Argonauts), and he was the protagonist of his own tragic story, which enjoyed much popularity in ancient and even modern art (cf. chapter 4). According to various versions, Orpheus was the son of the Muse Calliope ("Lovely-voiced"). His father was a Thracian king, or perhaps Apollo himself, and for some he was the brother of the poet Linus, whom Herakles unintentionally killed. Most famously, Orpheus's music had magical effects on people, animals, trees, and even on the gods (Figure 1.6, bottom). When his newly wedded bride, Eurydice, died by snake bite, he managed to make his way into the Underworld. Enchanting the watchdog Kerberos, as well as Hades and Persephone themselves, he was allowed to bring her back to life; but in a moment of weakness, the poet momentarily forgot the one condition he had accepted in the bargain, and he looked back at his beloved just before reaching the light, so she was dragged back into the dank Underworld forever. Other stories circulated about Orpheus, for instance that he was killed by raging Maenads or Thracian women, and that his head floated to the island of Lesbos where it became the source of an oracle (*Georgics* 4; Ovid's *Metamorphoses* 11.1–66; Apollodoros, *Library* 1.3.2).

Orpheus's knowledge of the Underworld and his gift for poetry and music inspired an entire poetic and intellectual, somewhat mystical movement (see Figure 1.6). Writings on a variety of topics were attributed to him, with most allusions and texts proliferating during and after the fifth century BCE, although some go back to an earlier date. Foremost among them were cosmogonies/theogonies captured in poems that we have largely lost, with titles such as *The Robe, The Net, The Krater, The Lyre*, and others. After Hellenistic times, other esoteric and pseudo-scientific texts were piled under Orpheus's authority too, including treatises on such a wide range of topics as magic, gems, plants, astrology, dressing and eating practices, and medicine. In turn, the main ideas of Orphic cosmogonies have to be teased out from various types of texts, which range from poems that circulated in Hellenistic and Roman times (*The Orphic Hymns, The Rhapsodies*), to quotations by the Neoplatonist philosopher Damaskios, which he attributed to earlier scholars, to ideas that modern scholars reconstruct from other scattered references. More rarely we have primary documents, such as the so-called "Protogonos theogony," to which I return later in this chapter. Cosmogonies ascribed to other figures, such as Aristeas, Epimenides, Abaris, Pherekydes of Syros, Dromokrites, Linus, Thamyris, Palaephatus, and others, are even less firmly attested, but indicate the cosmogonic genre was prolific and our knowledge of it abysmally limited (Bernabé 2003: 15–19; López-Ruiz 2010: 130–36; Graf and Johnston 2013: 167–86; Meisner 2018: 1–18).

In Orphic traditions, the order of the universe and the hierarchy of the gods was somewhat similar to that in Hesiod, but new elements were introduced, and the figure of Zeus and his descendants took on new twists. Combining and summarizing the main features of these cosmogonies, a pattern emerges: They all seem to expand on the stages of theogony preceding and following the traditional "succession myth," and Zeus's ascent known from Hesiod. At the "cosmic" end of things, they speculated on the first elements, something the natural philosophers were doing too at roughly the same time. Although these fragments do not reflect a unified Orphic cosmogony, several features are salient across them and contrast with the Hesiodic or mainstream mythology. In several of these Orphic fragments, Night appeared as the initial element or among the first elements, while water was the first element in one of them, and Chaos was almost absent. A new figure, Time, occupied various prominent places in most of them. Again, despite appearances, this Time/Chronos is not the same as Kronos, Zeus's father, although the Titan already in antiquity absorbed some features linked to time and eternity. This association is already palpable in Orphic texts, where Kronos receives titles such as "all-begetter of time, everblooming one" (López-Ruiz 2010: 158–64 for Kronos).

More surprising perhaps is the mention of an egg that emerges from Time or is made by him. From this egg comes a first king of the gods, called Phanes, meaning "Shining" or "Brilliant One." Depending on the version, he is also called Protogonos, or "First Born." After these unconventional elements, the traditional, Hesiodic sequence of kings of the gods follows, according to which Ouranos (Sky) is succeeded by Kronos, who is succeeded by Zeus. But another big surprise comes at the end of this sequence: Orphic texts place Dionysos after Zeus, adding an extra level to the traditional succession story and revealing a slightly different theology. Orphic and Bacchic groups, therefore, positioned Dionysos, Zeus's son with Semele or Persephone (depending on versions), at the end of cosmic evolution. It is essential to understand that this Dionysos is not only the god of wine and theater, and of revelry and mental alteration, but also a leader of *mystai* or initiates in mystery rites connected to the afterlife. It is unclear whether all Orphic cosmogonies featured Dionysos, but at least some did. This sequence is best attested in the Orphic *Rhapsodies*, a Hellenistic-period work that synthesizes earlier Orphic cosmogonies-theogonies that we know only from quotations and allusions by other authors. The full Orphic succession line, then, as reconstructed by scholars, would go as follows: Night, Chronos/Time, (from the egg) Phanes, Ouranos/Sky, Kronos, Zeus, and Dionysos (Meisner 2018: 38–39; overview in López-Ruiz 2010, 151–70, Table 3).

This position of Dionysos, however, did not result in the deposition of Zeus, as in previous stages of the succession of heavenly rulers (Ouranos to Kronos to Zeus). On the contrary, the trajectory of Dionysos was truncated by the Titans: Zeus, in the shape of a snake, had begotten Dionysos with his own daughter Persephone, on Crete; the baby was protected by the Curetes (like Zeus had been); at some point, Persephone was abducted by Hades; perhaps incited by Hera, the Titans painted their faces with gypsum, allured baby Dionysos with toys, then dismembered him, boiled his remains, and ate him; the Titans were punished by Zeus by means of lightning; but Dionysos's heart was saved by Athena and was born again, now from human Semele (a daughter of Kadmos in Thebes), which is why he is called "twice born." According to one version, Zeus created yet a new human race, the last one, from the ashes or soot left of the Titans, which contained Dionysiac matter as well. This is at least how the myth might have played out in the *Rhapsodies*, according to the most widely accepted reconstruction (West 1983; Bernabé 2004). This dismemberment-rebirth story is known as the "Zagreus myth" after the name given to Dionysos in some late Orphic allusions. Since the thread of this story is reconstructed from scattered sources far apart in date, scholars disagree on whether all of these elements belong in one story and constitute the original Orphic mythology that underpinned their theology and mystery rites (Meisner 2018: 237–78; Edmonds 2013: 148–59). Whatever the case, the *Rhapsodies* seem to proclaim Zeus as the ruler or accomplisher of "all things," Dionysos now ruling "in addition" to him. This is no small concession to the younger god's power, but we can also see it as a way for the Dionysiac Orphic followers to mythologize the fact that, historically speaking, *their* favorite god did not overcome his father, as Zeus remained the principal, highest authority among the Greek gods, in myth and cult (Meisner 2018: 276).

An important takeaway from the Orphic narrative about Dionysos's death is the idea that human beings have Titanic nature, and perhaps even Dionysiac nature (we will revisit this in chapters 2 and 4). In turn, the theme of the double birth of Dionysos circulated in other versions, independently of Orphic myth. In the mainstream mythology about the god, he was killed by lightning while still in his mother's womb, whence Zeus sewed the fetus's heart in his own thigh and Dionysos was born again. The background there was more "mainstream": the human mother, Semele, was impregnated by Zeus, and asked for him to dispel doubts of the child's paternity, as her siblings were skeptical and had slandered her. The idea was planted by a jealous Hera, knowing that showing Zeus's might would come in the form of lightning and kill mother and unborn baby (Euripides, *Bacchae* 1–9; Apollodoros, *Library* 3.4.3).

One of the most important aspects of Orphic mythology is that it revamped the figure of Zeus. In this cosmogony/theogony, Zeus is not only the established king; he acquires the Sky's generative power and recreates the entire universe on his own. There are references to this in the *Rhapsodies* and in the Derveni Papyrus, an extraordinary text dated to the fourth century BCE that contains a commentary on an earlier Orphic cosmogony, of which it quotes some lines (Betegh 2006; Santamaría 2019). Zeus does this either by swallowing Phanes/Protogonos or by swallowing the genitals of "the first-born king." This "king" is probably the same Phanes ("Brilliant/Shining"), also called Protogonos and Erikepaios, or perhaps he is the Sky, or both at the same time. As for the genitals, they are in either case understood as the Sun and the Sky's life force. This is how Zeus acquires his regenerative power. The first option (swallowing Phanes) is reflected in the *Rhapsodies*, and the second (genitals, or "reverend one") in the Derveni Papyrus. I quote from the *Rhapsodies*:

> *After retaining the strength of the first born (Protogonos) Erikepaios,*
> *he (Zeus) contained the body of all things inside his empty stomach,*
> *and he mixed with his own limbs the power and strength of the god,*
> *and for this reason, everything was formed again with him, inside*
> *of Zeus, the shining height of the wide aither and the sky, the abode*
> *of the barren sea and the glorious earth.* (*Rhapsodies*, Orphic Fragment 167)

Just as the castrated genitals of Ouranos/Sky in Hesiod had generated life on Earth, including the birth of Aphrodite, now Zeus captures the power of creation and becomes not just procreator of other gods and heroes, but a true cosmogonic creator, as the Derveni Papyrus's cosmogony shows (quoted below). As we can see here, even within a more pantheistic view of the universe concentrated in Zeus, the Sky god, this new recreator is still subject to incestuous sexual desires and is the actor of violent actions. His figure concentrates cosmogonic actions that were, in traditional myth, divided among Ouranos, Kronos, and Zeus, becoming himself both the castrator and generator of life:

> In him all immortal blessed gods and goddesses were joined,
> And rivers and lovely springs and everything else
> Which had come to be; and he became the only one.
> Now he is king of all and will be ever after.
> Zeus became the first, Zeus last, god of the shining bolts.
> Zeus the head, Zeus the middle, Zeus is formed from all things,
> Zeus breath of all, Zeus is destiny of all,
> Zeus king, Zeus lord of all, god of the shining bolt.
> Zeus engendered through ejaculation
> Persuasion and Harmony and heavenly Aphrodite,
> And he contrived Earth and broad Heaven above,
> And he contrived the great might of broad-flowing Ocean…
> In the middle the (moon) of equal measure everywhere,
> Which is manifested to many mortals over the immense earth.
> But when the mind of Zeus had conceived all the works,
> He wanted to unite in love with his own mother. (Derveni Papyrus, fragments 13–18[5])

But what is next? Is the succession over? The prominent place of Dionysos in Orphic myth might suggest it is not, but in the end the Orphic version of the succession still re-establishes that Zeus once

[5] Translation by A. Bernabé and M. Herrero, from López-Ruiz 2018: 55–56.

again managed to retain power. He does so thanks to some process of swallowing (his swallowing of Phanes, the Titans' eating of Dionysos) and unnatural appropriation of the birthing process, such as replanting Dionysos's heart in his thigh for his second birth; these are all themes with a long tradition in previous episodes of struggle for succession (Meisner 2018: 273–78).

Equally fascinating and much less somber is what the comic writer Aristophanes does with cosmogonic tradition. He had mocked natural philosophers, sophists, and Socrates in his comedy *The Clouds*. In 414 BCE he staged *The Birds*, in which these winged animals claim to be the true gods, as creatures who know the heavens firsthand. The chorus of Birds even venture a little cosmogony, according to which only Chaos, Night, dark Erebos, and Tartaros existed at first, and Night laid an unfertilized egg in the darkness, from which Eros (Love) emerged. From this winged entity that concentrated all the elements of the world, they, the Birds, were born (that is, from Eros and Chaos), before even Earth and Heaven and the famous Olympian gods existed (*Birds*, 693–703; see West 1994; Bernabé 2003: 85). In this way Aristophanes makes a humorous side-reference to the Orphic "cosmic egg," linking it to the aviary world and aligning his birds with that primordial force, Eros, who, like its Roman version, Cupid, was commonly represented as a winged archer. With his satiric cosmogony, Aristophanes mocks currents that were proliferating in his time, and along the way runs right into the proverbial chicken-or-the-egg problem.

To sum up, Orphic narratives broadened the possibilities of the imagined cosmic origins, while providing links with cultic groups tied to the figures of Orpheus and Dionysos. At the same time, Zeus was elevated to a theologically more complex plane, as a generative force at the center of the universe. This version of Zeus, in turn, resonated with the more abstract philosophical ideas about an all-intelligent God among philosophers of the time, especially Plato and the later Platonists (see chapter 4).

Building Community, Sustaining Belief

Oral tradition, memory, and a Panhellenic worldview

Not all cultures cultivate cosmogonies or pour them into written poetry. As we will see in chapter 3, the narration of cosmogony or theogony in epic form probably originated in Mesopotamia, from where it entered other literary traditions in the Near East and the Aegean. These creation stories had a deep effect in several aspects of society. We know, for example, they contributed to community- and shared-identity-building, helped promote and legitimate the idea of kingship and leadership at a time of formation of the Greek city-states, and these narratives also interacted with the world of ritual, especially in the case of Orphic cosmogonies that were the focus of initiation groups or mystery cults.

First of all, let us consider what the writing down of these creation stories meant. When Hesiod started his cosmogony and invoked the Muses for assistance, he was undertaking a task perhaps no other Greek poet had attempted: to sing not only the entire story of Zeus's ascension to power, but to start from the very beginning of the creation. The composition of long epics was made possible by the adoption of the Phoenician alphabet around 750 BCE. Greek poets had for centuries been building on orally composed poetry and poetic techniques (Parry 1971), but now, for the first time, they strung together larger clusters of mythological traditions, and even the poets' names became attached to these new versions (in Hesiod by the poet himself). The written transmission and circulation of these epics allowed the far-reaching spread and influence of a few privileged works. This was due to a combination of factors. Among them, their innovative engagement with the written medium, their appealing grand themes, and their sublime quality were essential, as well as their success in speaking to audiences of several generations in the context of growing Panhellenic trends and emerging city-states (Powell 1991; Raaflaub 1993;

Osborne 2009, 131–40). Once the few early epics became solidified in written tradition, they became points of reference, while others slowly fell into oblivion.

Hesiod's ambitious mythological tale and his claim to privileged communication with the Muses contrasts with the humble frame he sets for his poem: Hesiod presents himself as a shepherd-poet from an insignificant community in rural Boiotia (an inland valley west of Attica), and he features his local mountain, Helikon, as a proxy of Olympos and the place of revelation. Still, Hesiod is quick to leave his provincial landscape, and he shifts his narrative to a Panhellenic plane that was recognizable and relevant for all Greek speakers. When he invokes the Muses again, he describes them as Olympian (not Helikonian), and portrays them dwelling in Olympos and entertaining Zeus in his lofty palace (*Th*. 35–52).

Another strategy to make his account appealing to the broader Greek world is to avoid connecting his stories to particular places and local traditions, which is more easily done for cosmogonies than for human stories (see chapter 2). Exceptionally, he points to Crete as the birthplace of Zeus, to Cyprus as Aphrodite's home, and to Delphi ("Pytho") as the place where Zeus's rock substitute was deposited, but these were probably already famous landmarks in the Greek mythical-religious geography of his time. Hesiod's creation story, then, much like that of Homer's *Iliad*, provided a tool for cultural cohesion, consolidating and spreading narratives that were easily shared across Greek communities. This made his work a lasting success, which ensured its influence in the later traditions, thus perpetuating its relevance, in the kind of cycle that makes some works "classical." Part of the success of both the *Iliad* and *Odyssey* and of the *Theogony* was that Greek speakers from anywhere could feel represented: in the case of Homer's poems by the inclusion of Greek contingents from all across the Greek geography in the Trojan War and through the universality of Odysseus's travels through unknown wonderlands; in the case of Hesiod in the opposite way, thanks to the suprahuman, nonlocalized content of the stories.

How or how much these poems contributed to the rise and spread of Panhellenic culture and identity is a matter of discussion, but few would doubt that they were part of the process. Perhaps we need to look at later periods, to the time of the Persian expansion and invasion, for the articulation of a true Panhellenic identity (Hall 2002). But the fact remains that these early narratives were successful in part because they promoted common ground in the realms of religion, language, and worldview, amid the diversity and local traditions that characterized Greek communities, and the trend is palpable in the flourishing of Panhellenic sanctuaries such as those of Apollo at Delphi and of Zeus at Olympia from the eighth century onward (Hall 2002: 125–34).

The Muses themselves hold a key to poetry's social relevance. Cultural identity does not exist without Memory. The type of "catalogic poetry" that we find in the *Theogony* or in the *Iliad* shows the important role of oral poetry as a didactic tool in a world without formal schooling and limited literacy. These catalogues channeled the "gift of Mnemosyne," safekeeping and transmitting the community's cultural memory from generation to generation, in the form of thematically elaborated lists of characters. This aspect is also evident in Hesiod's *Catalogue of Women* and in his *Works and Days*, which feeds from the genre of "wisdom literature" and addresses topics related to agriculture, the calendar, marriage, and so on (see chapter 2). Catalogues also appear in Homer, whether in the famous "Catalogue of Ships" in Book 2 of the *Iliad* or in the series of ghosts of famous female characters Odysseus sees in *Odyssey* 11. In short, these epic poems and their myths were not only entertaining but also educational and instrumental in legacy-building, which in part explains why they stood the test of time. The fact that later on philosophers such as Socrates and Plato sternly criticize these stories, explicitly pointing to Hesiod's *Theogony,* as inappropriate educational tools for young malleable minds of their time (Plato, *Republic* 377d–78e) shows just how central they had become to the Greek belief system and worldview for centuries (see chapter 4).

Divine and human leadership

Peoples from all around the Mediterranean, including the Greeks, were used to the idea of kingship. In whatever modality, this perennial institution mapped onto the story of Zeus's ascent to power and his kingly figure. The language of royalty applied to both Titans and Olympian gods. Not all Mediterranean and Near Eastern cultures, however, mapped human institutions and power struggles onto their gods in the same way. For instance, this equation does not work so well in monarchic but monotheistic cultures like that of Israel, where the language of kingship is applied to God but there is no room for a succession myth or contested authority (see chapter 3).

Minuscule replicas of these kingly gods, human rulers also receive some attention in the *Theogony*. The Muses had two jobs, we learn: to praise and entertain Zeus and the gods up on Olympos, but also to inspire and grant authority to the voices of poets and kings among mortals:

> *Whomever the daughters of great Zeus honor,*
> *and (whomever) they behold when he is born among the Zeus-bred*
> *kings,*
> *they pour a sweet dew upon his tongue,*
> *and gentle words flow from his mouth; and all the people*
> *(85) from that moment look up to him as he resolves disputes*
> *with right judgment; and speaking confidently,*
> *he quickly puts an end even to a great quarrel.*
> *For this is why (we say) kings are sensible, because, when people*
> *are being wronged in the assembly, they (the kings) manage to*
> *restitute things*
> *(90) easily, persuasive as they are with their smooth words.*
> *And as he goes up to the gathering, they appease him as a god,*
> *with gentle reverence, and he stands out among the gathered ones.*
> *Such is the sacred gift of the Muses to men.* (Th. 81–93)

We do not know much about how communities were organized in the time when Hesiod's and Homer's epics were composed, beyond what we may deduce from archaeology and from cues in the poems themselves (Raaflaub 1993). It is fair to assume, however, that their audience was used to the idea of a single leader, who nonetheless took counsel with some sort of advisory body representing influential sectors of the community. Whether these kings, usually called *basileus*, were hereditary monarchs, tyrants imposed by political factions, or some other kind of leader or chief, they in turn looked up to the figure of Zeus. As we saw in Hesiod's story, the *basileus* of the gods ruled over immortals and mortals both by inheritance and by merit; he counted on the advice of a council of gods, who could check and even influence Zeus's impulses (if not bend his will).

As Greek communities became larger and more complex, and certainly by the seventh century BCE, we can start talking about the emergence of the independent city-state or *polis* as the main geopolitical unit across the Greek world, including the settlements abroad. These states usually comprised a well-developed urban nucleus and a surrounding territory of varying sizes (e.g., Athens governed over all of Attica). In a different model, some states were not structured around a single urban center, and these were called *ethnos/ethne*, or "ethnic group," "people" (e.g., Achaia, Thebes). In whatever shape, these growing communities saw the increase of rivalry and inequality, both among their inhabitants and among the neighboring states. The gods were crucial allies for any mortal who aspired to excel as a leader among his peers, whether in the assembly, in battle, or in athletic competitions, but also for those who simply wanted their fields, their cattle, and their enterprises at sea to prosper. This is the role Hesiod attributes, surprisingly, to the goddess Hecate, so long as she is propitiated properly "according to tradition" (whose tradition exactly we don't know). She usually features in Greek literature as a goddess of the night, crossroads, and magic, but in the *Theogony* she appears as a protector of the community and children, and the "most honored among the immortal gods" (*Th.* 411–52).

In these new communities, especially during the seventh and sixth centuries, myths started more and more to be the theme of artistic representation, whether in vase painting, temple sculptures, or other visual media. In rapidly evolving styles, artists used recognizable characters and vignettes to allude to entire mythical sagas. But epic poetry was the most detailed conveyor of myths, primarily experienced through performance, with recitation and music. Dining and household entertainment were a frequent context for these recitations, and the poets themselves played with these meta-poetic moments: Homer portrays bards moving the attentive crowds gathered at a banquet, and Hesiod brags about having won a poetic contest at a royal funerary game (*Works and Days* 654–69). This latter theme, in turn, resonates with the grand funerary games in the Homeric poems. But musical and athletic contests were also part of (nonfunerary) festivals and games in honor of particular gods, some of them acquiring Panhellenic scope, such as those at honoring Zeus and Apollo at Olympia and Delphi, respectively. Other poets like Pindar in the early Classical period, used myths in compositions that celebrated athletic victors, who were often aristocrats and rulers. These often elaborated on mythical themes that connected the victor to a mythological lineage, and through those allusions they bolstered the entire community's identity (e.g., Eisenfeld 2022).

Creation stories in particular had a role in providing a distraction from daily preoccupations. While they inspired kings, the Muses could do much for the common folk:

> For even if someone who holds sorrow in his recently battered spirit
> is parched with affliction in his heart, still when a poet,
> (100) servant of the Muses, sings of the famous deeds of men of old
> and of the blessed gods who hold Olympos,
> right away he forgets his troubles and does not remember
> his sorrows at all; for the gifts of the goddesses quickly turn them
> away. (*Th.* 98–103)

GREEK MYTHOLOGY

In other words, creation stories had a particularly soothing, even healing effect, as they brought into the present moment some of the magic of creation. It is not surprising, then, that we find cosmogonic and theogonic themes in texts that had to do with rituals and mysteries that unveiled special knowledge about life and death, as we see next.

Myth, ritual, religion

As Hesiod claims, creation narratives had the capacity to transport their audience to a mythical time. This idea is not unlike the *illus tempus* that Mircea Eliade described as a symbolic space that the mind yearns for and retreats into, a fully ahistorical moment where the insurmountable gap between humankind and the divine is momentarily bridged (Eliade 2005 [1954]: 76; Thompson and Schrempp 2020: 83–84). Hesiod made clear that poetry, and cosmogony in particular, can help someone put aside or forget their suffering, which is beautifully ironic, as the Muses are the daughters of Memory and the poet's memory aids (*Th.* 53 ff.). This quality of cosmogonies is nowhere more explicit than in Apollonius of Rhodes's *Argonautica*: taking his cue perhaps from Hesiod, this epic portrays Orpheus (an Argonaut himself) singing a cosmogony in order to stop the escalating quarreling among the heroes onboard (*Argonautica* 1.493–515). Moreover, in the short cosmogony the author experiments with an interesting combination of Hesiodic, Empedoclean, Orphic, and Egyptian traditions, which suits the author's intellectual environment in Hellenistic-period Alexandria. Orpheus sings of the emergence of natural elements without violent acts as the divine rulers succeed each other, attaining a calming effect that leaves the listeners spellbound even after he had stopped singing, "such an enchantment of a song he had left them."

Where the epics of Homer and Hesiod provided mythical nourishment for the people at large, Orphic theogonies were intended for a special circle of initiates: "I will speak to the truthful, shut your doors, profane!" warned the opening line of some Orphic texts (*OF* 1). Various elements of Orpheus's own back-story tied him with the mysteries of Dionysos (e.g., Apollodoros, *Library* 1.3.2). And Orpheus was associated in antiquity with the teachings of Pythagoras, who in turn influenced Plato and later Platonist and Neoplatonist philosophers, whence cosmogonic ideas left a mark on Western mysticism and philosophy (Bernabé and Jiménez San Cristóbal 2008; Graf and Johnston 2013; Edmonds 2004).

Archaeology has provided an exceptional window into other textual and ritual traditions involving Greek cosmogonies. The extraordinary text known as the Derveni Papyrus was found carbonized among the remains of a cremation burial dated to the mid-fourth century BCE (that is, contemporary with the end of Plato's lifetime). The scroll was excavated in 1962 in a tomb in northern Greece and is the earliest papyrus preserved in Europe. It also happens to contain the earliest surviving Orphic text, quoted along with extensive commentary. This document must have been greatly valued by the grave's occupant, as it accompanied him in the funerary pyre. It is difficult to date the text with precision, however, as the Orphic theogony quoted in the Papyrus is older than the commentary and must go back to the late sixth or early fifth centuries BCE, while both quoted text and commentary are probably older than the copy of this scroll itself. This testimony is priceless, as it shows the complex intellectual and ritual world surrounding the use of Orphic texts among initiates of these groups.

The Gold Tablets or Orphic Tablets provide another firsthand testimony of how initiates of so-called Orphic-Bacchic groups engaged mythology in their ritual practices. These were thin sheets or plaques of gold (*lamellae*), of very small proportions, inscribed in Greek (see Figure 1.6, top). They were found buried with individuals of both sexes, presumably initiates, hanging from their necks or kept in amulet cases or pouches. Thirty-nine of these tablets have been found so far, dating from around 400 BCE onward. The small

FIGURE 1.6 (top). "Bacchic-Orphic" Gold Tablet with Greek text, mid-fourth century BCE (note small proportions: 2.2 × 3.7 × 0.1 cm. or 7/8 × 1 7/16 × 1/16 in.). Source/Credit: Gift of Lenore Barozzi, donated to the J. Paul Getty Museum, 1975.
(bottom). Orpheus plays the lyre to wild animals; Roman-period floor mosaic from Tarsus, Turkey. Hatay Archeology Museum in Antakya. Source/Credit: Chris Hellier/Alamy Stock Photo.

From Chaos to Olympos

tablets were inscribed with texts that served as amulets and guides to the soul as it passed on to the Afterlife. The tablets functioned as memory aids for the soul, who required passwords and knowledge of specific landscape markers so as to arrive at the right place, where they would be received by Persephone and Hades. Most of the tablets are brief, consisting of keywords or brief formulae, while a few longer ones offer more detail. For instance, the soul is instructed to respond to underworld guardians with the sentence, "I am a child of Earth and Starry Heaven, but my race is heavenly." Another variation of this is the line that reads "I also boast to be of your happy race," along with similar formulations, which evoke divine and specifically Titanic origins. This may be an allusion to the Zagreus myth, whence human beings emerged from the soot of the slain Titans, or to the role of Prometheus and Epimetheus (sons of the Titan Iapetos) in the creation of the human race according to various myths (see chapter 2). The guardians will then grant permission for the deceased to drink from the "Lake of Memory" and join the spirits of other initiates of Dionysos, called *bacchoi* (cf. Figure 2.5). As a group, these texts reflect a set of beliefs and specialized knowledge shared by communities scattered, as the tablets are, throughout the Greek world, from southern Italy-Sicily to northern Greece (Graf and Johnston 2013).

Even more opaque but also connected with the world of Orpheus and Dionysos is a set of small bone plaques found in the ancient city of Olbia, on the Black Sea (today in Ukraine). These are dated to the fifth century BCE, so they are roughly contemporary with the oldest Gold Tablets. The Olbia plaques, however, were found all over the city, not in graves, and thus were probably carried around as amulets or special tokens of initiates. The texts engraved in them are telegraphic and only their carriers would understand what their message and power was, but they strongly suggest a connection with similar circles of initiates, as they contain the names of Dionysos, "Orphic(s)," and single powerful words: "life," "death," "truth."

We do not know much about these groups or their rituals, not least because they were by definition secretive (that is what "mysteries" means). Did they recite cosmogonies in a ritual setting? For how long and how did they use the written texts? Were there similar written amulets circulating on perishable materials? The accidental preservation of a single such document, the Derveni Papyrus, is enough to show that these groups were invested in mythical narratives and particularly in cosmogonies. Especially prominent in texts stemming from these circles are the role of Earth and Heaven and the place of Dionysos at the end of the succession myth, as well as myths of descent to the Underworld by figures such as Orpheus, Dionysos, Persephone, and Demeter, all of which lie behind Orphic fragments, the Gold Tablets, and the Olbia plaques.

In other words, cosmogony-theogony was used to connect cosmic beginnings and human ends, hence informing ideas of the afterlife and penetrating ritual practices. Some of the same myths will be connected to stories of origins of human beings too, which are the subject of chapter 2.

2

First Humans and Their Gods

A Tapestry of Stories

While in the *Theogony* Hesiod compiled views of the origins of the world and the gods, and the creation of woman, Hesiod skips the narration of the assumed "act two" of the creation, the fashioning of humans in general. By contrast, in Genesis and in other Near Eastern mythologies, this stage of creation takes a prominent position after the creation of the first elements and the gods (see chapter 3). Still, in Hesiod's universe, too, we find important ideas about the human condition and our place in the universe vis-à-vis the gods. Especially in the myth of the "Five Races," Hesiod shows Greek communities share with other cultures the idea that there was a break between a "before time," when early human beings interacted directly with the gods, and the historical generations of people, who live harsher lives cut off from divine company, and who interact with the gods only through prayer and ritual, save for exceptional epiphanies or divine interventions.

At first sight, then, Greek mythology is less invested in stories about human creation or anthropogony. It is difficult to ascertain why that is, but perhaps the stories were too many, or too local-looking and idiosyncratic to lend themselves to a unifying myth that would have appealed to the majority of a Greek audience and attained Panhellenic acceptance. As a speaker in one of Plato's dialogues puts it, "[I]t is easier, Timaeus, to appear to speak satisfactorily about the gods to other people, than (to speak) to us all about mortal people"

(Plato, *Kritias* 107a–b). For theogony or cosmogony it might be easier to find consensus, but for human societies the models may be infinite, just as a myriad of traditions would presumably exist about the origins of people and cities.

In the *Theogony* and *Works and Days*, the existence of human beings is a given. They are part of the background to the gods' more important quarrels. But there is a type of motif where human beings become momentarily relevant. Myths often contain mini-stories about the origins of rituals, or explanatory narratives that we call *aitia* or aetiologies (from the Greek *aition*, "cause," "explanation"). The *Theogony* itself, not otherwise too concerned with the world of mortals, contains two such *aitia*: first is the story that explains the ritual of animal sacrifice as first performed by the Titan Prometheus to trick Zeus and favor human beings, who thrived on meat consumption. The chain of events in this Prometheus story leads to the second mythical explanation: how the first woman and marriage came about.

The creation of the first woman and wife is narrated by Hesiod in both of his preserved poems, as we will see. At the same time, scattered allusions to an origin of men from Giants insinuate the human race was "the casual by-product of a violent cosmic drama" (Clay 2003: 98). But the *Works and Days* also offers the "Myth of the Five Races," where a sequence of types of human beings created or established by the gods illustrate their various qualities and flaws, their general moral decline, and their estrangement from the gods. Other ideas about the creation of people are linked to the story of the Flood and tied to local traditions of autochthony (origins from the earth or in one's own land), and yet other theories emerged from theological or natural philosophical speculation. In short, when it comes to human beings, stories of their creation are as varied as the scattered sources in which they appear. Greek myths of anthropogony offer a sharp contrast with the familiar tradition of Genesis, where the creation of humans is central to the creation narrative (and hence highly anthropocentric) and presented as universal.

Perhaps because of this lack of an overarching shared mythology of human origins synthesized in a "sacred narrative," Greek myths on this topic are strikingly peculiar and local. Or perhaps it is the other way around: because of the local attachment to peculiar traditions, poets like Hesiod may have intentionally avoided championing stories that would favor or contradict local versions or not easily fit within his Panhellenic narrative. We cannot even estimate how much variety we are missing, since we are limited to a few sources and variants favored by the few preserved authors. These in turn were revisited time and again by later authors, becoming popular and muffling the wider spectrum of narratives the Greeks were raised with. Sometimes we gain a glimpse of these through allusions in the visual arts and late written testimonies and commentaries. This chapter focuses on the earlier, more widespread sources first, principally Hesiod's poems, and then adds insights about some local and alternative traditions.

A Woman to Pay for the Fire

The creation of the first woman, named Pandora, is part of Hesiod's account of the entanglements of Prometheus with Zeus and with humanity. The episode appears in the *Theogony* (*Th.* 535–616), but it is more developed in *Works and Days* (*WD* 42–105), a poem that fits better in the genre of wisdom literature than epic. In it, Hesiod admonishes his brother Perses about finances and household affairs, agriculture, marriage, justice, and other aspects of life in human society. The story about early human beings is more at home in this poem than in cosmogonic myth, as the *Works and Days* deals with moral and practical matters. Hesiod's treatment of Prometheus and Pandora in both poems is very similar. It is clear that he draws from a single tradition, which he presents from different angles: in the *Theogony* the episode of Prometheus and the (unnamed) first woman is seen from the gods' perspective, while a human perspective calls for a more detailed and humanized story of the woman, now named Pandora, in the *Works and Days* (Clay 2003: 95–99).

Prometheus was a Titan's son. He challenged Zeus's authority repeatedly, and hence the Olympian order. And he does this by helping, and to some degree utilizing, human beings. Prometheus is the "Forethinking," "Predicting" one—that is what his name means. He acted as culture hero and a trickster god, much like Enki/Ea in Mesopotamia, Loki in Norse myth, and trickster gods in various world cultures. Prometheus is most famous for two feats: first, performing the first ritual of animal sacrifice (or manipulating the existing practice) to favor human beings, so they could forever obtain the more edible, nutritious part of the slaughtered animal. There are metaphysical implications to this act: as bread eaters and meat eaters, human beings remain forever mortal, biologically different from the immortals, and also tied to the need of agriculture and fire (Homer, Hesiod, and later Greek writers indeed characterize mortals as bread-eating beings; see, for example, Hesiod, *Theogony* 512) (cf. Figure 2.2). Second, Prometheus famously stole back fire for humans after Zeus had withdrawn it as punishment for the Titan's defiance during the sacrificial distribution. It is in this context, as a *further* punishment, that Pandora comes into the story, while this all happens in an entirely opaque setting. Hesiod places the episode in a particular junction, "when the gods and mortal people were sorting things out at Mekone" (*Th.* 535–36). The verb used (*krino*) can mean to "make a division," or "separate." What was the purpose of this encounter between men and gods? Where was this "Mekone" place, and what were gods and people "sorting out"? We don't hear. Perhaps Hesiod's initial audience was supposed to understand the allusion just by the mention of Mekone. Perhaps the answer is in front of us, and it was the occasion when the gods came to agree on a division of the sacrificial offerings, which is what happens in the story. It is also much debated why Zeus allowed Prometheus to trick him in the first place, even after he noticed what the Titan was doing. The issue of theodicy (divine justice) is relevant here: this situation provided for the perfect excuse to punish a potential rival, Prometheus, who now gains his excruciating eternal punishment. But it also allowed Zeus to reassert his power over human beings. The alternative, that Zeus only pretended not to have been deceived, is unlikely, as Zeus is portrayed as "all-knowing" and his will is the prevailing force in mythical stories.

Even though Prometheus's deceitful behavior backfired, his intention was to secure human livelihood. In the *Theogony*, this is articulated in the sacrificial division episode. He devises a trick whereby the meat is hidden under the animal's entrails (the disposable part of the victim), while the shiny, succulent fat of the animal covers only a heap of bones. Zeus, despite noticing the trick, chooses the fatty, deceitful portion, and so it was established that gods obtain the smoke from the fat and the charred bones of the offering, while people keep the animal's meat, essential for their livelihood (*Th.* 535–60; see Figure 2.1).

In the *Works and Days*, this or a similar deceit is only alluded to, but in both it causes Zeus to exact the next punishment: hiding

FIGURE 2.1 Painted wood panel (*pinax*) representing a sacrificial offering of a lamb and other products, accompanied by flute and lyre playing, sixth century BCE; from Pitsa, near Corinth, Greece. National Archaeological Museum of Athens. Source/Credit: Album/Alamy Stock Photo.

76 GREEK MYTHOLOGY

something himself, fire, which is the technology that made animal sacrifice possible in the first place. Zeus's intent is quite transparent: to preempt human progress and thus keep in check their ambitions and defiant arrogance, their *hybris*:

> *In fact, the gods hold back people's livelihood, hiding it from them;*
> *for you would otherwise easily work even in one day*
> *to have enough for one year, even without working;*
> *(45) soon you would place your steering-oar[1] on top of the fireplace*
> *and the work of the oxen would die out, as that of the hard-working mules.*
> *But Zeus hid it, when he became angry in his heart*
> *that crooked-minded Prometheus (Forethinking) had deceived him.*
> *It was for this reason that he devised sorrowful miseries for human beings.*
> (WD 42–49)

So when "benevolent Prometheus" stole back the fire and hid it to give it back to mortals, Zeus found another way to hinder human progress: woman. Pandora was exactly that, "an evil to pay for the fire, in which all of them will take pleasure in their hearts, while embracing their own suffering" (*WD* 57–58; cf. *Th.* 570), or, in short, "a beautiful evil in place of a good thing" (*Th.* 585). In a way, Pandora perfectly mirrors both Prometheus's sacrifice, since she is a deceitful offering attractively wrapped up, and the stolen fire, since she is at once necessary and desirable but also burning, unpredictable, and destructive.

There are some peculiarities about this Greek anthropogony. First, the story is about the creation of the first woman, not of human beings in general, which is not only oddly lopsided but defies basic logic: if Pandora was the first woman, who were those previous people, the ones meeting the gods at Mekone? Whom did they come

---

[1] This "steering oar" or "rudder" was a part of the plowing mechanism. In the *Odyssey*, Teiresias's ghost tells Odysseus that Poseidon will require of him to perform a hecatomb in such an inland place where people do not know about the sea and confuse an oar for a winnowing-fan, a similar wooden tool used to separate chaff and grain (*Od.* 125).

from? It is important to notice that they are called "people, human beings" (*anthropous*), not "men" (*andres*), even if traditional translations often resort to "man" and "mankind" as a generic. It seems clear that some people preexisted Pandora. Perhaps Pandora was introduced not as *the first* woman, but as a first "wife" (the word *gynaika* was used for both), or more generally an "upgraded," if more wicked version of existing women/wives, to complicate men's simpler existence (cf. Figure 2.6). Whatever the case, the subsequent "race of female women springs from this one," as Hesiod's story goes, which is supposed to explain the male's perception of women as deceitful and dangerously irresistible (*Th.* 589–90).

This female human being was made by hand, like a pot or a statuette. Just as in the widespread Near Eastern traditions, Hesiod chooses clay (literally earth mixed with water) as the prime material for creation (*WD* 60–61). She resembles the terracotta figurines made in Greece in Hesiod's time, often representing daily activities (cf. Figure 2.2). Moreover, she is a gift, and a double-sided one at that: her name means "All Gifts" or "All Gifted." Hephaistos, the craftsman god, conducts the operation, acting as a demiurge god aided by other Olympians who bestow gifts on this primeval woman: Athena gives her skill in crafts, Aphrodite makes her beautiful and desirable, and, to counter so much perfection, Hermes gives her a deceitful and "bitchy" character (*WD* 60–61; cf. *Th.* 571–84). Other gifts are bestowed upon her by the Graces, by Persuasion, and by the Seasons, to deceitfully adorn her lovely shape, all of it by Zeus's orders. In other words, she is a feminine "Trojan Horse," a cautionary tale for the ambiguity and potential danger of gift-giving and shiny appearances, just like the sacrificial portions.

In plastic arts, Pandora is represented coming out of the ground, which is appropriate as she has a nonhuman birth and is made of earth. As she receives her "gifts," Pandora is guided by Hermes to her new husband, who is none other than Prometheus's brother, Epimetheus. Pandora, therefore, is not given as a wife to a mortal man, but to a Titan god. Also, Epimetheus is not only Prometheus's

FIGURE 2.2 Clay figure of a women baking bread along the walls of an oven, from Cyprus, ca. 600–480 BCE. Source/Credit: Metropolitan Museum of Art, New York. The Cesnola Collection, purchased by subscription, 1874–76.

brother but also his "alter-ego." While Prometheus is cunning and "Forethinking" or "Predicting," Epimetheus's name means "Afterthinking" or "Afterthought." He is the obtuse, naïve, and short-sighted husband, unprepared for the complications to come. These complications turn out to be of disastrous proportions, as the first wife comes equipped with yet another deceitful wedding gift: a jar full of maladies and human pains, although it also contains Hope. The image here is of a storage jar or container (*pithos*), which is appropriate in the context of the set-up of a new household. Women were the primary administrators of the house's daily economy in ancient Greece. At the same time, the social stability signaled by marriage, and the surplus that marks a complex economy can be (like woman) ambivalent gifts.

First Humans and Their Gods 79

In another version that could have circulated early on alongside Hesiod's, Prometheus is himself the fashioner not of this female prototype but of human beings at large (*anthropoi*), formed "out of water and earth" (Apollod. *Library* 1.7.1; cf. Pausanias 10.4.4). In Plato's variation on the theme, "the gods" formed human beings "within the earth" using earth and fire, and elements mixed with earth and fire. Then Prometheus and Epimetheus are charged with giving them and other creatures their attributes and defense mechanisms (*Protagoras* 320ff.; see chapter 4). These stories, in any version, establish a bond between human beings and the Titans, in Hesiod a blood-bond, a theme that has ontological implications and is exploited in other creation stories. The lesson to remember, though, is that, just as the Olympian gods or their "employed" Titans were imagined as demiurges or "artisans" in human beginnings, they also had the power, which they exercised, to destroy their creation. I will return briefly to Prometheus's gifts to humankind in the last section of this chapter.

Creation, Destruction, and Human "Devolution"

The myth of the Five Races

After telling his brother Perses the story of Pandora in the *Works and Days*, Hesiod adds another one, to make the point that human beings deteriorated in overall moral quality and life conditions as time passed. It is a fairly common assumption across cultures that people of a faraway past were somehow simpler, in some way purer, and less corrupt (perhaps in parallel to the idea of a universe that evolved from simplicity to complexity). In other words, human beings draw further away from a time in which they lived closer to the gods or even *like* gods, after which divine kinship gradually wears off. This "yet another story" runs parallel to that of Pandora inasmuch as it

80   GREEK MYTHOLOGY

shows the worsening of the human position in the universe, despite the fact that "gods and mortal people have one common origin":

> *And if you want, I will top it off with yet another story,*
> (105) *one I know well too—and try to keep it at heart:*
> *how gods and mortal people have one common origin.*
> *Golden was, at first, the race of human beings,*
> (110) *which the immortals, who hold Olympian mansions, made.*

The Greek term translated as "race" (*genos*) applies to lineages, generations, or types of human beings, without the connotations of "race" in the modern sense. The race or generation of Gold was the first one, followed by those of Silver, Bronze, Heroes, and Iron (*WD* 107–201). Each of them is characterized by their relationship to the governing god, their character, and how they fare in the afterlife. They are identified with metals of different values, as a metaphor for their moral corruption and distancing from a state more similar to the gods. Only the perfectly linear sequence of degrading metals (gold-silver-bronze-iron) does not map onto a perfectly linear quality of the generations, and the race of heroes also seems to interrupt the sequence.

Summing up how these themes play out for each, first the Golden Race lived during the kingship of Kronos (who is often associated with a more primitive and idyllic state of things). It is not said how they were generated, only that they lived almost like the gods, without sorrows or labor. They are honored beneficiary spirits (*daimones*) after death, which makes them somehow immortal. The subsequent races of Silver, Bronze, and Heroes are *made* (verb *poiéin*) under Olympian rule and are progressively disappointing: The Silver Race was made by the Olympians (perhaps not yet by Zeus) but was immature, violent to each other, and impious toward the gods; they behaved childishly and did not reach maturity. They were covered by the earth, whereby they are still considered "subterranean blessed mortals." The Bronze generation that followed was made by Zeus himself "from the ash-trees." These were too strong and violent for their own good and exterminated each other without need for the gods' intervention. These "Bronze Race" people were meat eaters but not bread eaters, hence they are marked as warriors, not farmers; they did not toil the land like historical people but also had no civilization to speak of, and they were characterized by the use of bronze implements and houses. The ancient Greeks associated bronze alloy with the legendary past, before iron became common in the Mediterranean, which is in fact a convention among modern archaeologists, who distinguish between the Bronze Age (until around 1200 BCE in the Aegean and Near East) and subsequent Iron Age period.

The natural next step down the ladder of human "races" should have been the Iron Race, which reached into Hesiod's historical time. But the poet inserted a sort of appendix to the Bronze Race: a race of Heroes (literally "men-heroes"), also made by Zeus, and similar in strength to the Bronze Race. This race, however, comprised the heroes and "demigods" who died with glory in famous wars, such as the Trojan War and the Theban wars. Unlike their nameless predecessors, these heroes' names were remembered in the legends sung in epic poems (Agamemnon, Achilles, Hektor, Eteokles, Polyneikes, and many others). These and other heroic ancestors (presumably including nonwarriors and women too) went on to the Isles of the Blessed where they enjoy a privileged afterlife. The generation of heroes thus provides a dignified backdrop to Hesiod's world, and, through their connections with local royal lineages and traditions, the heroes provide a bridge between the historical and the mythical times.

When the story reaches the fifth and final race, that of Iron, we face Hesiod's "reality," in which all is work and gloom with little bliss, despite some good things mixed in with the bad. It would seem that Pandora's jar had already broken open, although the poet does not integrate these stories in a linear or unified narrative. Hesiod laments belonging to this race and to this time:

82 GREEK MYTHOLOGY

After this, I wish I did not have to be among the fifth group of men,
(175) but that I had died before or been born in later times.
For now indeed the race is of iron; and never during the day
do they rest from toil and hardship, nor by night, when they are worn out,
as the gods will give them troublesome worries.
Though, all the same, these will also have good things mixed with the
bad ones.
(180) But Zeus will destroy this race of mortal people too,
at the time when those who are born come out with gray temples.

The Iron Race has no divine creator but follows the race of Heroes. Despite the contrast in quality, this race may still be seen as a continuation of those heroic demigods. Now, however, devoid of any divine blood, moral corruption or degradation seems unstoppable. As befits a society characterized by their cruelty, envy, impiety, and lack of honor for parents, the Iron Race's prospects are devastating. Even Shame and Indignation (as personified deities), Hesiod predicts, will give up on human beings and will depart from earth to live with the Olympians. We humans are left to our own devices, although Hope may still be somewhere in storage, and we Iron people can still keep injustice in check and let the good Strife (Eris) guide us. This seems to be the main lesson or warning Hesiod is trying to get across his brother Perses (Most 1997). His misplaced priorities fall on the wrong side of the metal spectrum.

*

Whether Hesiod was inspired by motifs he had heard and where those stemmed from, this is a unique story within Greek tradition, a mythological "hapax." We find no other versions or independent allusions to it by Greek or later Roman authors, whose reworkings of it trace back to Hesiod. Distant parallels, however, can be glimpsed in the Iranian tradition about Zoroaster's vision of a tree with branches of gold, silver, steel, and iron representing the world's ages (Bahman Yasht 1.2–5, 2.14–22); in the biblical story about the dream of Babylonian king Nebuchadnezzar II, where the metaphor

First Humans and Their Gods   83

takes the form of a statue made of degrading materials from the metal head to the clay feet (Dan. 2.31–45); and perhaps in the more distant Indian motif of the ages (*yugas*) symbolized by colors and deteriorating in longevity and moral quality (West 1997: 312–19).

The story of the Five Races or Ages has been a favorite of readers and interpreters since antiquity, lending itself to elaborate and attractive interpretations. For some, the "races" represent the maturation phases of a human individual, from the near-divine newborn purity of the Golden Race to the childish character of the Silver Race, passing through the impulsive, violent teenage-hood of the strong Bronze Age. These Bronze Age brutes have their foil in the more perfected adulthood of the Heroes, all of it declining in the Iron Race that represents old age—it seems a more neutral "Middle Age" would remain unrepresented in this scheme. In a different structuralist reading of the myth, the story reflects the archetypical social occupations and orders of Indo-European societies: kings (Gold, Silver?), warriors (Bronze, Heroes), and farmers (Iron) (see Most 1997: 106–7 for an overview).

One of the most accepted modern readings focuses instead on the moral quality of the Five Races and the pattern that emerges when they are contrasted with each other. In this interpretation, the generations either represent *hybris* (arrogance, wrongdoing) or *dike* (justice). If the Golden Race people were just (*dike*) but the Silver ones were impious (*hybris*), the Bronze race people were certainly violent (*hybris*) while the Heroes were more pious and just (*dike*). A ring or chiastic structure thus emerges, with the Iron Race as a synthesis of both outside the pattern, exercising both *dike* and *hybris*, justice and injustice, as Zeus has given both good and evil as their lot to handle (Vernant 1983). Some scholars, in turn, have emphasized the continuity between Heroes and the Iron Race. The Greeks looked back at the Trojan War period as a fixed point in time at the end of what historians and archaeologists call the Bronze Age. So the Heroes provide a historical anchor to the Iron generations, connecting their communities to a heroic past and setting a model to aspire to, so long as the Iron Race had the willpower to avoid becoming completely unjust and be destroyed by the gods. While tiredly tilling

FIGURE 2.3 Woman on a threshing sledge in the countryside of Corinth, Greece, with the Acrocorinth and Temple of Apollo in the distance. Source/Credit: Pericles Papachatzidakis, *Threshing in Old Corinth with Acrocorinth in the Background, 1912–50*. ©Benaki Museum Photographic Archives.

the land with their iron and bronze tools, these generations still looked around to landscapes touched by the gods and heroes of old (see Figure 2.3). In short, we can see the Heroes as concrete "Bronze Age" ancestors, those whose names we know, and they provide a hinge between the purely mythological "races" of people of the historical time of Hesiod (Most 1997; Clay 2003: 81–99).

We can also notice how the human generations map onto the "succession myth," as their creation and existence falls along the line of divine rulers, at least the two main phases marked by Kronos (Gold—Silver?) and his son Zeus (Silver?—Bronze—Iron). In turn, this story alludes to a benevolent patriarchal facet of Kronos, not the one typified in the *Theogony*, where he is but the cruel father of Zeus and his siblings. As a father of the Golden Race, Kronos is here associated with an idealized primitive, "pre-Olympian" time that human beings dwell on with nostalgia. This is even more explicit in some lines of the *Works and Days* in which Kronos is said to rule also over the Race of Heroes, whose souls live in the Isles of the Blessed (*WD* 173a–e)—these lines may not have belonged in the original composition but were added at some point to the poem. There are also echoes of this "Golden Age" Kronos in the verses of Pindar, who sings to the souls of virtuous heroes, who "complete Zeus's road to the tower of Kronos, where Oceanic breezes blow around the Island of the Blessed" (2 *Olympian* 70–71). The Olympians of course bear the title of "Kronides" with pride throughout Greek epic poetry, and the patriarchal Titan was honored at Zeus's most famous sanctuary at Olympia. The trail of this tradition about Kronos continued as the Titan acquired even other positive connotations associated with time and prosperity in magical and Orphic texts (López-Ruiz 2010: 117–19, 161–67; see chapter 1).

The Flood and other breaking points for early humans

Once upon a time, perhaps inspired by a local catastrophe, the Babylonians told a story according to which the gods, upset at humanity's numbers and racket, sent a great flood. They failed to wipe out humanity because a special man received the help of a friendly god, who warned him and instructed him to build a floating home to save himself and his family. This mythology has achieved world fame thanks to its Israelite retelling, the story of Noah's ark in the Hebrew Bible, which adapted it to Israelite theology (more on this in chapter 3). But the trope also reached Greek ears, and we find a very similar flood story among the traditions about early humans, involving Prometheus too, running parallel to the narrative of the Five Races but somehow oblivious to it. No extant epic poem contains this story, but its protagonists, Deukalion and Pyrrha, are mentioned in fragments of the *Catalogue of Women* attributed to Hesiod. They also had roles in Pindar's poems and in lost Greek tragedies, so we know the story was certainly circulating early on (*Catalogue*

Book 1; Pindar, *Ol.* 9.42–46; Epicharmos' play *Deukalion*). The fuller narrative is presented in the summary of Greek myths made by one Apollodoros, sometimes called Pseudo-Apollodoros, in his *Library* or *Bibliotheke* of Greek myths (Apollod. 1.7.2–1.7.3).

It goes something like this: Zeus sends a flood, and Prometheus is again the natural culture hero and human ally. Who better than the Titan who helped human beings regain fire? Unlike in versions we will see in later chapters, the extant Greek story of the Flood does not specify what Zeus's motivations were to send the flood, only that he was about to destroy the "Bronze Age of men," whom we encountered in Hesiod's "Five Races" as that last prehistoric version of humanity before the Heroes and Iron Race. I will return to this Bronze Age's destruction a bit later. It was Zeus, as a Storm god, who took on the pouring of rain and flooding "over the greater part of Greece, so that all men were destroyed, except a few who fled to the high mountains in the area" (*Library* 1.7.2[2]). Prometheus's motivation, however, seems clearer and multiple: he might have wanted to help humans survive in general, as before, while challenging Zeus's authority, but he was also invested because of his family ties. One of those survivors was Deukalion, who was regarded in Greek tradition as a son of Prometheus (opinions about his mother varied). He had married Pyrrha, the daughter of Epimetheus and Pandora. Instructed by Prometheus to build a chest or a boat, Deukalion, however, did not do anything meritorious to be the chosen one; he was simply Prometheus's son.

Most of all, however, the Flood was a restart connected with genealogies of the Greeks. For one thing, this cataclysmic restart (*kataklysmos* is the Greek word for flood or inundation, literally "downpouring") was not imagined as a universal wipeout, but one confined to the Greek world. Moreover, the early testimonies of the story, fragmentary though they are, emphasize the genealogical aspect: Deukalion and Pyrrha begot children who populated Greece.

[2] Translated in Frazer 1921.

In other words, the descendants of the Flood survivors were not ancestors of all the world peoples, as we will see in Genesis, but just of the Greek tribes. The most important of them was their firstborn son Hellen.[3] He was associated with northern Greece (Thessaly), and he became the ancestor of the Hellenes (called after him) or "Greeks." His sons Doros, Xuthos, and Aiolos are the eponymous (i.e., "naming") ancestors of the three main tribal groups of Greek speakers: Dorians, Ionians, and Aiolians (Apollod. 1.7.3; cf. Strab. 8.7.1; Paus. 7.12). In short, the Greek tradition emphasized the role of Deukalion and Pyrrha as forefathers of Greek peoples, and their position at the top of a tree of Greek tribal and dialectal branches. These groups had distinct dialects and religious customs but were still bound by a perception of a common heritage and ancestry, which is one of the main functions served by mythology (Hall 1997: 41–51).

But later Greeks do not only descend from Deukalion and Pyrrha in this way. This couple in a way "sowed" an entire new population without coupling, using the earth's matter by throwing stones over their shoulders, from which males and females sprung, each from the stones thrown by the male and female partner. In this odd procedure they followed divine advice, either coming from Zeus or (in Ovid's version, see chapter 4) from mother Earth herself, through an oracle that instructed them to throw "the bones" of their great mother. Thus, they used earth's matter to make people spring from the earth, which provides a perfect pun between the words for stone (*laas*) and people (*laos*) in Greek, readily used by Apollodoros (cf. Pindar, *Ol.* 9.45–46).

Deukalion, therefore, appears in the *Catalogue of Women* not as a culture hero but because of his position at the top of Greek genealogy; after all, that poem accounted for the descendants of gods and mortals. Stories that establish mythical lineages thus provided an

---

[3] *Hellēn* is the base word for the Hellas and the Hellenes, not to be confused with Helen of Troy.

imagined bridge between the legendary and divine realms and that of mortal communities and families. These ties are crucial for group identities and instrumental for aristocratic and royal lines to promote their status. That is the case with particular heroes who were placed at the top of some lines. For instance, kings of Sparta and of the Argive region claimed descent from the sons of Herakles known as the Herakleidai, just as the kings of Aegina claimed Aiax, son of Telamon, grandson of Zeus, as their ancestor, and the Julio-Claudian family in Rome exploited the narrative of their descent from Venus through the Trojan hero Aeneas, to mention a few. In the case of Deukalion and Pyrrha, the genealogies they head are broader, Panhellenic, hence the importance of this myth. At the same time, the story combines the idea of the cataclysmic restart with a most literal image of autochthony, the indigenous origins (literally "in the same/your own earth/land"), here from the earth itself, an idea promoted by various Greek communities, as we will see.

But we cannot forget another implication of the story, clear and simple: that "gods and mortal people have one common origin," as Hesiod puts it in his opening of the Five Races story (*WD* 108). Some heroes might descend from Zeus or Venus or Poseidon, but humans in general have Titan "blood" running through their veins, if we follow the Prometheus and Deukalion narrative, with Pandora as their main female ancestor, a woman prototype fashioned by the gods. This thread is never forgotten in epic poetry, but it resurfaces in an interesting way in stories linked to Orphic cosmogony (discussed later in this chapter).

In the cosmological scheme of things, the Flood still works as a breaking point with an imagined primeval time when gods and human beings were on closer terms. What for human beings was an end was perhaps for the gods the start of a more desired order, that of an unchallenged Zeus. For the Greeks, the Flood is one of the expressions of the "paradise lost" theme pervasive in so many mythologies and religious traditions, including Hesiod's Five Races and the narrative about the Garden of Eden in Genesis

First Humans and Their Gods

(see chapter 3). But how these stories related to each other is unclear. For instance, if the Greek Flood was sent by Zeus to "destroy the men of the Bronze Age" (Apollod. 1.7.2), why then did Hesiod not mention the Flood as a cause for destruction of his Bronze Race? In the *Works and Days*, the Bronze people destroyed themselves due to their violent, arrogant nature, just as famous wars were the cause of the disappearance of the Race of Heroes, who seem a redeeming final version of the Bronze Race, and more dignified ancestors of the Iron one.

The theme of a cataclysmic end of the heroes (if not by flooding) is more explicit in an early epic tradition according to which Zeus destroyed this race of heroes because their "myriad tribes" were oppressing the earth. Pitying Gaia, the gods' ultimate ancestor and steady seat of immortals and mortals, Zeus devised the Trojan War with the intention that the "weight of death" would "relieve the all-nurturing earth of humankind." This was told in the *Cypria* (fr. 2), one of the poems of the Epic Cycle. These were a group of poems composed after Homer, which narrated all the famous events surrounding the Trojan War, from the Judgment of Paris and the kidnapping of Helen to the fall of Troy and the adventurous return (*Nostoi*) home of the surviving heroes.

Although the theme of impiety and arrogance or *hybris* is not explicit in the *Cypria*, the theme taints heroic behavior in the Homeric poems and the entire tradition about the heroes, such as later on in tragedy. Similarly, the tension between *dike* and *hybris*, as we saw, characterized the human generations in Hesiod. What is more, some have seen reverberations of a "destruction of the heroes by flood" in an episode of the *Iliad* in which the wall built to defend the Greek camp on the beach is destroyed by Poseidon and Apollo (*Il.* 12.1–35). The "Achaean wall" episode "takes on the characteristics of a cleansing event that restores the world of humans and the physical geography back to its primeval state of silence and flatness" (Doak 2012: 127; Scodel 1982). Apollo and Poseidon destroy the wall, not only because *they* are protectors of Troy, whose magnificent

90   GREEK MYTHOLOGY

walls would eventually come to dust, but because the building of this Greek wall itself was an act of *hybris* (*Il.* 7.448–51). The mechanism of destruction is most relevant: they divert entire rivers, causing a flood, although later, in a different passage, Apollo is depicted scattering the wall just like a child playing with sand on the beach, in one of Homer's most universal images (*Il.* 15.361–64). In short, with more or less explicit moralizing emphasis, these and other episodes in Greek epic reveal a tradition in which the Bronze Age or the age of heroes or demigods (*hemitheoi*) came to an end by a divine plan, whether by great wars or cataclysms enacted or allowed by Zeus (Doak 2012: 123–33).

Now, why Zeus might want to please Gaia by alleviating her burden is another, untold story. True, Gaia and Ouranos are the primordial couple, and they give advice or oracles to the succeeding divine rulers, Kronos and Zeus, but it was Gaia who tried to destroy Zeus by begetting Typhon, his last cosmic enemy. Perhaps she knew that with Zeus humanity would grow and thrive and become an insufferable, destructive burden on her, one that not even Zeus (despite his own misgivings and sabotages) could mitigate. In any case, from a human perspective, the gods were less invested in human generations as time passed, and that was Hesiod's lesson.

A note on the gods and humans of the *Homeric Hymns*

Five of the *Homeric Hymns*, the longest ones, narrate the gods' encounters with people at some undefined early time. But who and *when* were these people? Scholars have drawn a correspondence between these humans and those of the Bronze Age (Clay 1989), but it is difficult to map them onto each other in a direct way: unlike Hesiod's Bronze Race, the human societies of the *Hymns* live in regular towns; they eat bread, which requires agriculture; they are not mere worriers but shepherds and traders, even pirates; and we know at least some of their names. In reality, there is no hint as to where these humans of the *Hymns* fit in the grand mythical-historical timeline. We can assume they are post-Diluvian and at least in one case pre-Trojan war characters (Anchises, Aeneas's father, in the *Hymn to Aphrodite*). But in reality they are not marked that way, or framed in relation to other myths (except, again, Anchises). And perhaps that is precisely the point, that these are not intended as human but as divine epics, each capturing one moment or process in the gods' trajectory: in these hymns, some gods are still finding their place among their divine piers (Apollo, Hermes, Demeter, and Persephone), while others depict one single divine adventure or misadventure, as in the case of Aphrodite.

In the grand scheme of divine-human relations, there is an inescapable contrast between the heroic world of the Homeric poems and that of the *Homeric Hymns*, where the gods are aloof and only reached by regular means of religion: prayer, sacrifice, and divination. The hymns celebrate the gods' occasional visible and terrifying manifestation to people by epiphany, but it is a humble, troubled world that the gods visit at different mythical points. Moreover, while the *Hymns* merge family and cosmic drama (Clay 1989) and celebrate the gods' "journey for power" (Penglase 1994), the interventions of the gods on Earth also have utilitarian consequences. For instance, Demeter establishes her new cult center and rites at Eleusis (*Homeric Hymn 2: to Demeter*) and Apollo his main oracle at Delphi (*Hymn 3: to Apollo*), Aphrodite gains a new lineage through Aeneas's conception on Mount Ida (*Hymn 5: to Aphrodite*), and Dionysos seems content with testing and terrorizing mortals (*Hymn 7: to Dionysos*). The *Hymns* seem to confirm that, despite their "common origins," the gap between gods and people has but widened and become insurmountable, except in those moments provided by poetry and storytelling, which reenact famous heroic and post-heroic encounters (see new rendition of Greek hymns in Powell 2021b).

Other Human Births: Myths of Autochthony and Orphic Tales

Myths of autochthony were popular among the ancient Greeks. As we saw, in one story human beings sprung from the "bones of the earth" that Deukalion and Pyrrha threw over their shoulders. Yet in another one they sprang from teeth of a slain dragon, sown on the earth. This motif appears in the foundational story of Thebes. Kadmos, a Phoenician prince, arrived there searching for his sister Europa, who had been kidnapped by Zeus in the form of a bull and carried over his back to Crete. Following a cow (a foil to Europa's bull?), he was led to the place in Boiotia where the Delphic oracle said he would establish a new city, the future Thebes. But he and his companions were confronted with a local dragon. From the teeth of the slain monster sprung the Spartoi or "sown men" (not Spartans), who emerged from the ground fully armed, like Athena from Zeus's head. Behaving as Bronze-Race men of sorts, these Spartoi turned against each other violently, easily prompted by Kadmos as he threw stones in their midst. Five of these autochthonous warriors survived and became the ancestors of the main families of the new city (Apollod., *Library* 3.4.1–2).

Boiotia and its main city, Thebes,[4] seem particularly tied with myths of human origins, some of which acquired Panhellenic status: Deukalion and Pyrrha's landing after the Flood and their subsequent repopulation is connected with Mount Parnassos, on the western end of Boiotia, and Hesiod himself was from Boiotia, where presumably some of his myths of early humans had evolved. In turn, from the lineage of this Kadmos and his divine wife Harmonia (daughter of Ares and Aphrodite) came an entire Theban saga of famous sons and daughters with their own stories, including Semele, who begot the god Dionysos with Zeus. Thebes was also the cradle of Herakles and the tragically famous king Oedipus. We can only wish the

---

[4] Boiotia is the region inland and west of Athens and Attica. See Map 2.

First Humans and Their Gods

ancient long epics about Thebes had been preserved, but we have only mention of a poem called the *Thebaid*. It is probably because of Thebe's proximity and rivalry with Athens that we have access to part of its mythical heritage, to the extent that it became part of Attic culture, and Theban myths became popular materials for Athenian tragedies (e.g., Aeschylus's *Seven against Thebes*, Sophocles's *Oedipus King* and *Antigone*, and Euripides's *Bacchae*).

In another myth, people sprung up from the earth at Colchis on the Black Sea, also from the teeth of a dragon. This was not coincidental; we are talking about the same dragon slain by Kadmos at Thebes, some of whose teeth were given to Jason as part of the seemingly impossible tasks of retrieving the famous golden fleece in Colchis before returning home with his companions the Argonauts. These "sown men," therefore, behaved exactly like the Theban ones, and Jason likewise tricked them with stones into turning against each other (Apollod., *Library* 1.9.16–28). Rocks and bones are entangled in these stories: people can emerge from stones (bones of the earth), or from dragon's teeth (bones of a special, perhaps magical kind), and stones cast intentionally by heroes can cause birth and death (note also the pun between stones and people mentioned previously).

Other ancestral figures in Theban mythology stress autochthony, especially the local heroes Amphion and Zethos. They were sons of Zeus and Antiope, the beautiful daughter of a local river. Their story anchors Thebes in a local mythical landscape as well, but is not connected to the creation of people, as Kadmos's myth is. But the traditions of anthropogony at Thebes exemplify another broader trend, which we will see in Athens as well: autochthony and foreign origins could combine in one tradition. For instance, the Thebans were "Kademeian children" with a tinge of Eastern origins, since Kadmos was a Phoenician prince, but they were also autochthonous, descendants of the "sown" Spartoi (for these Theban myths, see Gantz 1993: 467–88).

Myths of autochthony were also dear to the Athenians and other groups. For instance, Homer describes the inhabitants of Athens as "people of greathearted Erechtheus, whom once Athena, daughter of Zeus, raised, but the lifegiving land bore him" (*Il.* 2.547–48). This is a reference to the tradition about one of the very earliest kings of Athens, named Erechtheus or Erichthonios, who emerged from the earth and had the body of a serpent. The story is connected with the attempted rape of Athena by Hephaistos (foolish attempt), whose seed fell on the ground instead. Depictions show the baby brought forth by Gaia from the earth. Bearing the mark of his chthonic origins in his serpentine body, he was received by Athena, the tutelary goddess of Athens. As often occurs in Greek myth, supernatural events lead to tragedy: Athena placed the hybrid baby in a chest guarded by two snakes, but the daughters of the king, Kekrops, disobeyed the goddess and looked into the chest. Chased by the snakes or by Athena, depending on the version, they ran away and jumped off the Akropolis.

The sources for this Athenian myth are sometimes confusing and reflect a swarm of popular stories that are difficult to streamline (Gantz 1993: 233–38). For instance, we know that the legendary king Kekrops also had the body of a snake (for unknown reasons). As a crawling, earthy, and self-regenerating creature, the snake is connected to the idea of autochthony.[5] The names Erechtheus and Erichthonios, assigned to various legendary kings of the same line and sometimes for the same character, derive from the word for earth, *chthon* (the same root as in "chthonic"). The building known as the Erectheion (see Figure 2.4) on the Akropolis of Athens paid homage to the city's patron gods, Athena Polias ("city protector"), Poseidon, and Hephaistos. Among its many cultic landmarks, it held a live snake (associated with the autochthonous ancestors), an olive

---

[5] In Greece or in the Near East, the snaky body is also the choice for primeval monsters, such as the storm god enemies, Typhon, Tiamat, and others (see chapter 3), and "dragons," which are but giant snakes (from the Greek *drakon*, "snake") that have to be overcome in foundational stories. Some of these led to anthropogony from the soil, as in the case of Kadmos and Jason, and in other cases the clash led to the foundation of a new cult, as when Apollo slew the giant primordial snake Pytho at Delphi.

FIGURE 2.4 Temple known as the Erechtheion, west side (finished in 406 BCE). Source/Credit: Wikimedia Commons.

tree (Athena's symbol), and trident marks left by Poseidon on the rock, from which salty water sprung. But the temple was also dedicated to the city's founding heroes. By its name itself (after Erechtheus/Erichthonios), the complex commemorated the legendary kings of Athens, and it included the tombs of the hero Boutes and of the kings Erechtheus (who shared an altar with Poseidon) and Kekrops, whose daughters were also honored there. Adding layers to its civic symbology, the Classical-period structure sat on top of the Mycenaean palace, a prehistoric site of royalty if any memory of it remained (Pedley 2005: 198–99).

Myths of autochthony sometimes run parallel to migration narratives or genealogies that imply such migration, such as the spread of Dorian, Ionian, and Aiolian tribes from Deukalion and his son Hellen's line. The Athenians had their share of this Panhellenic genealogy connected to the Flood, which established a kinship between the different Greek groups. In particular, the Athenians belonged in the Ionian tribal grouping, which in the *Catalogue of Women* was represented through the marriage of Xouthos (Hellen's son) to a daughter of one of the Athenian legendary kings, also called Erechtheus (Hesiod fr. 10a.20–24). At different points in Athenian history, one narrative or the other was highlighted in literature, depending on whether the author wanted to emphasize difference or kinship with the broader Ionian-speaking world (Hall 1997: 51–56).

The second, and even more famous, temple preserved on the Athenian Akropolis is known as the Parthenon, dedicated to Athena Parthenos ("Virgin"). It stood on and by the remains of previous temples of the goddess and eponymous patroness of the city (while the Erechtheion was a tribute to the human, or semi-human, foundational figures of the city). These monuments were connected through foundational narratives more intensely than we previously thought. In a recent reinterpretation of the Parthenon sculptural program, Joan Connelly has argued that the famous Parthenon friezes allude directly to these legendary Athenian kings and their tragic story—in particular to the story that one or all three of Erechtheus's daughters died on behalf of the city in order to stop a dragging war, which also led to the establishment of the first priesthood to Athena on the Akropolis. The little-known story is one of "ultimate sacrifice that resonates with those central to foundational myths in Judaism and Christianity and in other cultures" (Connelly 2014: 335–36). This myth was possibly fundamental in the city's identity, despite being scantly attested in texts. Recent additional fragments of a tragedy *Erechtheus* by Euripides, however, has aided the reconstruction of the myth and its link to the ritual and mythical cityscapes of classical Athens (Connelly 2014: esp.126–48). If this interpretation is correct, the viewer would be presented with several mythological levels, compacted in this monument: from the local, foundational myth (in the frieze), to Panhellenic myths involving heroic wars against Trojans, Centaurs, and Amazons in the metopes (also the fight between gods and Giants), to the theogonic level, with the representation of the birth of Athena on the east pediment, over the main entrance of the building.

The rivalry between Athena and Poseidon for the patronage of Athens was featured on the Parthenon's west pediment, reflecting cultural and civic identities in tension, the local and the Panhellenic: Poseidon represents the sea-born inclination of Athens, shared with the Ionians across the Aegean, while their patron goddess Athena and her olive tree represent their unique local character and their pride in craftsmanship and intellectual prowess. In the contest for the city's patronage, it is Athena who defeats Poseidon, the land versus the sea, but the city remained driven by both centripetal and centrifugal forces. Hephaistos is a third leg in this local set of divine patrons, representing the city's industrious nature and reliance on "making," not only trading (cf. chapter 4). Appropriately, the god was also said to be born from the earth, like Erichthonios, in one version of his genealogy (Gantz 1993: 233).

Like Erechtheus/Erichthonios, other local founding figures were thought of as "earth-born" (*gegenes* is the word Herodotus uses, Hdt. 8.55). So were the first king of Lakonia and that of Miletos, and the first inhabitant of Arcadia, called Pelasgos. In fact, "Pelasgians" became a term used by historians for the original (autochthonous) inhabitants in the Peloponnese, Attica, and other areas of the Aegean in general (Map 2). Insects could also be associated with anthropogony. This is the case in a tradition about Achilles's soldiers, the Myrmidones from Phthiotis in Thessaly, who were said to originate as hard-working obedient ants turned into soldiers by a god, all probably because their name brought to mind that of the insects (Ovid., *Met.* 7.650–60).[6]

Rivers and springs were usually divinized and associated with nymphs. Nymphs were lesser nature divinities whose number could increase as much as needed to animate ancient landscapes. But

---

[6] Although not rising to the level of anthropogony, the Athenians were especially attached to cicadas as an earth-born insect that symbolized their autochthony. The summer insects appeared in tokens issued in Hellenistic-period Athens, and, according to Thucydides, distinguished Athenian men before his time wore cicada adornments in their hair (Thuc. 1.6.3).

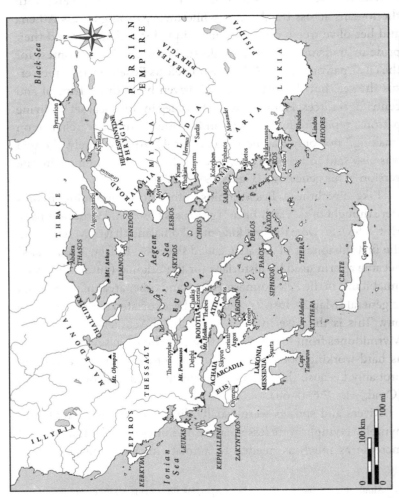

MAP 2 Greece and the Aegean in the Archaic-Classical periods. Source/Credit: Map by Alliance USA.

First Humans and Their Gods 99

sometimes heroes were themselves born from or gave their names to local rivers, such as the first king and fire-bringer hero Phoroneus of Argos, a sort of local Prometheus, who was born from the Inachos River (Paus. 2.15.5; see Hall 1997: 53). In turn, Hesiod makes his Bronze Race come from ash trees (*WD* 145), perhaps referring to the Ash-Tree Nymphs or Nymphs Meliai, who were born from Ouranos's severed genitals in the *Theogony* story. This might reflect a pre-Greek, Indo-European tradition linking human origins with trees and stones, a basic pair connected to origins and divine knowledge in Hesiod and in Near Eastern mythology (López-Ruiz 2010: 62–72; Nagy 1990: 181–201). Similar tropes surface much later on in Virgil's *Aeneid*, when one character (Evander) says that the Latin peoples were born from "tree trunks and hard oaks" (*Aen.* 8.314) and another (Latinus) that they were descended from Saturn directly (*Aen.* 7.202). By the Archaic period, in any case, pre-Socratic thinkers sought explanations for human beginnings that stayed away from these divinized landscapes and natural elements. Still, philosophers such as Anaximander postulated people's origins in fish or fish-like animals, and Plato returned to divine agency, but they put a very different spin on those traditional tropes about origins (see chapter 4).

Finally, we return to the connection between human origins, the Titans, and Dionysos (see Figure 2.5). As we saw in chapter 1, the so-called Zagreus myth was central to Orphic theogony. According to the generally accepted reconstruction, the Titans had devoured infant Dionysos (called Zagreus), whereupon Zeus had stricken them with lightning. Human beings were then born "from the soot of the smoke that arose from them," and Dionysos was reborn from Zeus. While allusions to Dionysos's dismemberment appear in earlier literature, we only have one source that ties this theogonic event with the birth of a new human race. Olympiodoros, a Neoplatonic philosopher writing in sixth-century CE Alexandria, brings the story into his commentary to Plato's *Phaedo*, where Socrates alludes to a secret myth that provides an argument against suicide, namely, that "the gods are our guardians and we people are one among the

FIGURE 2.5 "The Victory of Dinysos" in a Roman-era mosaic, with the god carried by panthers and accompanied by winged Nike ("Victory") and a Maenad (Bakche). Zeugma Mosaic Museum, Gaziantep, Turkey. Source/ Credit: Wikimedia Commons.

properties of the gods" (*Phaedo* 62b). Olympiodoros thinks Plato is referring to the Orphic myth of Zagreus, which was tied to the Orphic-Bacchic mysteries. He puts together the story from oblique and vailed references in earlier literature (or some sources we don't know) and adds the previously undocumented idea of the birth of humans from the mix of Titanic and Dionysiac matter, hence concluding that

> we should not commit suicide on account of our bodies being Dionysiac. For we are part of him [Dionysos], to the degree that we are composed from the soot of the Titans after they had eaten his flesh.[7]

[7] Olympiodoros, *Commentary on Plato's Phaidon* 1.3, on *Phaidon* 62b; 41 Westerink = OF 304 I, 318 III, 320 I.

Because this anthropogony from Dionysos is not attested earlier, some scholars have doubted its existence in Orphism (Edmonds 2013: 375–90). But most agree that there are grounds for the reconstruction of an earlier Zagreus myth, since other aspects of the Dionysos death and rebirth are attested (Meisner 2018: 248–53). The problem is that Orphic texts, including their summary in the *Rhapsodies*, are only preserved in scattered allusions, and details told in the mysteries were secretive by definition, which explains why they come to light in later sources. If the birth of people from this Titan-Dionysiac matter was indeed part of the earlier mythology, however, we would have yet another, more direct tie between human beings and the rebellious Titan gods, to which a superior divine element was added through Dionysos, son of Zeus. In any case, the connection between humankind and the gods, especially the Titans, has deep roots in stories of human origins, as we saw in the myths of Prometheus-Pandora and the Five Races. Whatever the version, something made the initiates who used the "Bacchic-Orphic" Gold Tablets (cf. Figure 1.6) call themselves "the sons of Earth and Starry Heaven," that is, Titans.

Sacrifice, Marriage, and the Question of Hope

In the introductory lines of the *Works and Days*, Hesiod invokes the Muses and calls on Zeus to listen to his poem. This time, however, the topic is not Zeus's lineage and struggles with the gods, but advice on human matters, in the form of admonitions and exemplary stories that Hesiod tells his brother Perses, and by extension all of us interested in reflecting on what life in community means and the hardships of the human condition. Still, the will of Zeus is always the ultimate factor, for a simple reason:

> *Through him mortal men are with or without fame,*
> *spoken of or unspoken of, thanks to great Zeus.*

102   GREEK MYTHOLOGY

> For easy he makes one mighty, and easy he crushes the mighty one,
> easily he reduces the conspicuous and makes the inconspicuous thrive,
> and easily he straightens the bent one and bends down the arrogant,
> Zeus, who thunders up high, who inhabits the highest dwelling.
> Pay heed to me [o Zeus], watching and listening, and you yourself [Zeus]
> set straight the ordinances justly; as for me, I will proclaim truths to
> Perses. (WD 3–10)

Zeus, in other words, controls the wheel of fortune, the seemingly capricious reversals that can raise the humble and crush the powerful, an idea we can see almost universally in literature, and expressed in the Hebrew tradition in very similar wording, as in the poem known as "The Song of Hanna" inserted in the second Book of Samuel:

> For the Lord is a God of knowledge,
> And by him actions are weighed…
> The Lord kills and brings to life, he brings down to Sheol and raises up.
> The Lord makes poor and makes rich;
> he brings low, he also exalts.
> He raises up the poor from the dust;
> he lifts the needy from the ash heap,
> to make them sit with princes…
> The Lord! His adversaries shall be shattered;
> the Most High will thunder in heaven.
> The Lord will judge the ends of the earth;
> he will give strength to his king,
> and exalt the power of the anointed. (I Samuel 2:1–10[8])

The power of these thundering gods, Yahweh and Zeus, is described similarly. They grant justice on earth and protect human leaders— whomever they choose to. The connection between kings in heaven

---

[8] Translations from the Hebrew Bible follow the NRSV (New Revised Standard Version), sometimes slightly modified.

First Humans and Their Gods 103

and kings on earth was an obvious move in a largely monarchic society (this was highlighted also in the role of Hekate in the *Theogony*). There were also alleged descendants of demigods walking the earth, and claim to a divine line legitimized houses of kings and founding figures in many Greek cities. But there is a more general tie that pertains to all mortals: whether as descendants of Pandora and Epimetheus, or the children of Deukalion and Pyrrha, as members of devolving generations created by Kronos or by Zeus or sharing in the Titan's lineage, Greek stories return to the idea that mortals and immortals perhaps share a common origin.

Sacrifice

Despite their possible points in common, the partition of the sacrificial meal by Prometheus illustrates the inexorable difference between gods and human beings: mortality. The gods are *athanatoi* and *aphthitoi* ("deathless" and "unperishable") while humans are but decaying creatures, slaves to the need to feed themselves, "bread eaters" (*sitophagoi*) (*Od.* 9.191; cf. *Il.* 13.32) and "mere stomachs," as the Muses called them (*Th.* 26). The gods do not eat bread or drink wine, only nectar and ambrosia. Likewise, they do not have blood as humans do, but a substance called *ichor*, as Homer explains, "and that is why they are bloodless and are called deathless" (*Il.* 5.340–42). There is a virtue in human attachment to bread and cooked meat: an enraged Achilles is accused of eating raw flesh, hence he is deemed untrustworthy (*Il.* 24.207–8), and the monstrous Cyclopes live without agriculture, and hence are represented as lawless, without a community and without respect for the gods, even if they are themselves half-divine (*Od.* 9.105–35) (Kitts 1994). More generally, rites of animal sacrifice and, as importantly perhaps, stories about them were about boundaries, they "affirmed the central (mediating) position of humanity between gods and beasts" (Buxton 1981; Detienne and Vernant 1989). Cannibalism occupies an exceptional place in the spectrum of mortal meat-eating, bringing humans closer to animals and symbolizing a transgression of human and divine order, as we can see in the story of Lykaon (see chapter 4), or in those of entire accursed mythological lines, such as those of Pelops and the House of Atreus.

It is no coincidence that animal sacrifice, fire, and marriage, then, occupy the spotlight in the only myths involving human beings in the *Theogony* and *Works and Days*, besides the story of the "Five Races." Sacrifice and marriage are social institutions that articulate and sanction two basic needs: food and sex, both indispensable for the survival of the human species. Sacrifice was not only religiously relevant as an offering to the gods, but it was inseparable from the cooking and communal consumption of meat from domesticated animals. It represented a sedentary socioeconomic order that evolved from that of hunting and gathering. Connected to it, fire is not only essential for the performance of animal sacrifice; the manipulation of fire distinguishes early humans from their fellow animals. Fire makes possible cooking meat, forging metals, and warding off cold temperatures and wild life. If biological anthropologists are right, perhaps it led to a change of diet that allowed hominids to devote less energy to digesting and more to developing their large brains (Wrangham 2010).

As Zeus intended when he hid fire from mortals, without fire there was no sacrifice and no cooking of meat to begin with. Hence Prometheus was the quintessential ally of human progress, which positions him somehow as a challenger of Zeus's authority. The punishment Prometheus suffered for his intervention is one of the most famous in mythology: he was tied to a high rock, where an eagle would devour his liver every day, after it regenerated at night (Apollod., *Library* 1.7.1). He was at one point liberated by Herakles. A lesson for human beings is, perhaps, that pleasing the gods, whether to secure their support, prevent their negative intervention, or pay them back for their favors, requires a ritual and familial structure, which are also ingrained in mechanisms of survival of the species.

First Humans and Their Gods 105

But there is another side to this development: if there is no species, there is no worship, and the gods cannot be pleased, so perhaps they lose their raison d'être altogether. That interdependency became quite explicit in the *Homeric Hymns*.

Marriage, strife, and hope

Through the story of Pandora, Hesiod reflects on the hardships of human life in his society, including marriage. Hesiod expands on Pandora's role as the prototype of women and wives in the *Theogony* (*Th*. 590–612), where he makes clear that from her comes the entire "race" or "family" (*genos*) of human women. On the cosmogonic plane, women are, like marriage, a sort of trap laid out by Zeus. Marriage is a necessary constraint on a presumably better, freer existence, a necessary social norm. Hesiod admits not marrying can be as bad as marrying an exploitative wife, and good things come with the right marriage too. But there is an upside of all this: predictability. The technology of fire makes agriculture and food processing possible, and marriage offers sanctioned and predictable sex and procreation. Technological advancements and social constrains mark the toiling existence of the Iron Age, but they allow this "race" of humans to not entirely depend on the gods, so far as they can sustain their own mechanisms and strategies of protection and survival. Prometheus, "Forethinking," and his gifts literally represent predictability and prevention, in contrast to his brother Epimetheus, "Afterthinking," who is pure impulse, pure reaction. Of course, this may be just what Zeus wanted, and the reason he allowed Prometheus to challenge him and to help mortals, so as to justify Zeus's subsequent "punishment by marriage." In a calculated way, this new state of existence meant humankind could cope with life while it kept them sufficiently insecure and dependent on Zeus, ensuring the continuous worship (with fire) of the god of law and justice. He was,

FIGURE 2.6 Vase-painting representation of a bride preparing for her wedding and receiving a container of cosmetics or jewelry; attributed to the Eretria Painter, ca. 440 BCE–415 BCE; from Attica, Greece. Source/Credit: British Museum, Creative Commons.

perhaps, now more necessary than ever in a more complex and frustrated society.

With Pandora's dowry came the maladies of the world, concentrated in a *pithos*. This is a container in which one might have stored olive oil or grain or wine, even though it is popularly represented as a box in modern reception of the story (see Figure 2.6: the wedding scene contains a meta allusion, as the ceramic container with the painting was probably gifted to a young woman at her wedding in real life). In Hesiod's story, Pandora opens the jar and sets loose all the evils of the world, leaving only Hope hidden in the jar. In this way, Pandora falls into the common trope of female irresponsible curiosity, just as Eve in Genesis (cf. chapter 3), only here not contravening a divine prohibition. But we should hear it from Hesiod himself, following the stealing of fire and the creation and endowment of Pandora (*WD* 90–100):

(90) *For before this the tribes of men used to live*
far apart from evils and apart from harsh pains
and from distressful diseases, which now give death to men.
[For in anguish mortals quickly turn old.]
But woman scattered them, after she lifted the great lid of the jar
(95) *with her hands. And so she conceived miserable sorrows for humankind.*
Only Hope remained there, in its indestructible home,
under the rim of the jar, and it did not fly away;
for, before it could, she put the lid back on the jar
by the plans of the aegis-bearer, the cloud-gatherer Zeus.
(100) *But another thousand miseries roam about among human beings.*

Hesiod repeats the somber fact that *it is not at all possible to evade the mind of Zeus* (WD 105). This is what Zeus wanted, somehow. But the presence of Hope (*Elpis*) in the jar is one of the most puzzling images in early Greek literature. Hope, we read, was hidden under the rim, and stayed there. What does this mean? If Hope is a good thing, what was it doing in the jar in the first place? Is Hope an evil, namely "false hope," or is it kept there as a remedy to attenuate so much misery? Or, on the contrary, did it perhaps stay there by the will of Zeus, so we do *not* even have hope? Most scholars lean toward the reading that Hesiod meant a crippling, "blind hope." This is what Aeschylus implied when his Prometheus says it is his fault that mortals do not foresee their own doom (death), as he caused "blind hopes" (*typhlas elpidas*) to dwell within people's hearts. Here is the exchange with a Chorus of Oceanids (daughters of another more submissive Titan, Ocean):

Chorus: *Did you perhaps transgress even somewhat beyond this offence?*
Prometheus: *Yes, I caused mortals to cease foreseeing their doom [death].*
Chorus: *Of what sort was the cure that you found for this affliction?*
Prometheus: *I caused blind hopes to dwell within their breasts.*
Chorus: *A great benefit was this you gave to mortals.*

108   GREEK MYTHOLOGY

Prometheus: *In addition, I gave them fire.*
Chorus: *What! Do creatures of a day now have flame-eyed fire?*
Prometheus: *Yes, and from it they shall learn many arts.*
Chorus: *Then it was on a charge like this that Zeus—*
Prometheus: *Torments me and in no way gives me respite from pain.*
Aeschylus, (*Prometheus Bound* 249–58[9])

Others take the word *elpis* to convey neutral "anticipation" of good or bad things. But the ambiguity remains: If it is a purely negative quality, it is not clear why Hope did not fly out of the jar to plague the world with the other evils. We seem trapped in a circular reflection of what is better, to feel or not to feel anticipation or hope (is it worse to risk frustration or to lose motivation?), and perhaps that was exactly what Hesiod wanted. It is still not out of the question that this *elpis*, "hope, expectation," may be a gift to human beings, surreptitiously mixed in by Zeus himself with the evils, stored in the clay container for us to preserve along with other resources we might need when hard times arrive. As the first wife stores both good and bad things for the household, she may be imagined also as the one who can first access Hope when things go south. Hope can be the only resource available for a family or an individual in the face of unpredictable illnesses and disgrace that come their way (entire populations who lack health insurance might relate, with hope to avoid illnesses as the only resource they have been left with). Perhaps Zeus allows Hope to remain in the household storage as a resource against the unpredictability that Epimetheus represents.

In Homer we find a similar metaphor of storage jars (*pithoi*) containing good and bad destinies (*Il.* 24: 524–33). After sharing with Priam (the father of Hektor) a bout of grieving, Achilles makes this reflection about the inevitability of human fate and the futility of grieving:

[9] Translated in Smyth 1926.

For there is no advantage to be won from chilling lamentation.
(525) Such is the way the gods spun life for unfortunate mortals,
That we live in unhappiness, but the gods themselves have no sorrows.
There are two jars that stand on the door-sill of Zeus.
They are unlike for the gifts they bestow: a jar of evils, and jar of blessings.
If Zeus who delights in thunder bestows a mix of these
(530) on anyone, sometimes he meets with evil, other times with
good fortune.
But when Zeus bestows from the jar of sorrows, he makes him
a failure, and evil misery drives him over the shining
earth, and he wanders respected neither of gods nor mortals.[10]

Another ambiguous notion, that of Strife (Eris), looms large in the *Works and Days*. The poem, after all, is motivated by the quarrel between the two brothers, Hesiod and Perses, who were entangled in an inheritance litigation. According to Hesiod, there are two types of Strife on Earth: There is the blameworthy, oppressive, and cruel Strife, which fuels wretched war and conflict, and there is a praiseworthy Strife, the one that arises from envy of your neighbor's prosperity and stirs people (the farmer, the builder, the poet, anyone) to work harder, a Strife that is "good for mortal people" (*WD* 11–26). This productive competition represents the often-cited agonistic streak in ancient Greek society, fostered by more inclusive and engaging political framework of the city-states and by the display of virtue and wealth at Panhellenic sanctuaries and festivals, among other factors. The good and bad Strife can be blamed for booms of extraordinary artistic, scientific, and intellectual achievements we owe to the Greeks, as well as for the inter-polity conflict that devastated these same communities in long wars.

*

[10] Translated in Lattimore 1961, modified.

110 GREEK MYTHOLOGY

In the end, the poems of Homer and Hesiod share a sense of human helplessness before the gods' power and manipulation. After all, "it is not possible to evade the mind of Zeus" (e.g., Homer, *Il.* 1.5; Hesiod, *WD* 105). But even in the worse circumstances, it is possible to seek and hope for improvement (good Strife), displace envy with compassion, and, when possible, find enjoyment in life's simple things. In his encounter with Priam, Achilles comes to accept the mortal condition and feels empathy toward the old man, in whom he sees his own father, who will one day mourn him too (*Il.* 24.440–676). Their exchange contains a type of wisdom we find already in the Mesopotamian *Epic of Gilgamesh*. It is also in an encounter with an old wise man, the survivor of the Flood, Ut-napishtim, that the young hero finds a similar humbling lesson. I quote the key lines in this excerpt of Tablet X:

> *"[Why (?)] have you exerted yourself? What have you achieved (?)? You have made yourself weary for lack of sleep, you only fill your flesh with grief, you only bring the distant days (of reckoning) closer. Mankind's fame is cut down like reeds in a reed-bed.... Nobody sees Death, nobody sees the face of Death, nobody hears the voice of Death. Savage Death just cuts mankind down. Sometimes we build a house, sometimes we make a nest, but then brothers divide it upon inheritance. Sometimes there is hostility in [the land], but then the river rises and brings flood-water. Dragonflies drift on the river, their faces look upon the face of the Sun, (but then) suddenly there is nothing [etc.].*[11]

With these images the wise old man expresses the futility of conflict. A more positive but similar "carpe diem" reflection circulated in the Old Babylonian version of *Gilgamesh*. This time it is uttered by a woman called Siduri, an independent tavern-keeper. In contrast to the tale of Pandora, Siduri makes the gift of family and women a

---

[11] Translated in Dalley 2000, *Epic of Gilgamesh*, Standard Version, Tablet X.vi.

First Humans and Their Gods

desirable thing to keep you grounded in the day-to-day appreciation of life, as she speaks thus to a worn-down Gilgamesh:

> *Gilgamesh, where do you roam? You will not find the eternal life that you seek. When the gods created mankind, they appointed death for mankind, kept eternal life in their own hands. So, Gilgamesh, let your stomach be full, day and night enjoy yourself in every way. Every day arrange for pleasures. Day and night, dance and play. Wear fresh clothes. Keep your head washed, bathe in water. Appreciate the child who holds your hand, let your wife enjoy herself in your lap.*[12]

Hesiod was especially concerned with the loss brought about by family divisions and strife, and he composed the *Works and Days* around this theme. At the heart of the poem is the point that material resources were once easily given by the gods but are now scarce; it is no wonder that most of our energies focus on how to acquire them, administer them, and protect them. Perhaps Hesiod could have used Siduri's words to diffuse the fraternal conflict and also remind Perses that we only live once, and we must find happiness in the midst of all those divine-inflicted human obstacles and distractions.

---

[12] Translated in Dalley 2000: 150.

3

Facing East

An Eastern Mediterranean Context

Classical scholars have for centuries read Greek and Roman literatures in tandem and studied them as part of a single foundational corpus of texts, which formed a canon for European culture. The literatures from the ancient Near East[1] followed a very different path, since most of their texts were only discovered in the nineteenth and early twentieth centuries, at a time when orientalist views, colonialism, and European race ideologies exacerbated the divide between "East" and "West." The Hebrew Bible was an exception, as a body of literature stemming from the Levant that had made it into the Western canon through its adoption by Judaism and Christianity. After a century of archaeological and philological work and half a century of interdisciplinary debate, we have learned how much we miss by reading Greek myths as if they had formed in a cultural airlock (e.g., Bernal 1987; Burkert 1992; Lane Fox 2008; West 1997— West's book *The East Face of Helikon* inspired this chapter's title). Since Greek speakers settled in the peninsula that extends from the Balkans to the Aegean in the early second millennium BCE, they became increasingly immersed in a world shared by people

---

[1] For the sake of simplicity, I use the traditional term "Near East" to refer to the cultures of Anatolia, the Levant, Mesopotamia, and also Egypt. In more specialized scholarship, Egypt (in North Africa) is not grouped with the Near East. There is a movement to avoid "Near East" altogether as a Eurocentric term, using Middle East, West Asia, and North Africa instead for these regions and their ancient cultures.

112

who spoke other languages and worshipped other gods. They had already fused with pre-Greek inhabitants of Hellas when they became close neighbors with Near Eastern groups from Egypt, the Levant, and Anatolia (see Map 1). As communications increased during the first millennium, aided by a renewed literacy and Greek colonization of areas east and west of the Aegean, Greek speakers and Near Eastern groups knitted closer networks in areas of intense contact, such as the Levant, Crete, Euboia, Cyprus, and even southern Italy.

When we bring Near Eastern creation stories to the fore, classical myth becomes part of a richly textured canvas. Greek stories stand out against a much deeper background of similar themes, articulated in earlier iterations by various neighboring cultures, each according to its own traditions and theologies. The very idea of "classical" mythology and the "classical culture" is transformed by the exercise of comparison. Opening up Greco-Roman mythology to the influx of ideas and literary tropes from the broader Mediterranean world helps us appreciate this heritage in a fresh way, not as an immutable or impermeable block of referential works that represent Western culture, rigidly handed to us through Alexandrian, Roman, medieval, and later scholarship, but as part of an evolving tradition, whose literature was richly integrated into a wider network of religions and mythologies, only a tiny part of which has been salvaged for posterity. As Mondi (1990: 144) summarized it, the comparison between Greek and other eastern Mediterranean and Near Eastern myths opens up "a more extensive nexus of mythic themes and ideology common to Greek and Near Eastern thought. In essence, it increases for our consideration the number of realizations of a mythic idea."

In this section I focus only on particular themes that provide evident overlap or offer most interesting contrasts. These Near Eastern stories represent mythologies that the Greeks themselves were in dialogue with, and indeed they shaped some of the adaptations and innovations that made the Greek stories what they are. Second,

114   GREEK MYTHOLOGY

some of these narratives were "classical" in their own terms in the ancient Mediterranean world, meaning they circulated widely and became canonical, producing imitations and adaptations, so that their influence was enormous in later traditions. Some of them have had direct impact in Western culture independently, especially those in the Hebrew Bible. But most came out of oblivion only with their discovery and decipherment in the nineteenth and twentieth centuries. Such is the case of Egyptian and Mesopotamian texts, and even less-well known Hittite and Ugaritic epics. These recovered narratives have given us access to new universes of literature and mythology, and it is fascinating to uncover the ways in which Greek myth-telling, knowingly or not, interacted with these contiguous traditions. Lastly, there came a time when the entire Near East became enveloped in Hellenistic and Roman cultures, and versions of Greek myth were overlaid on a millenary literary and religious heritage. As we will see in chapter 4, centuries of cultural and intellectual adaptation produced fascinating narratives that fused Near Eastern and Greek traditions, including classical themes, such as the succession myth or the Flood, now reinterpreted through new philosophical and religious lenses.

Primeval Elements and Modes of Creation

In the beginning when God created the heavens and the earth,
the earth was a formless void and darkness covered the face of the deep,
while a wind from God swept over the waters.
Then God said, "Let there be light"; and there was light...
—Genesis 1.1–3

These lines open the Book of Genesis, providing what, in the long arc of history, has become the best-known cosmogony in the Western world. The Hebrew Bible redactors presented a polished narrative that they attributed to the founding figure, lawgiver, and prophet

Moses. In fact, they encoded not one but two more or less harmonious versions of the creation in Genesis 1 and 2, which convey different details and vary in their emphases. It is practically impossible to know exactly when (or how, or by whom) these lines were fixed, but we know that by the time the Torah was put together as we know it, it contained collected, collated, edited, and rewritten materials spanning many centuries and literary genres, which had evolved in different periods and contexts (Alter 2011). Some of the long narratives, songs, and passages deepen their roots in the Late Bronze Age (ca. 1550–1200 BCE); most were gestated during the ensuing centuries of the early Iron Age (twelfth–ninth centuries BCE); and others still later on, even during the captivity of Jews in Babylon in the sixth century and after. With all its originality, this monotheistic cosmogony integrated and adapted elements inherited from the ancestral lore passed down in the region of Syria-Palestine for centuries, and more broadly from the Canaanite, Mesopotamian, and Egyptian backdrop against which the Israelites were constructing their unique religious worldview (e.g., Carr 1996; Niditch 1997; Cross 1998; Smith 2002). In these motifs we also will find parallels and contrasts with the Greek traditions discussed in chapters 1 and 2.

The first lines of Genesis show creation in action, right away. There is no proem or preamble, no invocation of some external inspiring voice, no Muses or justification of the narrator's authority. There is no need to track the genealogies of the gods (no theogony), as there is only one god in this cosmogony, the god of the Israelites. He is called Elohim or Yahweh, depending on the tradition the passage is drawing on. The first name means "God" (literally "Gods," as Elohim is a plural form), and the second is of obscure etymology but it was read as "The Lord" or "Adonai." We can remember how the Geek cosmogony of Hesiod laid out the first primordial elements that simply "existed" and that set the universe in motion: Chaos, Earth, the Underworld, and Love. In contrast, the first sentences in Genesis present the creation as a methodical, symmetrical, logical action by an intellectual, detached god, Elohim.

This orderly emphasis is consistent with the formal repetitive style of the Priestly source (P) of the Pentateuch or Torah, which uses the name Elohim and is especially concerned with legal and ritual order as well as genealogies. The creation narrative in these opening lines of Genesis contrasts with those in Genesis 2–3, attributed to different redactors. This source is known as Yahwist or Jahwist (J), as in it the Israelite god is called Yahweh. As we will see, this second account centers on the divine-human conflict (the Eden story) and the complications of human free will. As Robert Alter (1996: 7) states, "[w]hatever the disparate historical origins of the two accounts, the redaction gives us first a harmonious cosmic overview of creation and then a plunge into the technological nitty-gritty and moral ambiguities of human origins." As he also points out, it may be that the redactors deliberately combined these accounts as literary expression of a subject that was "essentially contradictory, essentially resistant to consistent linear formulation" (Alter 2011: 145).

The Genesis 1 creation contains primeval elements: the heavens and the earth, a "formless void and darkness" (*tohu-wa-bohu*), akin to the Greek concept of *chaos*, wind ("a wind from God"), and water. The prominence of water in this primeval scenario, as well as the mention of heaven and earth, harkens back to a Mesopotamian tradition preserved in the Babylonian creation poem. This epic is known mainly from the copies compiled in the Neo-Assyrian palace library, in the seventh century BCE, which makes this version roughly contemporary with the poetry of Hesiod and parts of the Hebrew Bible. But the story goes back to at least the late second millennium BCE, when experts believe the epic known as *Enuma elish* was composed. The first words of the poem, "*Enuma elish...*," serve as its "title," following an ancient method, in this case meaning "When on High"—in the Hebrew Bible, too, the first words of each book were used to refer to it, such as "*Be-reshit*" ("In the beginning") for Genesis, etc. It is worth quoting the first lines of *Enuma elish*:

When the skies above were not yet named, nor earth below pronounced by name, Apsu, the first one, their begetter and maker Tiamat, who bore them all, had mixed their waters together, but had not formed pastures, nor discovered reed-beds; when yet no gods were manifest, nor names pronounced, nor destinies decreed, then gods were born within them. (*Enuma elish*, Tablet I[2])

The skies and earth are mentioned first, but only to say they had no name yet, just as other realms of the world had not been named yet and therefore were unclassified, unordered, and to all effects nonexistent. A straight correlation is drawn between names and ontology, between language and organization. The same philosophical principle is present in Genesis 1, as Yahweh creates from his intellect and brings realms of nature into creation and defines them. A more physical image appears in Genesis 2:4–5: "In the day that the Lord God made the earth and the heavens, when no plant of the field was yet in the earth and no herb of the field had yet sprung up." Here Yahweh plans out the world as an artisan or a landscaper. The image is even stronger in the passages that follow in which he "fashions" human beings as a painter or sculptor does, an action described with the verb *yatzar*, "to design," "to craft." In Greek myth, the bestowing of names on the elements is not problematized; the Sky, Earth, and the rest all come into the cosmos with their names, and when we use the word "cosmos" we are using a Greek term that means "order, arrangement" and also "adornment."

Returning to the importance of water, we can note that in *Enuma elish* the primeval gods are themselves the waters: a male god, Apsu, and his female partner, Tiamat, represent the sweet and salty waters, respectively. Apsu becomes the underground sweet waters, vanquished by the subsequent gods (see Figure 3.1). Tiamat, in turn, the salty and trouble-causing waters, will become the primeval

---

[2] Translation from Dalley 2000 (*Epic of Creation*), p. 233.

FIGURE 3.1 The Mesopotamian god Ea sitting on his throne over the waters of Apsu, receiving another god. Impression of engraved cylinder seal from Ur (Akkadian period, ca. 2350–2150 BCE). Source/Credit: Drawing by Esther Rodriíguez González.

enemy that the Storm god Marduk fights and overcomes later in the story. This clash and his victory present the opportunity to recreate the universe at his will, which he does from the remains of Tiamat, as we will see. At the very beginning, it is from these waters that the gods were born and multiplied. The waters are the point of departure and, consequently, they will also be the means of destruction, in the form of a great flood.

Each poetic tradition copes differently with the problems of starting a cosmogonic narrative. Hesiod does it by spending more than a hundred verses invoking the Muses and setting the stage, and perhaps inventing a new concept, *chaos*, as an image of that first generative moment. The Babylonian tradition of *Enuma elish*, meanwhile, resorts to a paradoxical statement about things not existing by name while they are named in the text; the poet conjures an image of emptiness and lack of definition by mentioning what was not there or defined yet (López-Ruiz 2012). We can also notice how time-markers move the narrative: "when," "in the beginning," "then" "not yet." Paradoxically again, time is difficult to grasp and poses a problem even for quantum physicists (cf. chapter 1). Time is as much a product of our perception of experience as it is an independent quantifiable thing. It is not an element, but time and space seem to constitute the fabric in which all elements exist, at least in our minds (Buonomano 2017). As noted in chapter 1, there is no Time god in Hesiod, nor in the known Mesopotamian cosmogonies, which is especially counterintuitive in the case of Greek epic, where abstract concepts are so often personified and deified. The time frame, instead, is marked by the first moment ("in the beginning," "when on high"), and by the continuous sequence of events that follows.

That said, the association with time and eternity was embedded in the attributes and epithets of the Israelite and Canaanite gods, and eventually a Time or Eternal god surfaces in Orphic and Phoenician cosmogonies (López-Ruiz 2010: 151–64; see also chapter 1). Moreover, arranging or ordering time is a deliberate divine act in both the Babylonian and the Hebrew accounts. When Babylonian Marduk recreates the universe after defeating Tiamat, he "sets up constellations," and related to these astral points of reference he "designated the year," and within it the twelve months and the days of the year (Tablet V). Day and Night are also elements in Hesiod's *Theogony*, as are the moon and the sun, both natural light sources and astral markers of the cycles of days, months, and years. Similarly, in Genesis 1, time organization is taken one step further when God creates the arbitrary time-measure of the week, articulated around the Shabbat, the seventh day reserved for resting, deliberately set by example by Elohim after his six-day creation work (Gen. 1:1–2:2). We have inherited this time-unit in the Western world from the

Israelite calendar *via* its Christian adoption (for instance, the Romans divided their months into three ten-day periods). As Jack Sasson (2008: 498) remarked, "by opening the long story of his people on a drama divinely choreographed to display the birth of a consecrated seventh-day that is uniquely Hebraic, the Hebrew editor could have found no way more appropriate to glorify the special link between his people and Yahweh—a rapport that is the principal theme in Hebraic historiography."

Although *Enuma elish* is the most extensive and best known among Mesopotamian creation myths, it was one among many other traditions in this region, each with varying solutions for these questions. Stemming from different cities, many were not preserved due to the cultural dominance of Babylon, whose texts were more broadly reproduced and circulated. Proof of such diversity comes from the *Theogony of Dunnu*, coming from a small city called Dunnu in Babylonia and composed ca. 1000–750 BCE. In this creation story, the gods represent aspects of nature and also basic human activities in early sedentary communities: Plough, Earth, Sea, Cattle, Flocks, River, Herdsman, Pasture-and-Poplar, and so on. The story is not so much interested in the creation process or the ordering or definition of elements. Instead, the myth is structured around the relations among these personified entities and their violent competition for power, in a repeating cycle of succession whereby the male characters kill their fathers and marry their mothers or sisters. The vicious circle is only broken when, in the New Year, Hayyashum deposed his father but "did not kill him, and seized him alive," and "ordered his city to imprison his father." (Dalley 2000: 280). The story, much like the *Theogony*, marks a break with the old order and power dynamics and welcomes a new era of civic relations and justice among the gods, at least up to that point (we are missing the end of the text).

It is not far-fetched to assume that the idea of narrating the creation is first rehearsed in Mesopotamian epics, whereby the genre traveled and inspired versions in Israelite and Greek cultures. In Egypt, for instance, we do not find anything similar, nor any mythical narratives in general. The Egyptians no doubt had myths, stories attached to their religious entities and ideas, but they did not express them in linear narratives, whether epic poems or some other form. A few stories might be considered mythical because they contain supernatural elements and divine interventions (e.g., the *Story of the Two Brothers*, the *Tale of the Shipwrecked Sailor*). But, overall, cosmogonic ideas and episodes involving the gods must have circulated orally and are known through allusions only. These appear in hymns, prayers, and the vignettes preserved in the spells transmitted in *Pyramid Texts*, *Coffin Texts*, and the *Book of the Dead* (see Figure 3.2). Thanks to these as well as iconography, we can tease out some fundamental motifs connected to creation stories (Pinch 2002; Shaw 2004).

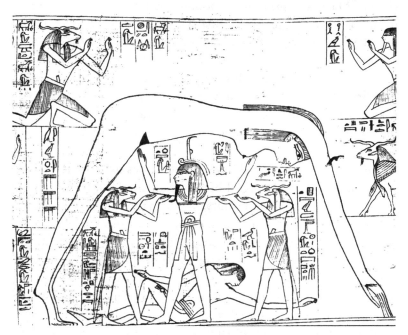

FIGURE 3.2 Cosmological scene from the *Egyptian Book of the Dead*, representing the gods Nut (Sky) and Geb (Earth), with Shu (Air) standing in between them. Greenfield papyrus from Deir el-Bahari, Thebes, Egypt, eleventh-century BCE. Source/Credit: The Print Collector/Alamy Stock Photo.

122   GREEK MYTHOLOGY

The configuration of the pantheon in Egypt varied by city, each of which privileged particular divinities. Scholars reconstruct at least two different cosmogonic traditions, stemming from the main centers of Heliopolis and Memphis. In the Heliopolitan tradition, the main creative entity is Atum (Re-Atum), the creator Sun god. He rose out of the primeval waters (Nu/Nun), and the primeval mound emerged also from the waters, for him to stand on. In *Coffin Texts* passages, Atum is called the "self-created god," while the emergence of the creator is represented in many different ways, such as from an egg that existed in the waters' womb-like environment, or from a lotus flower, or from a cow, or as a bird on the first earth mound (Pinch 2002: 59). Atum then separated light and darkness, and introduced order, structure, and justice, represented by the principle of Maat. The primordial mound upon which he stood was a pyramid-shaped stone and the first place the sun's rays reached (this is evoked by the shape of pyramids and obelisks). Atum then created the gods Shu (air, male) and Tefnut (mist or moisture, female) "with his hand"—that is, issuing his sperm in an act of parthenogenesis. This first couple of gods in turn begat Geb (Earth, male) and Nut (Sky, female), which are often represented framing the cosmos with the ground and celestial ceiling separated by their father Shu (Air) (see Figure 3.2).

Geb and Nut, Earth and Sky, are themselves the begetters of the other main gods: Osiris (god of the dead, afterlife), Isis, his sister and wife (goddess of love, fertility, revival in the afterlife), Seth (god of the desert, storms, war, chaos, etc.), and his sister-wife Nephtys (goddess of night, death, rivers, etc.). With the previous gods, Atum, Shu, Tefnut, Geb, and Nut, these all form the "Great Ennead of Heliopolis." The main mythological narrative involving these gods relates the rivalry between Osiris and Seth, leading to the death of Osiris, and his partial revival, as well as the begetting of Horus by Osiris and Isis. Horus eventually prevails as the next Sky and Sun god associated with Egyptian kingship. But this takes us far from

Facing East

cosmogony proper and into the sphere of the "succession" narratives that I return to later in this chapter.

We find early allusions to the Heliopolitan cosmogony in the *Coffin Texts*, dating back to the early second millennium BCE (Middle Kingdom). In one of these texts, the "Hymn to Life," Shu (air) is celebrated as a source of life. Speaking in the first person, the god says:

> *I am the one who made the sky light after the darkness; my skin is the pressure of the winds which come out behind me, from the mouth of Atum. My efflux is the storm cloud of the sky, and my smell is the rage of the dusk. The length of this sky is for my strides, and the breadth of this earth is for my foundations.*
>
> *I am the one whom Atum created, I will be a place of infinity, because I am the eternity who has begotten millions of millions! I am the one who repeats the ejection of Atum, who came out from his mouth when he used his hand, who has prevented his saliva from falling down to the earth.* (Excerpt from "Hymn to Life," *Coffin Texts*, Spell 80[3])

In this passage we can appreciate the different literary medium in which these creation stories appear in Egypt. At the same time, familiar patterns emerge. Just as in Greek and Mesopotamian tradition, the primordial gods personify realms of the universe and nature, and the gods are generated by couples through an implied sexual union. This reproduction comes after a first parthenogenetic impulse, by Atum, the Sun, a theme we saw also in the case of Gaia and Hera in Greek tradition. The separation of Heaven and Earth is also a shared motif, which in Egypt is not represented by a violent act of castration, as in Greek and Hurro-Hittite myth, as we will see. We can also appreciate the importance of the primeval waters, while the prominence of the Sun in its various divine forms is more peculiar and permeates Egyptian religion.

---

[3] Translated by Diego Espinel, in López-Ruiz 2018: 27.

124   GREEK MYTHOLOGY

If we look into the cosmogonic tradition from Memphis, however, we find a very different scheme. The god Ptah, who was the central deity of Memphis, is "the one who creates the totality and caused the gods to come into being," as written in the Shabako Stone. This is an eighth-century BCE document, which purportedly reproduces an older document, in which Ptah is represented as a demiurge god. He creates "through his heart and his tongue."[4] This is a theme we have encountered in the Genesis narrative and in the Babylonian *Enuma elish*, where existence is brought about by words and names, the structure of thought and language. While the Memphite cosmogony makes Ptah the creator of the Ennead of Gods, it also alludes to Atum's "semen and hands" as his creative power.

In parallel with the physical images and sexual overtones of some of these motifs, in Egyptian sources we can also find a more theologically abstract discourse. This is especially the case in texts that evoke a unifying generic "god" as creator of the universe, the sky and the Earth, the animal and vegetable realms. In the *Teachings for Merikare*, preserved in papyri and ostraca from the New Kingdom, this god's creation provides for human beings, who are "the cattle of god" (López-Ruiz 2018: 29). This motif states more than half a millennium earlier than Socrates the same idea that the gods are overseers and even owners of the human race, as we saw in the quotation from Olympiodoros about the *Phaidon* in chapter 2.

Kings in Heaven

Long ago, in former years, Alalu was king in heaven. Alalu was on the throne, and powerful Anu, their foremost, (that) of the gods, stood before him, and kept bowing down at his feet, and kept putting drinking cups in his hand. ("Song of Birth," excerpt[5])

---

[4] Translated by Diego Espinel, in López-Ruiz 2018: 24–26.
[5] Translations from the "Song of Birth" by M. Bachvarova, in López-Ruiz 2018: 155–58.

In the first decades of the twentieth century, Hittite texts were for the first time available to the public. They provided a sensational academic breakthrough, not least since one of them contained what was seen as an "oriental forerunner" of Hesiod's *Theogony* (Barnett 1945; Güterbock 1948). The script and language had been deciphered in 1915, thanks to the vast archive of cuneiform tablets excavated at the ancient empire's capital, Hattusa (in today's central Turkey), which contained not only mythological texts but also ritual and administrative documents, dating to at least ca. 1200 BCE when the city was destroyed and abandoned. Hittite mythology and literature, in turn, had absorbed older Hurrian traditions from northern Mesopotamia, adapting their myths and assimilating their gods, such as Kumarbi and the Storm god Teshub (Tarhun/Tarhunt in Hittite and Luwian texts).

The lines quoted above belong to the "Song of Birth," a theogony that accounts for the rise to power of the god Kumarbi, his birth, and his birthing of other gods. He was the central figure in a number of epic poems in which he seizes power from the older Sky god Anu and tries to defeat the Storm god Teshub/Tarhun by means of new supernatural enemies he brings into existence. These stories form what is known as the Kumarbi Cycle. The narrative of the "Song of Birth" opens with the succession of kings in heaven in intervals of nine years. Each time, the god's cupbearer and right hand is the one who challenges and succeeds him on the throne. Alalu was king first, a god whose identity is obscure. He might be connected to the Underworld (as he goes "down to the dark earth" in the story), but the name is also similar to that of the first human ruler mentioned in the *Chronicle of the Single Monarchy* from the city of Eridu in Mesopotamia, called Alulim (Bachvarova 2021: 189). All we know is that Alalu was dethroned by Anu, who is the Sky god, well known (and adopted) from Mesopotamia. Kumarbi, the principal Hurrian god associated with grain and prosperity, represents the next generation of gods. He not only defeats Anu but does so by castrating him with his own mouth, whereupon he becomes pregnant with other

126   GREEK MYTHOLOGY

entities and especially with the Storm/Weather god Tarhun (Hurrian Teshub). Here are the key lines:

> *As just nine years were counted off, Alalu was king in heaven, and in the ninth year Anu went in battle against Alalu. He defeated him, Alalu, and he ran away before him, and he went down into the dark earth. He went down into the dark earth, while Anu seated himself on the throne. Anu was sitting on the throne, and powerful Kumarbi kept giving him to drink. He kept bowing down at his feet and putting drinking cups in his hand.*
>
> *As just nine years were counted off Anu was king in heaven, and in the ninth year Anu went in battle against Kumarbi. Kumarbi, the seed of Alalu, went in battle against Anu, and Anu was no longer able to withstand the eyes of Kumarbi. He broke away from Kumarbi and from his hands. He ran, Anu, and he set off for heaven. Kumarbi assaulted him from behind, and he grabbed Anu (by) the feet, and he dragged him down from heaven.*
>
> *He bit his butt-cheeks and his manliness fused with Kumarbi's heart like bronze. When Kumarbi swallowed down the manliness of Anu, he rejoiced, and he laughed. Anu turned back to him and began to say to Kumarbi, "Did you rejoice before [yo]ur heart because you swallowed my manliness?*
>
> *"Don't rejoice before your heart. I have put a burden inside your heart. First, I have impregnated you with Tarhun, the august one."*
> ("Song of Birth," excerpt)

This text became paradigmatic of the succession myth or "kingship in heaven" motif, as it was called by scholars. Divine rivalry for power is articulated in the image of the courtly political tension between the king and his acolyte. The cupbearer is a highly symbolic figure attached to political power in the Hittite court. We know, for instance, of a title of "Chief of the Wine (Stewards)" given to high military commanders (Bryce 2002: 23), and of a "cupbearer" who was married to the Hittite king's sister and was involved in a plot to

Facing East 127

kill the king (Van de Mieroop 2007: 120). Assyrian kings also named a "Chief Cupbearer" (*rab shaqe*) among their highest officials (Van de Mieroop 2007: 257–59), a title that underlies Isaiah's *Rabshakeh* (Isa. 36:2) as "chief of the officers." The Persian king also counted the cupbearers among his closest, most trusted court members— being poisoned or not depended on them. So Herodotus mentions one Prexaspes, "whom he (Cambyses) held in particular honour, who brought him all his messages, whose son held the very honourable office of Cambyses' cup-bearer" (Hdt. 3.34.1–35.4; see Briant 2002: 264, 310–11). And the mythological-literary reverberation of this sort of intimate courtly position surfaces in Greek myths too: we can think of Tantalos, welcomed in Olympos and expelled when he tested the gods by serving them human flesh, or the child Ganymede, forced into being the lover and cupbearer of Zeus, or the succession conflict among Oedipus's sons, triggered by their failure to serve their father appropriately at the table (*Thebais*, frs. 2 and 3).

Most striking from the Greek standpoint, however, is the very particular motif of the castration of the Sky god by Kumarbi. The image provides a surprising parallel for the castration of Ouranos/ Sky by Kronos. Just like in Hesiod, the castration is a neutralizing action that becomes a creative action. In the Greek story, minor gods and giants were born from Ouranos's genitals as their flesh and blood (and semen?) came into contact with the earth, and Aphrodite from their contact with the sea (see chapter 1). The Hittite text is badly damaged, but the fragments indicate that Kumarbi indeed became "pregnant" with Anu's seed and, after a gestation period, gave birth to several entities. The broken text does not preserve how this happens; perhaps from his head, or perhaps from a mountain on which Kumarbi spits the sperm. Among the generated entities are the Storm god Teshub/Tarhun, the great River Tigris (Aranzah), and Teshub's brother, the god Tashmishu. Other epic stories that completed the Kumarbi Cycle show the rivalry between Kumarbi and his successor Teshub/Tarhun. In the preserved texts, we learn that the younger Storm god fights and overcomes two rivals created by Kumarbi: the snake monster Hedammu (a child of Kumarbi and a daughter of the Sea god), and the monstrous rock Ullikummi (engendered by Kumarbi and the rock Ubelluri, inside which the monster is gestated). In these challenges, the Storm god receives help from some divine allies and from human beings (Bachvarova, in López-Ruiz 2018: 154–76).

The Hittite epic is not so much a cosmogony as a theogony focused on the succession between king-gods, following a pattern closely comparable to that in Greek myth. The entire sequence moves from a Sky god (Anu) to a grain/prosperity god (Kumarbi), to a Storm/Weather god (Teshub/Tarhun), hence mirroring the Greek scheme of succession between Ouranos, Kronos, and Zeus (see Table 1). But there is a big difference: the Greek narrative follows a family pattern, with the throne taken over by the youngest son each time. In the Hurro-Hittite myth, Anu is not the son of Alalu. Instead, Kumarbi, his successor, is called "the seed of Alalu." Then, Kumarbi himself bears the seed of Anu as a consequence of the oral castration act and becomes the begetter (but not biological father)

TABLE 1. Succession of primeval and ruling gods in Babylonian, Hittite, and Greek myth.

Enuma elish	Hittite Kumarbi Cycle	Hesiod's Theogony
Apsu and Tiamat (sweet and salty waters deities)	Alalu (underground deity?)	Chaos, Gaia, Tartaros, Eros (Void, Earth, Underworld, Love)
Anu (Sky)	Anu (Sky) (castrated by Kumarbi, by swallowing)	Ouranos (Sky) (castrated by Kronos with sickle)
Ea (wise god; helps humans)	Kumarbi (helped by Ea; grain god)	Kronos ("crooked minded," grain god)
Marduk (Storm god)	Teshub/Tarhun (Storm god)	Zeus (Storm god)

of the next great god, Teshub. This succession scheme challenges the idea of linear genealogy of gods, in contrast with the *Theogony's* streamlined and orderly father-to-son succession, where legitimacy is not in question, but how power might be rightfully sustained or usurped by the different kind of god-rulers is. While the Hittite succession story echoes the Near Eastern tradition of king lists (Bachvarova 2021: 188), perhaps its nonlinear structure was meant to highlight the intricacies and unpredictable fates of rivalries among royal family members or dynasties.

How is it that the *Theogony* and the Song of Birth contain such similar themes? We are not dealing with an isolated oddity like the castration motif (odd enough as it is), but with parallel motifs embedded into larger narrative structures that also largely mirror each other. There is little room for coincidence here, and the similarity must reflect the adaptation of tropes across cultures that shared similar mythological and religious frameworks and categories (e.g., Mondi 1990; López-Ruiz 2014b). The channels through which these stories circulated are difficult to pin down, and may range from oral transmission to literary knowledge of specific texts, any time between the Late Bronze Age and the Iron Age, when versions of the Hurro-Hittite myth may have circulated among Luwian speakers in Anatolia. It is also possible too that stories containing some of these motifs circulated among Aramaic and Phoenician speakers, who were in contact with Greek groups in the first millennium BCE (Bachvarova 2021: 229).

The Hittites are in the company of the Greeks as speakers of an Indo-European language who were geographically, economically, and culturally enmeshed in the networks of the Near East since the Bronze Age. And, indeed, stories such as these illustrate the prevalence of the motif of divine fight for power in both Near Eastern and Indo-European lore (Watkins 1995). This theme also forms the backbone of other Near Eastern epics. With different stages and intergenerational dynamics, the common thread they share is the emergence of the Storm or Weather god as the ultimate ruler representing the

130   GREEK MYTHOLOGY

new cosmic order. In the Babylonian epic *Enuma elish*, the creation of the gods leads into a story of struggle between the higher gods, Apsu and Tiamat, and their offspring. Apsu had been threatening to destroy his own offspring and his offspring's offspring, represented by Anu/Sky, his child Ea, and other gods. Led by Ea, the wise god, Apsu is stripped of his crown and murdered, becoming the deep waters on which Ea now sits enthroned (see Figure 3.1).

In *Enuma elish*, the epic battle, narrated in all cosmic upheaval, is initiated by revengeful Tiamat (the primordial sea goddess), represented as a fish-dragon monster with an army of hybrid creatures and dragon warriors. None of the gods dare face her, except one, the young god Marduk. He is the son of Ea and Damkinu, and steps up as a valiant hero, chosen to lead the next generation. Marduk controls weather, especially the four winds (a gift from Anu), and his cosmic weapons include a net to capture Tiamat, a mace and a bow, a storm-chariot led by stallions called "Slayer," "Pitiless," "Racer," and "Flyer," and the "flood-weapon." Marduk is described as the most perfect of the gods, all-perceiving and all knowing, and "superior in every way. His limbs were ingeniously made beyond comprehension, impossible to understand, too difficult to perceive" (Tablet I).[6] Once more ancient cosmogonic-theogonic narratives stress the limits of words and human concepts.

Marduk is also celebrated as a *recreator* of the universe: Using his defeated enemy, he first arranges Earth's geography out of Tiamat's carcass. Fittingly for a cosmogony that started with waters and ended with the Storm god's victory, Marduk takes control of the waters, sending one half of Tiamat into the sky's vault, where the heavenly waters are guarded (Tablets IV). He opens springs from her eyes, and rivers are born from them, including the Tigris and Euphrates (the same words are used for "eye" and "spring" in Semitic languages), and he forms mountains from the udders of Tiamat, the original mother (Tablet V). As a cosmic arranger, Marduk sets up

---

[6] All *Enuma elish* translations from Dalley 2000; López-Ruiz 2018: 7–22.

Facing East 131

constellations and organizes time cycles, the twelve months of the year, marked and structured by the phases of the moon, which he created as "the jewel of night to mark out the days" (Tablet V). Marduk then turns to the creation of human beings and also of their cities (Tablet VI). He gives the order to build Babylon (*Bābilim*), which means the "Gate of the gods." Similarly, he instructs the gods to create "primeval man" out of the blood of Qingu, who is sacrificed for this purpose. The lover and second partner of Tiamat, Qingu, had received his position of power from her and had incited the war. This anthropogony makes people descendants of a rebellious lesser god, a theme that appears also in the Flood epic (*Atrahasis*).

If we look back at Orphic myth, we find striking points of convergence between these motifs: The Orphic Hymn to Zeus, as we saw, recentered the entire universe around the Sky god, who became a regenerative force. Moreover, an Orphic anthropogony tied human beings to the remains of the rebellious gods of old, the Titans, pulverized by Zeus in that story (in the *Theogony* they were only imprisoned in Tartarus; see chapter 2). Even the castration motif took a new form in the Orphic fragments, where Zeus swallowed the phallus of the Sky (Ouranos), instead of severing his genitals with a sickle, as Kronos did in the *Theogony*. In all cases, whether it is the castration or the destruction and dismemberment of Tiamat, the violent acts are also life-generating and allow Sky-Storm gods to become creative celestial forces. *Enuma elish* culminates with the recitation of the fifty names of Marduk, whose name is substituted by the Assyrians of the first millennium BCE by that of Assur, their equivalent main god, in their renditions of the Babylonian poem. This list is the capstone of the poem's glorification of the Storm god as the usher of world order around Babylon, which remains the cultural and religious capital of Mesopotamia even when Assyria rises to political and military power.

In terms of a "succession myth" pattern, the arc of this story is not exactly linear or predictable. Marduk flexed his supernatural muscles not in a conflict with the previous generation of gods (as Zeus,

132 GREEK MYTHOLOGY

or Teshub/Tarhun), but with the primeval goddess Tiamat and her army. She represents the salty waters in their destructive force, while the champion who defeats her, Marduk, is the god who brings rain and fertility, time and order—if anything, he is a foil to Apsu, her initial partner, who represented the deep sweet waters. The generational gap is enormous, but so is the reach of the forces of chaos, which are ever-present and in tension with the need for stability and cyclical regularity in the universe. A similar generational clash plays out in the final fight between Zeus and Typhon in Hesiod's *Theogony*, since Gaia, the ancestral mother of the gods, is the one who begets the monster with Tartaros, the deep Underworld. While Gaia's motivations are not explicit there, the Typhon motif acquires new, more primeval undertones when compared with the Tiamat-Marduk conflict.

In the Late Bronze Age epic of Ugarit, in North Syria, we encounter another narrative centered around the Storm god, Baal. He is the principal Canaanite god, perhaps best known for the biblical attacks on his worship as a bull lingering among some of the Israelites. This Canaanite epic was composed sometime in the thirteenth century BCE, before the city was destroyed, like Hatussa and other cities of the Near East, in a chain of disasters that marked the end of the Bronze Age (Cline 2014). Ugaritic texts were discovered at the site of Ras Shamra (Ugarit) in 1929. They were written in clay tablets and in a Northwest Semitic alphabet and a language related to those of the later Phoenicians, Aramaeans, and Hebrews. Alongside other Ugaritic poems and ritual texts, the epic known as the *Baal Cycle* constitutes a fundamental testimony of the cultural-religious background of Syria-Palestine that preceded (and in some areas overlapped with) the emergence and consolidation of Israelite religion in the first millennium BCE (Parker 1997; Cross 1998; Smith 2002).

To highlight the main themes that we have been following in this chapter, once more the epic narrates the struggle of the Weather/Storm god, to attain his rightful position. But the narrative is, once more, full of original character and peculiar to this poem. Baal is only

Facing East   133

one among the new generation of gods fostered and overseen by an ever-present older, patriarchal figure, the god Ilu or El (meaning literally "God," the same word under El/Elohim, Allah). In this tradition, moreover, the god representing this older generation is not overthrown, but rather seems to be willingly handing the throne to the younger gods, all of whom are called "beloved of El." As a revered patriarchal figure, El is sometimes represented in art as a seated, bearded, god[7] (not a smiting figure as Baal or Marduk and others, as in Figure 3.4), and he maintains an important role in the passing of the scepter to the next ruler. Baal will be enthroned, but not without several fights, much help from Anat, and a final arbitration by El, expressed by the Sun goddess Shapsh.

In order to obtain the throne, Baal demands to have his own palace built on Mount Saphon (as Zeus on Mount Olympos), which the craftsman god Kothar-wa-Hasis builds for him. The texts feature the disagreement between the engineer god and Baal about whether to place a window or "clerestory" in the palace. Baal refuses at first, but later decides to install a window. The metaphor makes the window into "a rift open in the clouds," an opening for "his holy voice"— rain and thunder. From the royal palace on Saphon, the god's "utterance" reaches and terrifies the world below. But Baal is called to confront two main contestants to the throne: the gods Sea (Yam/Yammu) and Death (Mot/Motu). The Ugaritic tradition departs from the multigenerational succession pattern, presenting instead the contenders as equals among Ilu's protégées. This scheme is not entirely absent from the Greek mythical universe, if we recall the passing mention in Homer of how Zeus, Poseidon, and Hades had distributed the realms of the universe by lot among themselves: The Sky, the Sea, and the Underworld (*Il.* 15.187–93, cf. *Hymn to Demeter* 85–87). This is a very different scenario than the one presented in

---

[7] See, for instance, the seated statuette from Late Bronze Age Megiddo at the ISAC Museum (https://commons.wikimedia.org/wiki/File:El,_the_Canaanite_creator_deity,_Megiddo,_Stratum_VII,_Late_Bronze_II,_1400-1200_BC,_bronze_with_gold_leaf_-_Oriental_Institute_Museum,_University_of_Chicago_-_DSC07734.JPG).

Hesiod's *Theogony* (chapter 1), which underscores that strands of Greek mythology that are not as developed in the extant epics could also be thematically close (even closer) to Levantine epics in various ways.

The ensuing fight between Baal and Yam fits into the theme of the Storm god's defeat of watery chaos, which takes the shape of a dragon-like entity: the enemy here is called "Sea," "Prince Yam," "Judge River," but also "Dragon," "Serpent," "the twisting one," the "tyrant with seven heads" (Meier in López-Ruiz 2018: 181). The resonances of the battles between Zeus and Typhon and between Baal and Yam are evident. Some thoughts on the symbolic and cultural position of these Storm gods in these adjacent cultures might help us better appreciate the success of this theme. Zeus is the Indo-European god of the bright sky and daylight (the name of Zeus, accusative *Dia*, genitive *Dios*, comes from Proto-Indo-European *djeus, and shares its root with the word for "day"). In the second millennium, Greek speakers settled in the Greek peninsula and the Aegean. These incoming (pre-)Greeks were originally not familiar with the sea; their word for the sea, *thalassa*, was borrowed from the indigenous Aegean inhabitants. They joined the older complex societies in the Fertile Crescent, where the first agricultural communities had learned millennia earlier that their cultivation of the land depended on retention of rain water and control of irrigation and river flooding. For the Mesopotamians, in turn, the sea was a distant threat, not the advantageous and necessary bridge across cultures and economies that the Greeks and Canaanites made it into. In this new context, their Sky god Zeus's personality acquired traits of the eastern Mediterranean Weather gods, mirroring his Hittite, Babylonian, and Canaanite counterparts. The Greek "cloud-gatherer" is perhaps closest to Baal, the "cloud-rider," also known as Adad/Hadad in the Levant.

In order to defeat the snaky, watery enemy, both the Semitic and Greek gods received weapons from allied gods, such as the lightning-bolts gifted to Zeus by the Cyclopes, and the two maces Baal obtained from Kothar-wa-Hasis, the craftsman god. It is in fact possible that the figure of Typhon stems from this Canaanite mythology. His name may have somehow traveled westward from Baal's mountain, Saphon/Zaphon, the "Olympos" of the Levant, which towered over the land of Ugarit and over the Mediterranean Sea. It was there that Baal defeated his serpentine enemy Yam/Sea. The Greeks themselves placed the clash between Zeus and the serpentine Typhon in this very mountaintop in North Syria/southern Turkey, known to them as Mount Kasios and to the Hittite-Luwian speakers as Hazzi (today Jebel al-'Aqra'; see Figure 3.3; cf. Figure 1.4 for Zeus) (Apollodoros 1.6.3; Güterbock 1948: 131; Lane Fox 2008: 188–98: López-Ruiz 2010: 109–13).

The Israelite god assimilated some of Baal's mythical features, especially in his representation as a thundering "smiting god" and victor over the seas and over the serpentine Leviathan. The Canaanite and other Storm or Weather gods are often represented in smiting

FIGURE 3.3 Photo of Jebel al-'Aqra', the Mt. Saphon of Ugaritic texts (the "Olympus of the East"), at the border between Turkey and Syria, seen from the north, with 1,717 m./5,633 ft. of altitude. Source/Credit: Wikimedia Commons.

position, wielding their weapons, such as a mace, axe, or rod, and a lightning bolt or thunderbolt (see Figure 3.4, cf. Figure 1.4). His name and mythical role continued the Canaanite tradition about Yam, called Litan or Lotan in the Ugaritic epics (an antecessor of Hebrew Leviathan), and the poetic tropes of the fight against the sea enriched

FIGURE 3.4 (left): Basalt stele with relief representing the Hittite Storm god Teshub/Tarhun, ninth century BCE; from Babylon, Iraq. Archaeological Museum of Istanbul. Source/Credit: Zev Radovan/Alamy Stock Photo. (right): Storm god Baal ("Baal with Thunderbolt") carved on a limestone stela from Ugarit, Syria, fifteenth–thirteenth centuries BCE. Louvre Museum, Paris. Source/Credit: Wikimedia Commons.

Facing East   137

the representations of Yahweh's power (e.g., Ps. 29, 74:13, Job 7:12, 26:12, 38:8; Leviathan: Isa. 27:1, Ps. 74:14, Job 3:8, 4:25). The following verses from Psalm 29 could be read as much as a praise to Canaanite Baal as a song to Yahweh in his guise of cosmic victor:

> (3) *The voice of Yahweh is over the waters;*
> *the God of glory thunders,*
> *Yahweh, over the mighty waters.*
> (4) *The voice of Yahweh is powerful;*
> *the voice of Yahweh is full of majesty.*
> (5) *The voice of Yahweh breaks the cedars;*
> *Yahweh breaks the cedars of Lebanon.* (Ps. 29:3–5)

In our own days, when countries are increasingly battered by heat waves, fires, floods, and hurricanes, we can easily imagine the power of the images invoked in these stories, and why the narratives about these gods and their opponents were so resilient. Baal and Yam (Zeus and Typhon, Marduk and Tiamat, Teshub and Hedammu), represented the nurturing and destructive qualities of water: the rain and controlled flooding or irrigation, which fostered agriculture, and the permanent danger of stormy seas and hurricanes.

The exception that confirms this pattern, once more, is Egypt, whose geological makeup is as different as its mythology. For the Nile peoples, agriculture did not depend on local rains (what rains?) but on the regular inundation of the Nile, a recurrent event tied to the monsoon rains much further south at the river's source. Instead, the Sun in his various forms dominated Egyptian religion. The Egyptians also articulated differently the struggle between chaos and order, connecting it to the cycles of day and night, the victory of light over darkness. The idea of a serpent monster, however, is also cosmically important in Egypt. The Sun (Re) also fights against a serpent enemy, Apep, who threatens to overturn the set order. Every night, Re confronts the monster as he sails through the Underworld driven on his solar boat; and every night, aided by Horus, he

138   GREEK MYTHOLOGY

overcomes the threat. As light returns at dawn, it signals the renewal of order. Instead of narrating the establishment of order in a primeval past when Zeus or other gods acquired their power and dominions (as if in a divine historical timeline), the Egyptians took a cyclical approach to the divine struggle. In their worldview, cosmic creation was defended and chaos averted every single night and day. The Egyptians did not need to look back at a long-lost Golden Age, since the "reign of the sun god, the lost golden age of Egyptian myth, was reenacted every night" (Pinch 2002: 93).

The most famous Egyptian story (in popular culture at least) is that of the struggle between Osiris and Seth, and then Seth and Horus. This is a succession myth of sorts. The most extensive version comes from the Roman-period account in Plutarch's *Isis and Osiris*, but allusions to the ancient myth surface in texts and depictions throughout Egyptian history, from Old Kingdom Pyramid texts to papyri from the Middle Kingdom and later (e.g., López-Ruiz 2018: 143–45). The story confronts members of the same generation, in this case the brothers Osiris and Seth. Although Osiris is killed by Seth's trickery, he is partially revived by Isis as a mummy and becomes king in the realm of the dead. Seth is ultimately defeated by the younger Horus, begotten by Isis and (dead) Osiris, but remains as a powerful force representing the desert and chaos, while Horus is established as ruler of the sky and Egyptian kingship. The victorious god, whose main form is that of a falcon, is not a Weather god but a sort of synthesis of the Sun gods and the personification of political rulership over the united land of Egypt. If we try to superimpose (as the Greeks did) this division over the Greek or Ugaritic tripartite scheme of the Sky/Storm god, the Underworld, and the Sea, the odd god out would be Seth, which shows that the Egyptians placed the desert in the position of watery chaos or the sea. This explains why, in Plutarch's version, which synthesizes Greek and Egyptian mythologies, Seth is translated into Typhon, the watery-fiery enemy of Zeus.

A God Creates, a God Destroys

Creation and destruction in Mesopotamia

"When the gods instead of man did the work," opens the poem known as *Atrahasis* (Tablet 1). There was a time when the gods tilled the land and dug canals for irrigation, even manipulating and "digging out" the streams of the Tigris and the Euphrates. In the land between the two great rivers (that is what "Mesopotamia" means in Greek), the beginnings of humankind were tied to the labor of the gods. In a case of extreme anthropomorphism, not only did the gods create humans in their image, but they did so with a specific purpose: Specifically, human beings came into the picture as third-tier laborers, to replace the lesser gods (called Igigi), when the "the load was too hard, the trouble too much." The Igigi had themselves lifted the burden from the great gods Enlil/Ellil, Anu, Ea/Enki, and others. This is the situation at the opening of the *Atrahasis*, a Babylonian epic, which begins with the creation of humans and ends with repeated attempts by the supreme god Enlil to wipe them off the face of the earth, the last of which is the Great Flood.

This epic of creation and destruction is preserved in three Tablets in its Old Babylonian Version (OBV), dated to around 1700 BCE, supplemented by fragments from the first millennium (Standard Babylonian Version). The story is also separately narrated within the *Epic of Gilgamesh* (Tablet XI). "Atrahasis" is the name of the central human figure in the story, the "original Noah." His name means "exceedingly wise." In the *Epic of Gilgamesh*, however, the same character is named Ut-napishtim, "he who found (eternal) life," known as Ziusudra ("Life of long days") in Sumerian, a name that lies behind the Xisuthros of Hellenistic sources (attested in Berossos's *Babyloniaka*; see Dillery 2015). The story, originated among the Sumerians in the third millennium, is one of the most ancient mythical narratives preserved in the human record. Most strikingly, some

140　　　　GREEK MYTHOLOGY

versions of the Sumerian king lists use the Great Flood as a historic "peg," before and after which they situate kings of various cities; some even mention Ziusdra in Shuruppak as the king after the Flood. It is no wonder that it was in a land marked by dry climate punctuated by flooding that affected crops that the Flood acquired mythical proportions. It became rooted in the Mesopotamian collective memory "as a primeval cataclysmic Flood that wiped out all life on earth and brought humanity to the verge of extinction," and we find allusions to this primeval event broadly in other types of Akkadian literature (e.g., in poetic, historiographical, and magical texts) (Wasserman 2020: 1; see his study for all the sources). From this story stems a lineage of later flood narratives among groups in the eastern Mediterranean, each adapting it to their worldview, as we see in the stories of Noah and of Deukalion and Pyrrha (see chapter 2).

Other tropes about early humans narrated in *Atrahasis* have become highly engrained in Western imaginary. A central one is that people were made out of clay. They were not made like vessels, however, as in later familiar myths, but like mud bricks, the essential building blocks for the first sedentary urban civilizations of the Fertile Crescent. In fact, exactly like bricks, they were made out of pieces of pinched clay. The fourteen pieces were divided in two groups of seven, to create males and females, set right and left of a finished mud brick, perhaps akin to a birthing brick. In this extremely ancient account of the creation, the first male and female human beings came to life as equals, formed exactly in the same way from identical pieces of clay, whereupon they grew up and "chose each other" as mates (see Figure 3.5).

The creation procedure would sound familiar to listeners of all walks, an image that invoked their own building labors and the brick houses that witnessed their lives, from birth to death. The great god Enlil/Ellil entrusted Nintu, the "womb goddess" (also called Belet-ili, Mami, and Mistress of the Gods) to "create primeval man, that he may bear the yoke, the work of Enlil, let man bear the load of the

FIGURE 3.5 Clay model of a nude couple making love on a bed, from Mesopotamia, ca. 1800. Source/Credit: Trustees of the British Museum.

gods!" (Tablet I).[8] But there is more. This basic clay matter from which humans were made was forever complicated by an added ingredient. Nintu mixed the clay with the flesh and blood of a sacrificed god, a minor god who possessed intelligence. We saw the same theme in the *Enuma elish* when Marduk created humankind by slaughtering Qingu, the lover of Tiamat. The Igigi gods, who had until then been doing the labor, happily contributed to the mix by spitting on the clay, now a mix infused with further life by the gods: "Let us hear the drumbeat forever after," they said, as the rhythmic sound of the human heart started, and "let their ghost exist so as not to forget," referring to their origin from a slain god.

---

[8] Quotations of *Atrahasis* are from Dalley 2000; cf. López-Ruiz 2018: 74–90.

142 GREEK MYTHOLOGY

What went wrong, then? Why the onset of destruction? We are given a reason, if one that shows the capriciousness and omnipotence of the supreme gods: "The country was as noisy as a bellowing bull." Enlil was restless, tired of the racket made by the over-spreading humans. Determined to reverse the effects of his creation, Enlil sends various disasters on to human-folk. The more powerful the god, the less labor imposed on him, so Enlil charges other gods with sending disease and draught and famine to annihilate the noisy men and women on earth. In one chilling passage the poem describes how starvation breaks not only social norms but family ties, pushing people into cannibalism: "When the fifth year arrived, a daughter would eye her mother coming in; a mother would not even open the door to her daughter.... When the sixth year arrived, they served up a daughter for a meal, served up a son for food" (*Atrahasis*, Tablet 2). These destruction bouts happened at intervals of 600 years. Each time, the god Enki/Ea (whom we saw as father of Marduk and a "wise god" in *Enuma elish*) helped people every time by informing his protégé Atrahasis about which god they needed to appease to put an end to each disaster. Atrahasis lives for a thousand years (impossible longevity is also a feature of ancestral characters in the Hebrew Bible) and has a special relationship to "his god" Enki/Ea: his "ear was open to his god Enki: he would speak with his god and his god would speak with him."

The last of these trials was the Flood (Tablet III). Adad is commanded to send it, as Storm god akin to west Semitic Hadad and Canaanite Baal. Forced to swear an oath to not speak to Atrahasis this time, Enki deploys his trickster mind and makes his message heard by speaking to the walls of the wise man's reed hut ("reed hut, make sure you attend to all my words! Dismantle the house, build a boat"). The hero warns his community, together they build a boat, as instructed, and he invites them in. Both animals and his family come on board. While it is not clear how many people accompanied Atrahasis, some mortals weather the storm and survive the cataclysm, which lasted seven terrifying days:

Facing East 143

> *The face of the earth changed. Adad bellowed from the clouds....No one could see anyone else, they could not be recognized in the catastrophe. The Flood roared like a bull, like a wild ass screaming the winds [howled]. The darkness was total, there was no sun.* (*Atrahasis,* Tablet III)

Enlil was furious at the survival of life, and Enki took the blame. Not deterred by the internal divine drama, as soon as the boat reached dry land, the gods still rushed to the smell of the burned sacrifice offered by Atrahasis. The womb goddess Nintu called out the gods' hypocrisy and harshly denounced their attempt to destroy her creation. It was a madhouse. In the end, the gods consulted in an assembly and decided to let humanity survive and nature run its course. No more genocides. Instead, it was decided to let Nintu establish some natural ways to diminish the rate of the population growth, such as miscarriages, stillbirths, and infant mortality, and devoting entire groups of women to a "temple life" that restricted their childbearing.

The *Epic of Gilgamesh* transmits another version of the same story (Tablet XI). This version fills some gaps and provides an even closer precedent to the story of Noah told in Genesis. It is the survivor of the Flood himself, Ut-Napishtim, who tells Gilgamesh how he alone among men is immortal, and neither Gilgamesh nor any other hero or commoner can aspire to the same fate. After they survived the Flood and Enlil overcame his frustration, the great god himself resolved to bless him and his wife and make them "as gods are," perhaps so they could bear witness to these unique primeval events. In the Gilgamesh version, for instance, Ut-Napishtim describes the making and measures of the boat or "ark," and we read that he includes in his crew all kinds of animals, besides his "kith and kin" and "all kinds of craftsmen." The description of the deluge is particularly expressive: Ut-Napishtim describes how even "the gods cowered, like dogs crouched by an outside wall," the goddess Ishtar "screamed like a woman giving birth," and the Mistress of the Gods wailed at the destruction of her children, who were dissolving in front of their eyes like clay in the water, filling the sea "like fish spawn." When the storm has passed, Ut-Napishtim sends out a dove, then a swallow, and finally a raven, who finds land and does not come back. When he and his crew land and make the required sacrifice, the gods, in this version too, gather around it "like flies," while the womb goddess also reproaches Enlil for trying to destroy her people without consultation or warning. Even in this very hierarchical pantheon, the gods are supposed to respect each other's realms of authority.

This Mesopotamian myth is less familiar to most readers than the Noah story, and yet it vividly expresses tropes that become familiar in later adaptations. The scenario described in the Babylonian creation myth of the *Enuma elish* provides a certain logic to the flood destruction too. The gods attempt to end by water what had begun in water. In a perfect circularity, the first elements contained the potential for the end and new beginning of life. The Hebrew Bible adopted this narrative almost to the letter, put to the service of the Israelite monotheistic or monolatrous creed (Genesis 6–9). Their adaptation placed considerable strain on the original plot, however, as the concentration of all divine action fell on one god. In the well-known Genesis story, "when men began to multiply on the face of the earth" (Gen. 6:1) and their generations became morally corrupted, the Israelite god decided to destroy them. But then he then decides to save some of them. This change of heart takes the place of the conflicting agency of multiple gods in a polytheistic narrative (e.g., Enlil orders a punishment, while Enki helps humans and the mother goddesses objects, etc.). But such a trope is not unprecedented in polytheistic systems either. For instance, in *Atrahasis*, Enlil changed his mind and allowed people to survive in smaller numbers, and the Egyptian god Re-Atum decided to recall the destruction of the rebelling humanity, which he tried to enact through the goddess Hathor (*Book of the Heavenly Cow*; López-Ruiz 2018: 92–94; see also Pinch 2002: 74–75).

Egyptian gods, who created other gods by word and thought, or without a mate, are also attributed the creation of humans. Although anthropogony does not feature much in Egyptian texts, some of them mention that humanity had come out from the tears of the eye of Atum (or Re-Atum), the primordial Sun god in the Heliopolitan tradition. This motif brings back the theme of creation from a water-based substance, whether we think of Atum rising from the primeval waters or creating other gods from his bodily fluids, be it semen or spit. The reason of this anthropogony is moving: The god cried people out into existence, because he was "alone with the primeval waters in inactivity."[9] In parallel, other allusions to creation highlight the loneliness, sorrow, and imperfect existence of the human race (Pinch 2002: 67; see 66–68 for more sources).

Anthropogony and the Great Flood in Genesis

The biblical tradition of Genesis 1–3 also portrays the divine creator as a demiurge. He fashions a first man and woman deliberately, as if creating artwork, not by "genetic" reproduction. Two different traditions are presented in Genesis, however. In Genesis 1, humankind is created by a distant and powerful god through his word and thought. Man and woman appear at the end of a series of other elements in the universe, all separated from the preexisting, indiscrete waters: light, the sky, dry earth, and animals. God places animals and plants under human oversight for their own consumption (Gen. 1:26–30). This narrative is interested in order, boundaries, and symmetry (typical of the Priestly source) and closes a complete and round creation process with the seventh day of rest (Gen. 1:1–2.4). Genesis 2, in turn, presents another method of creation and reflects a different

---

[9] Translation by A. Diego Espinel, "Hymn to Life" from the *Coffin Texts*, also mentioned in the *Book of the Heavenly Cow*; see López-Ruiz 2018: 27, 92.

perspective. Here God's artisan work is done by hand, using clay as prime material, just as in the Mesopotamian *Atrahasis*. This clay is also animated with life, thanks to the input of the divine, when Yahweh infuses his breath into it. God creates human beings in his image, just like in the first version, but the differences between the two accounts are stark: in Genesis 1, man and woman are created equal, while in the second narrative man is created first, establishing a clear hierarchy. God shaped the first man "from the dust of the ground" and placed him in the newly planted garden of Eden (Gen. 2:7–8). Then God created animals and allowed man to name them (2:19–20). This first man is referred to as *'adam*, literally an "earthling" (whence Adam), in an intended pun with the matter he is made of: dirt, earth (*'adamah*) (Sasson 2022). The name is sometimes used as a generic for "humankind." But Adam is no common man; he is given a creative position himself, that of naming and classifying nature, which is a fundamental part of the cosmogonic process in Genesis 1 and in the broader Near Eastern tradition.

While man is exalted to this function as the "right hand" of the creator himself, the creation of the first woman is subordinated not only to his creation but also to that of animals. Like them, she is instrumental, a solution for man's solitude and lack of help to oversee animals and plants. She also solves the problem of the lack of a sexual partner to continue creating human beings. Marking this hierarchy too, and in a theme we have not seen in other creation stories, the first woman is formed differently from man, out of his own rib, surgically extracted by God. She who becomes the birth-giver is herself born from a male human, by divine intervention (the motif recalls Zeus's parthenogenesis of Athena and other divine birthings).

Adam's position is puzzling, then: As a source for the non-natural appearance of another human being, Adam seems elevated to a lower-scale cosmogonic position. But Adam is most of all God's tool or material source for the creation of woman, more like when the Mesopotamian gods deployed clay to make the first people, only using his flesh, itself made of earth. His dominant position as first

Facing East

human, arranger, and even creator, still stands. He names the first female companion simply "woman," which in Hebrew is the grammatical counterpart to "man" (*'ish*, "man"; *'ishah*, "woman") (Gen. 2:23). Later, however, he finds for her a less generic name, Eve, *Hawwā*, connected to the Semitic root for life (*hyw*, cf. *hayyim*), for she is a source of human life, "the mother of all the living" (Gen. 3:20). She has, after all, tasted the forbidden fruit from the Tree of Life. Her name is only established after this transgression happens and the couple has been expelled from Eden, as they join the fate of other mortal creatures to harshly live, reproduce, and die (Sasson 2008: 503).

It is surprising how central human beings are, overall, in the Israelite creation account of Genesis, in relation to the creation of the entire cosmos. In contrast with the more cosmic opening in Genesis 1, the syntax of Genesis 2 especially pulls us immediately into the human realm: "In the day that the Lord God made the earth...then the Lord God formed man" (Gen. 2:4–7). The god of this anthropocentric account (attributed to the Yahwistic redaction) is more proximate to human beings and concerned with them. But he is also a more emotional and severe figure, one that expresses love and anger; in other words, more human. The account continues with the famous episode situated in the Garden of Eden, in Genesis 3, which brings us back to the "paradise lost" or "Golden Age" motif we visited in the Five Races and the Prometheus-Pandora stories in Hesiod (see chapter 2). The Garden of Eden represents this special but tense relationship with his human creation, which sets up the tone for the subsequent unique but conflictive relationship between the God of Israel and his chosen people (Sasson 2008). Yahweh allows temptation and punishes disobedience, intent on keeping the first man and woman from growing too arrogant in their progress. The disobedience in tasting the fruit from the tree planted in the center of Eden, the "Tree of Life" or "life-giving tree" symbolizes human rebellious nature and free will, their obsession with the possibility of immortality (Gen 2:9; Sasson 2022). After the failure of this first couple to keep in line with the boundaries imposed by Yahweh's rules, they gain self-awareness, but not without a price. This self-awareness is represented as a sudden shame in their nakedness, a nakedness that is only a sign of vulnerability now that they are outside of the Garden, when they are forced to join the other animals and find ways to protect themselves (Sasson 2008: 503; see Figure 4.2).

By way of comparison, we can remember how Zeus also knew what lay behind Prometheus's sacrificial trick and still let it proceed. This transgression was necessary for the larger plan of Zeus. Like the Heroes and the people of the Iron Race, Adam and Eve and their descendants now entered the course of history, so to speak, when the clock of time, marked by labor and aging, starts ticking. The cycle of human survival and their struggle with nature (human and otherwise) was unstoppable. At Eden, the blame was passed around, from the man to the woman, from the woman to the snake, but God punishes them all, cursing the snake and laying out a grim future for the human couple. He demotes each of them to a lowly, suffering version of their initial nature, and, like the people created in *Atrahasis*, they are bound to work the land for survival. The "Golden Age" is gone, and with it the possibility of an existence in which the divine is within reach.

This mythical garden was imagined "in the east" (Gen. 2:8). The reference to the four rivers that flow from the garden, including the Tigris and the Euphrates, points to Mesopotamia as a source of traditional cosmogonic lore. The "Tree of Life" motif resonates with broader Near Eastern mythical and symbolic traditions, especially with mythologized aspects of the wilderness and primeval purity. Before becoming Gilgamesh's inseparable friend in the *Epic of Gilgamesh*, the wild man Enkidu (called a "primitive man") lived care-free and shame-free in the wilderness until he spent time with a woman (Shamhat), and thus became "domesticated" and alienated from animals and nature (Tablet I). A sacred beautiful paradise was inhabited by the monster Humbaba in the same epic. In a similar vein, the famed Gardens of Babylon were designed to bring the magic and purity of nature into the heart of civilization, allowing the king to be imagined as the master of both realms (Dalley 2013). In turn, many of these foundational stories introduce women as the corrupting element. Ironically, femininity is traditionally associated with irrational or emotional behavior, the raw physicality of the reproductive cycle, and other traits associated with nature. However, in these "paradise lost" narratives she falls in the other side of this dichotomy. Whether Shamhat, Pandora, or Eve, she represents the "domestication" of man, in the sense that she complicates a previously happy, careless existence. These misogynistic narratives blame primeval women for the onset of institutional and social responsibilities and constraints, including marriage and everything that made human society "castrating" for the male partner.

Greek and Israelite flood stories share their predilection for genealogies. Some Near Eastern myths portray the creation of human beings in bulk, without an explicit gender hierarchy (e.g., *Atrahasis*). But Genesis 1 and 2 place one couple (or one man and then one couple) at the very origin of humankind. The cosmogonic moment is thus tied to all the generations of Yahweh worshippers and humans at large, all passing through the funnel of the Flood and its survivor Noah. Adam and Eve and their male children, Cain and Abel, reproduced and humans multiplied. (But how did they reproduce, if there were no previous women on Earth? As in the Greek story of Pandora, the logic of demographics is not relevant.) In turn, the Genesis redactors hardly reconcile the various genealogical traditions. Thus, Noah, and hence the surviving humankind, descends from a different line out of Adam, from a third son, named Seth (Gen. 5:3), who was begotten: "in his own likeness, after his image." Again, this first human's creative action is worded as an emulation, in human scale, of that of Yahweh.

After the Flood and Noah's survival with his family, God accepts the first sacrifice on dry land, and blesses the survivors despite his disappointment with human corruption and wickedness. Both the

150 GREEK MYTHOLOGY

Mesopotamian and biblical narratives establish the ritual role of early humans through these first, postdiluvian sacrifices, although the instrumentalist approach to human creation is more evident in Mesopotamia, where Marduk creates humans to take up the work of the gods (Alter 2011: 29). The element of moral judgment, however, is an innovation of the biblical tradition, missing in the Mesopotamian story, where the capricious annoyance of Enlil led to the Flood and their salvation was aided by other gods' interventions (principally Ea/Enki). Once more, a monotheistic theology called for creative adaptations that have theological consequences, here introducing theodicy or divine judgment. Whatever the case, here too the supreme god "resets" the creation through a return to water. A new genealogy begins through his children Shem, Ham, and Japheth, whose descendants will fill the entire Earth (Gen. 9:18–19). They come to represent all strands of Semitic and other peoples, outlined in the "Table of Nations" in Genesis 10 (Darshan 2013).

Noah concentrates the functions of the helper and the survivor, of Atrahasis and Prometheus: since there are no divine intermediaries in the Genesis Flood story, the agency in saving humanity lies on Yahweh, who sends Noah instructions, and on Noah himself. Noah is thus presented as a culture hero, fitting within the genre of mythological etiologies, whereby key human characters are inventors and culture bringers. Then, just like the Flood survivor Atrahasis/Ut-napishtim, he makes the first sacrifice that marks this new era (Gen. 8:20–21). As its fragrance pleases Yahweh, he is moved to forgiveness, and to bless Earth's fruits and the new generations. The first ancestors, Adam and Eve and their children, had been presented as the first to wear clothes and to become shepherds and farmers. But Noah is "the first to plant a vine" (Gen. 9:20) and the first wine maker. Fittingly, Noah is also the first drunken character in the Hebrew Bible (presumably the first ever), in an episode of strange connotations that leads to Noah's cursing of one of his children (Ham/Cham) after he sees the father naked. The cursed child represents the future line of "impious" Canaanites. The episode of Noah's drunkenness turns on its head a motif that is represented positively in older mythologies. The underlying Canaanite ethos is especially expressed at Ugarit, where various tests stress the duty of the children to protect the honor of their father and physically help him if he is overcome by wine at the banquet (Zamora 2006; see "El's divine feast," "Aqhat epic": Parker 1997). Once more, the broader Near Eastern perspective helps us appreciate how the monotheistic narrative elevates Noah to a mythically powerful position, that of the "drunken god" or king, who issues curses that will affect entire future peoples.

*

A complex layering of mythological traditions comes to the fore in other moments of the Israelite account. The Flood story opens with perhaps the most polytheistic sounding lines in the Hebrew Bible, as it sets the episode in a time when "the sons of God(s)" took wives from among the daughters of men:

> *The Nephilim were on the earth in those days—and also afterwards—*
> *when the sons of God(s) went to the daughters of human beings, who*
> *bore children to them. These were the heroes that were of old, warriors*
> *of renown. Yahweh saw that the wickedness of humankind was great in*
> *the earth.* (Gen. 6:4–5)

This miscegenation seems to have marked the turning point when moral corruption grew among the people at large, and Yahweh decided to act upon it. This is one of the instances where the name "Elohim," conventionally translated "god," might retain the plural meaning embedded in its morphology; hence we could read "the sons of gods" and capture a glimpse of the pre-monotheistic traditions behind this story, in which many supernatural beings were involved. The motif of the giant-human interbreeding, in turn, is fleshed out in extra-biblical or apocryphal writings such as the books of Enoch (see chapter 4). And a polytheistic background is intimated in other texts, such as in Yahweh's fear that man might become like "one of us" (Gen. 3:22, 11:7), or in the allusions to divine assemblies or councils and "hosts of heaven" and messengers of Yahweh, even if an internal heavenly hierarchy is always implied (e.g., Psalm 82.1; 1 Kings 22:19–23).

Bringing us closer to Greek mythology, the prediluvian breed mentioned in Genesis 6 is semi-human, in other words, closest to the Homeric-Hesiodic demigods, whose "race" also marked the transition between the "before-time" and the historical time of the "Iron Race" (see chapter 2). These demigods are called Nephilim in the biblical passage (Gen. 6:4) and appear here and elsewhere as a primeval race of human beings that inhabited Canaan and were later extinguished, either by divine intervention or by their own violent nature, much like Hesiod's Bronze Race (e.g., Num. 13:33; Deut. 2.10–11; see Doak 2012; Smith 2014). All of these passages resonate with mythological and theological threads that were alive in the regions where the Israelites formed their own traditions, including not only Canaanite lands but those beyond (Smith 2002).

Near Eastern Cosmogonies in Practice

Every month of March, the Assyrians celebrated the New Year in the Akitu festival. For over a week, the capital and the court teemed with envoys from vassal-states close and far-off (whether client states or annexed provinces), who came to pay their respects to the king and renew their oaths of allegiance. At the height of the Neo-Assyrian Empire, in the late eighth–early seventh centuries BCE, these territories encompassed not only upper and lower Mesopotamia (i.e., Assyria and Babylonia) but also large portions of Syria-Palestine, which included Phoenicians, Israelites, and other peoples, as well as a good part of Egypt and southeast Anatolia. It is possible that leading figures from further afield, including Greek speakers, were drawn to this imperial event. In front of this international audience, the Babylonian epic of creation, known as *Enuma elish*, was recited, as had been done before by the Babylonians, among whom the poem originated. In the Assyrian version, the god Marduk was replaced by Ashur, the patron Storm god of the Assyrians, with whom the king strongly identified as head of his own human cosmos.

The oral performance of the creation narrative had a powerful effect that reverberated through the empire, a message that married myth and political propaganda. Those present not only celebrated the New Year, but the poem took them on a journey as far back as the collective memory of Babylonian culture could reach. Perhaps those most enthralled with the narration felt they could grasp for a moment that initial emptiness and the imagined state of harmony among the first gods and their creation, a mythical moment suspended outside human time (Eliade 2005). At the same time, the image of Marduk/Ashur as an arranger and rearranger of the cosmos out of the remains of his defeated enemy resonated with the empire and was conveniently projected on to the presiding king, who thus reasserted his own hegemonic position as keeper of the balance between chaos and order on Earth (Bidmead 2002).

A ritual object from the land of Sumer encapsulates this cosmic view (see Figure 3.6). The "Warka Vase" was found among ritual artifacts belonging to the temple of Inanna, the goddess of love, fertility, and war, and stems from Uruk, one of the first known cities and likely the birthplace of writing. The reliefs capture a hierarchical cosmology, with registers representing, from bottom to top, the waters, plants (reeds, grain), female and male sheep, men (perhaps servants/slaves) carrying agricultural products, and priestly or kingly figures amid cultic elements associated with Inanna—hence moving from water, to domesticated nature, to the lower working strata of society, to the ruling class and the gods.

This is just a well-documented example of the intersection between myth, religion, and political ideology. In Archaic Greece, we saw how in the kingly yet politically savvy figure of Zeus, Hesiod

FIGURE 3.6 Alabaster vase, known as the "Warka Vase" (three ft./1 m. tall), from ancient Uruk, southern Iraq, ca. 3000 BCE. National Museum of Iraq. Source/Credit: Wikimedia Commons.

set an example for leaders of his time in the competitive world of emerging city-states. As he made clear in his verses, their success depended in part on their good rapport with the appropriate gods and on the support from their community, a shift from the oppressive

Facing East   155

rule exemplified by Zeus's predecessors, Ouranos and Kronos (see chapter 1). In the Hittite world too, mythical tropes and epic poetry were incorporated in festivals and ritual actions of importance to the community's well-being and prosperity. For instance, in Anatolia, the story of Illuyanka, the "eel-snake" monster that was vanquished by the Storm god Tarhun-Teshub, was connected with the Hattic *purulli* festival of the land celebrated in spring. Excerpts of this and other broadly circulating poems were embedded in ritual and magical texts, including verses adopted from the *Epic of Gilgamesh* (Bachvarova 2021: 78–110, 252). Similarly, at Ugarit in Syria, the king and the palace had a central role in sustaining and enacting the ritual cycles that assured the stability of the state, and ritual texts and incantations against snakes and other evils incorporated snippets of mythical texts, especially the *Baal Cycle*, as well as short mythical vignettes, often known as "paramythological texts" or "*historiolae*" (Pardee 2002).

In their representation of primeval times, Near Eastern texts such as the *Enuma elish* and *Atrahasis* also transmitted ideas about class and power relations, tied to the emergence of complex, urban, and agricultural states in Mesopotamia in the third millennium BCE. In contrast, epic poems such as the Hurro-Hittite *Kumarbi Cycle* and the Ugaritic *Baal Cycle* are not at all concerned with human beings and their labor issues, although some other of their mythical stories do feature human characters. These epic narratives instead highlight the rivalries among the gods and portray diplomatic and court tensions among the lofty sovereigns. In a political reading of the *Baal Cycle*, its mythical narrative projects on the divine order the kind of interpolity competition proper of the Canaanite kingdoms of the Bronze Age, who were minor players in a larger "game of thrones" dominated by the Egyptian, Hittite, and Assyrian imperial projects. The epic, after all, represents Baal and his rivals Yam and Mot as peers on the same footing; their struggle plays out under the nose of the patriarchal figure of Ilu, who remains seated on a distant throne but ultimately directs the negotiations to favor Baal. Ilu in this scheme might represent the imperial power (Hittite, Egyptian) under whose purview the smaller states of the Levant and Anatolia lived their regional politics (Tugendhaft 2018).

The representation of Baal as a struggling head of state is just one example of the discursive and symbolic connection between divine and human kings. Moreover, "[t]he ideology of kingship embodied in the personality of the Storm-god" (Bachvarova 2021: 260) was widely adopted and easily transferable across cultures that shared similar religious and political taxonomies. More generally, the association between divine and royal power is virtually a universal mechanism of power construction and legitimation throughout history. In the Mediterranean world, we can think of everything from symbolic connections between religious and kingly institutions (e.g., Catholic and Anglican monarchies), or societies where statesmen were charged with central ritual offices essential to the community's well-being (e.g., monarchs of the Canaanite, Hittite, and Assyrian realms; or the *archon basileus* in Athens), to more general ideas of divine protection of a king or his dynasty articulated through stories about founding figures (e.g., Akkadian, Persian, Greek, Roman kings), to straight identification of the king with a god (e.g., Egyptian Pharaoh as Horus) and divinization and cult of the king (e.g., Pharaonic Egypt, Roman imperial cult). But, just like human kings, and to various degrees, divine monarchs did not act alone. Divine councils appear in Near Eastern, biblical, and Homeric narratives, sometimes leading to collaboration and negotiation about earthly affairs, but often resulting in the planned destruction or genocide of humanity at large (the Flood) or of a people. In such a way were the fates sealed for the cities of Troy, Sodom, Ebla, or Ithaca (Louden 2006: 207–9; Bachvarova 2021: 139–42). In a circular self-feeding cycle between reality and fiction, human communities project their power structures onto the anthropomorphized divine scene, and in turn these narratives imbue human politics with a mythologized, authoritative veneer.

We have seen cosmogony deployed as a self-standing primeval narrative centered on the gods, and only laterally concerned with early humans (*Enuma elish, Atrahasis,* the *Theogony*). But sometimes the balance shifts and creation stories appear set as preamble to historical narratives. This is the case of the Hebrew Bible. A continuous line connects the primeval narrative of Genesis to the early history of Israel, taking us from nonverifiable (i.e., "mythical") into recorded (i.e., "historical") characters and events. The choice is not accidental but a way of signaling the unique relationship of Israel with its God in historical terms since the beginning of time (Sasson 2008). The model grew roots the Levant, where we will find Roman-era authors adopting this model, connecting cosmic beginnings and history, in their own writings about the Jews and about the Phoenicians (see chapter 4). On a smaller scale, some traditions preserved in surrounding cultures connected historical times with narratives about city foundations or destructions (the Trojan War for Greeks and Romans, the foundation of Rome, etc.).

In the Near East, mythological narratives that explained aspects of human life proliferated. These stories are far from limited to the connection of the gods with meteorological phenomena and the agricultural and fertility cycles. While primeval gods create the larger cosmic order and living matter, the subsequent generations of mythologized human beings act as first inventors and culture heroes, including those who made the first sacrifice; who invented clothes, agriculture, the vine and wine; and a long list of creators of other technologies and areas of culture. In Genesis, Adam and Eve and their children were not only progenitors of the human race but culture bringers. Their sons, Cain and Abel, are the first farmer and the first shepherd, and their descendants, Jabal, Jubal, and Tubal-Cain introduced nomadic husbandry, the arts of the lyre and pipe, and metalwork (Gen. 4:22), while another primeval man, Noah, had his own role in establishing animal sacrifice, and was also the first to produce wine and become drunk, as already mentioned (Darshan 2013).

In the Mesopotamian *Theogony of Dunnu*, the first gods represent the innovations of agriculture and husbandry, with names such as "Plough" and "Cattle-God," and in the story of Adapa, a Sumerian sage from the antediluvian era was all-knowing and refused immortality, setting the course for humanity to remain mortal (Dalley 2000).

Since the role of culture heroes or inventors was applied to either gods or early humans, the category became useful in trends of rationalization or "historicalization" of mythological figures in antiquity, especially the view that the gods were early humans divinized for such contributions (this is known as "Euhemerism"; see chapter 4). The image of the primeval culture hero could also be projected forward onto historical royal figures as means to increase their mythical aura. Most notoriously, the Assyrian king Sennacherib (late eighth to early seventh century BCE) portrayed himself as a founder or refounder of cities. His manipulation of the waters and nature evoked the epic past associated with Babylon and its creator the Storm god Marduk. Thus, Sennacherib's flooding of Babylon was narrated as a controlled real-life version of the primordial Flood, even borrowing language from the epics, and the famous "Hanging Gardens of Babylon," designed and sited by the king in his own palace, probably in Nineveh, were yet another symbolic recreation of primeval flourishing and transformed his political center into a new Babylon (Dalley 2013).

*

Circling back to Babylon, then, we turn from the political to the personal ritual use of cosmogonies. As previously mentioned, the prosperity of the community and the crops, and hence of the family nucleus, was guaranteed by the recitation of the creation epic in the New Year festival. At a private level, then, verses evoking the creation moment in similar terms could ward off pain or illness, as preserved cuneiform tablets show. The most broadly cited text is an incantation "Against a Toothache," also known as "The Worm and the

Toothache," which "weaponizes" cosmogonic language similar to that of *Enuma elish* against a particular physical malady, including instructions for the performer of the ritual:

After Anu created heaven,
Heaven created earth,
Earth created rivers,
Rivers created canals,
Canals created swamps,
Swamps created the worm,
The worm came weeping before Shamash,
His tears flowing before Ea.
What will you give me as my food?
What will you give me as my drink?
I will give you ripe fig and apple.
What good are a ripe fig and an apple for me?
Heave me among the teeth and set me in the jaws, to suck
the blood of teeth, to chew the roots in the jaws.
[Diviner:] *Insert the needle and seize the foot (of the worm,*
and say)
"Because you said this, worm, Ea should strike you with his
mighty hand!"
(This is) an incantation against toothache; its ritual is
second-grade beer ... and oil you will combine; you must recite
the incantation three times and place (the medication) on
his tooth.[10]

In the realm of private life, mythological themes enriched funerary texts of different types and periods. Beyond the more famous story of Osiris, mythologically connected with death, the afterlife, and mummification, acts of creation and recreation found a special place in the Egyptian funerary texts. For instance, the appearance of

---

[10] Translation from Sasson 2008: 491; cf. Foster 1995: 411–12.

160 GREEK MYTHOLOGY

allusions to Atum and other generative forces in mortuary texts fits within "the conceptual framework of Egyptian creation myths where the myriad things of the created world are continuously brought into being from a unitary source" (Nyord 2021). To a different degree, we also see the use of cosmogonic themes in Greek funerary texts. We can think of the "Orphic/Bacchic" Gold Tablets, written as guides or amulets for the dead initiates, or the Orphic cosmogony referred to in the Derveni Papyrus, also buried with its reader and becoming itself a funerary object (see chapter 1). In short, just as primeval elements fed into our living world, the reverse was intuitively possible—that death is a sort of return to the primeval creation.

Traveling Myths

The crossover between creation motifs and ritual opened paths for the exchange of mythological stories between Greek speakers and those of various eastern Mediterranean areas. Some contexts would have been especially fertile for these encounters. For instance, religious festivals in which epic poetry and hymns might have been recited and where international audiences might have been present, such as at Greek Panhellenic sanctuaries or festivals in Mesopotamian centers themselves. Festivals and rituals, in other words, acted as spaces of contact among cultures (Bachvarova 2021: 219–65). Thinking about these contexts, Walter Burkert placed religious specialists and "charismatic" leaders at the center of the question of adaptation of Near Eastern cosmogonic myths by Greek speakers. A figure such as Epimenides of Crete (seventh–sixth century BCE), captures this idea: according to tradition, he composed a theogony (now lost) and also performed a ritual purification of Athens due to the "Kylonian pollution." This was a case of "blood guilt" resulting from the Athenians' violent reaction and the killing of supplicants after an attempted coup led by Kylon in 632 BCE in Athens

Facing East 161

(Hdt. 5.71; Thucyd. 1.126). But we know nothing else about the wise man's performance: Did his purification ritual include cosmogonic verses?

In the traditions about other figures, such as Empedokles, Pythagoras, Pherekydes of Syros, or Mopsos, aspects of mystical-philosophical revelation, religious-ritual leadership, and sometimes cosmogonic speculation seem to merge. As much as we remain in the dark regarding their real role in the interweaving of Greek and Near Eastern cosmogonies, it is significant that their biographies connect them to the eastern Mediterranean, as they were associated with Cilicia, the Levant, Egypt, and Crete. At least they provide personal names for the many cultural intermediaries that were involved in this phenomenon that shaped Greek cosmogony and mythology (Burkert 1992: 42; López-Ruiz 2010: 171–202). These individuals and others we do not know about may have channeled mythical narratives across physical and cultural realms, although this was not the only channel nor perhaps the principal one (Bachvarova 2021: 200–206).

We cannot neglect the likely role of less formal and less erudite storytelling as an important way of transmission of stories, sometimes even across cultures and languages. We are reminded by Plato, for instance, of the role of mothers and nurses in transmitting stories to children, as well as by listening to prayers and other rituals (Plato's *Laws* 10.887d). Already in the *Homeric Hymn Aphrodite* (113–16), a nurse is attributed the role of teaching a foreign language, and with it for sure children songs and stories, to the aristocratic woman that the goddess pretended to be when she met her lover Aeneas. Foreign nurses, mothers, teachers, lovers, merchants, and many other actors would all have been part of the traveling lives of myths that connected Mediterranean communities far and wide.

4

Resilient Myths

The lover of myth is, in a sense, a lover of wisdom, for myth is composed of wonders.
—Aristotle, *Metaphysics* A2, 982b11–19[1]

Hidden in Plain Sight

When we use expressions such as making a "titanic effort" or being burdened by a "Sisyphean task," or when we call some tropical cyclones "typhoons" and use Gaia (Ge) as the geological name of our mother planet, we are engaging with Hesiod's *Theogony*, whether we know it or not. Few images are as emblematic of New York as the colossal statues of Prometheus and Atlas at Rockefeller Center, chosen to symbolize the inventiveness and ambition of early twentieth-century industrial North America. Atlas holds the world's weight somewhere by the Hesperides, at the edges of the known world; Prometheus carries the stolen torch, challenging Zeus in his eagerness to bring progress. The Titan was old and rebellious, and, just like America, aspired to be a beacon of innovation. Not far from this Prometheus, the glasswork on the door of the General Electric building of 30 Rockefeller Plaza shows a bearded god-figure that could well represent Yahweh or Zeus over the proclamation:

---

[1] Translated in Brisson 2004: 29.

FIGURE 4.1 Zeus- or Yahweh-like figure in glass, at door of the Rockefeller Center General Electric building, New York. Source/Credit: Photo by the author.

"Wisdom and Knowledge shall be the stability of the times," a quote from Isaiah 33.6 (Morales 2007: 33) (see Figure 4.1).

The colossal bronze statue of Lady Liberty in New York Harbor was erected to welcome those sailing into the New York in 1886, her torch and sun-ray crown a beaconing light for the thousands of migrants seeking opportunity. These attributes were borrowed from previous colossal statues representing Sol/Helios, such as the famous Colossus marking the main harbor of the island of Rhodes, which became one of the "Seven Wonders" of the ancient world. A famous Roman version was erected by Nero and gave the name to the Colosseum that was built in its place later on. In her neoclassical form, Liberty stands as a new, female colossus for a Western cosmopolitan harbor. At the same time, she resembles the prominent statue of Athena Promachos on the Akropolis, visible from afar, as a Defensor of her city; but, instead of lance and shield, Liberty holds a written scroll representing the Declaration of Independence, and the broken chains at her feet celebrate the abolition of slavery in the previous decade.

These early "American icons" are some of the most recognizable among the myriad of allusions to Classical mythological figures found not only in New York but all over the Western world. Classical allusions multiplied with the boom of neoclassical art in the eighteenth and nineteenth centuries, which accompanied the Enlightenment and the extension of education, based largely on the Greco-Roman canon, to a growing industrial class. Ancient Greek gods and heroes became symbols, shortcuts for Western principles tied to modern progress; they were chosen because they were deemed universal and inspiring regardless of race or religion, even if the societies and elites that most promoted this heritage did not always live up to those ideals.

If we think of the presence of Classical mythology in modern culture, however, cosmogony and anthropogony might not be the immediate "go-to" place. Our minds may drift easily toward the stories of famous heroes like Herakles, Odysseus, Aeneas, and others, or toward famous female characters like Helen, Antigone, Medea, or Penelope, not to mention the Olympian gods and goddesses. The Judgment of Paris, the sack of Troy, or Oedipus's tragic self-recognition have certainly been tropes of literature and art throughout European history much more frequently than those narrated in Hesiod's *Theogony* or the Orphic poems. The fates of heroes, their flaws and endurance, and their fantastic deeds and enviable closeness to the gods provide attractive models to convey human troubles and aspirations in all ages. Programs such as Theater of War Productions[2] have brought Greek tragedies to veterans who can see

---

[2] https://theaterofwar.com.

aspects of their own unspeakable suffering expressed in the timeless words of tragic figures of the Trojan War, such as Ajax and Philoctetes. Their pain and sense of abandonment was elevated to Greek tragedy and awoke empathy for fifth-century BCE Athenian audiences (all too experienced in war themselves) and for readers in subsequent centuries. In the end, Homer's *Iliad* and *Odyssey* are easily among the greatest literary creations of all times, the type that continue to connect with universal audiences in their representation of grief, love, pride, longing, resilience, and other fundamental aspects of the human experience (see, e.g., Fletcher 2021).

Creation stories are not as apt for human re-enactment. And yet they are inspirational in different ways, and they have their special place in ancient and modern reception. To begin with, they are the scene of grand divine battles, when gods and cosmic monsters fight for power and establish the world order. That is a selling point. Also, the framework of Greek theogony is ever present in the reception of myth, for two reasons: First, the generations of heroes and founding figures operate within the cosmogonic frame; they are part of a world order and timeline that linked the divine and human planes. For instance, Herakles, the Trojan War heroes, and other foundational figures could be matched with Hesiod's "Race of Heroes" in the grand scheme of things, acting as intermediaries between the divine and human communities. We can see this also in the opening lines of one of the Sumerian poems about Gilgamesh. This hero, called "Bilgamesh" in Sumerian, is the oldest known in recorded literature, and he was the most famous in the ancient Near East. In one of the oldest poems about the hero, his story is framed in cosmogonic-anthropogonic terms, in lines that reverberate in the *Enuma elish* and other cosmogonies: Gilgamesh (Sumerian Bilgamesh) comes just after the cosmos and human society, symbolized by temples and bread-making, had taken shape:

In those days, in those far-off days,
In those nights, in those distant nights,

166 GREEK MYTHOLOGY

In those years, in those far-off years,
In olden times, after what was needed had become manifest,
In olden times, after what was needed had been taken care of,
After bread had been swallowed in the sanctuaries of the land,
After the ovens of the land had been fired up with bellows,
After heaven had been parted from earth,
After earth had been separated from heaven,
After the name of mankind had been established... (Sumerian poem
Bilgamesh and the Netherworld, lines 1–10[3])

Second, precisely because cosmogonies deal with the origins of the
world and the gods, or, at most, primeval people, they were the perfect medium for theological and philosophical exploration. The traditional view of the Greek gods and their myth-history could be
rejected in favor of a philosophical model of the divine, or it could be
mined for symbolic meaning through allegorical explanation, but
Zeus and his extended divine family remained a point of reference
for centuries even as Roman religion and eventually Christianity
spread in the ancient Mediterranean and increasingly changed the
relationship toward those stories and their gods.

The brief overview I offer in this last chapter will follow some of
the winding paths of cosmogonies and their transformations. As we
will see, our basic modes of interpretation and appropriation (e.g.,
political, artistic, philosophical, entertainment-driven) were already
modeled in antiquity. In other words, when we read or retell ancient
myths, generally, we are not in dialogue with authors who created
ancient versions from scratch, but with poets who set their minds on
interpreting and adjusting existing traditions to their own times and
mind-sets.

---

[3] Translated in George 2003: 178–79.

Death or Renewal

Greek myth travels far and wide

Creation and epic stories had accompanied Greek groups across the Mediterranean since at least the eighth century BCE, when their trade routes and colonies expanded across the Mediterranean and the Black Sea. Greek speakers had already settled earlier on in western Asia Minor and Cyprus. But it was with the military and political expansion led by Alexander the Great at the end of the fourth century BCE that Greek culture was channeled even farther in an unprecedented way: As the Hellenistic kingdoms parceled out Alexander's conquests, Greek language, institutions, and literature were adopted throughout the Near East. The overlap of cultures cut both ways. Now Greek speakers and their stories inhabited Babylon and Damascus, while Aramaic speakers from Mesopotamia or Syria, with their traditions, were pulled to new establishments with Greek names such as Alexandria, Antioch, or Philadelphia.

In this "Greek-wide-web," mythology followed a bifurcated path, whether it was received through a more traditional or a more philosophical perspective. In the more "traditional" path, art and literature continued to represent the gods and their myths much in the customary way, following the famous poets, who had become authoritative sources over the centuries. Homer, Hesiod, and the Classical Athenian tragedians continued to be the backbone of education and recreation in Roman times and later. Along this axis, ancient Greek myths also inspired new poetry, some of which became part of our Classical canon as well. We can think of the Hellenistic-period librarian and poet Apollonius of Rhodes (third century BCE), or the most famous Augustan-era poets Ovid and Virgil. Myths were also compiled and digested for educational or entertainment purposes, in works such as Hyginus's *Fabulae*, written in Latin also in Augustan times (ca. 64 BCE–17 CE), or the *Library*

(*Bibliotheke*), written in Greek by one Apollodoros (also called Pseudo-Apollodoros) at an unknown date, perhaps in the second century CE.

The second path usually runs parallel to but sometimes intersecting the "traditional" reception of myth in art and literature, but, in reality, it was equally rooted in pre-Classical and Classical culture. The skeptical view of the traditional stories about the gods was introduced already by the pre-Socratic thinkers and natural philosophers in the sixth century BCE. The philosophical criticism and reinterpretation of myths continued without interruption in the Athens of Socrates and Plato and beyond, not deterred by the resilience of the traditional representation of myth in art and literature, not to mention in the largely oral world of common folk, which left barely any written trace.

I will turn to philosophical interpretations in the next section. But, staying with the "mainstream" path for now, myths never lost their ties to religious landscapes and ritual life, and these traditional narratives were a pillar of education. Learning meant reading, memorizing, and emulating older Greek literature, especially Homer and Hesiod. In the now expanded Greek world, this heritage was also essential to sustain and nourish a shared Hellenic identity abroad, which, moreover, sustained the colonial project, just as later it underpinned the Roman empire superimposed on it. The process of collecting "world" literature and curating a corpus that would become canonical or "classical" had precedents in ancient Mesopotamia, but it took on a new intensity in the Greek world with Alexander's successors, the Ptolemies, at their capital of Alexandria in Egypt. The Hellenistic-period figure of the "benefactors" (in Greek, *euergetes*), who invested their fortunes to promote economic and cultural life, did much to spread the type of globalization where Greek literature had a central place.

While Greek culture was a colonial tool for the Hellenistic kingdoms, it was also an instrument for local communities and emerging powers, such as the Romans, to bring aspects of their own heritage

Resilient Myths 169

to others into the international arena (Errington 2008). Translation was a crucial part of this process. As Irene Vallejo (2022: 229) puts it, "the Ptolemies weren't content with just to map the unexplored world but wished to open the way into the minds of others," and, indeed, we might say that "European civilization was built on translations—from Greek, Latin, Arabic, Hebrew, from all the different languages of Babel." What the Hellenistic centers and later the Romans were doing with earlier Greek literature—learning it, copying it, rewriting it, translating it—was already done by the Akkadians from Babylon with the earlier Sumerian language and literature, and by the Assyrians with older Akkadian literature from Babylon, as exemplified in their long relationship with the epic *Enuma elish* (Charpin 2010). We do the same when we study "Classical" myths, as we harness their masterworks for educational purposes and turn their mythical figures into modern symbols.

Cosmogonies offer a few examples of these receptions. By the third century BCE, the territories conquered by Alexander were under the rule of his former generals and the dynasties they established. The Seleucid kingdom or empire (named after its first ruler, Seleukos I Nikator) was the largest of these administrations. It covered Syria and Mesopotamia, as well as a vast territory further into Central Asia, whose borders fluctuated at various times. Toward the beginning of this new rule, in the early third century BCE, the historian Berossos wrote an account of Babylonian civilization (*Babyloniaka*), in which he incorporated Mesopotamian mythological culture heroes within the historical timeline of Mesopotamia. Thus, he bridged the mythological and historical pasts, in a fashion not unlike what we find in the redaction of Genesis. We only have access to some of its fragments (that is, selected quotations by later authors) but enough to see, among other features, that he wrote about the sage Oannes, a half-fish, half-man amphibian entity and a version of the sage Adapa, known from earlier Mesopotamia texts. Berossos stresses how this character gave humanity wisdom, including writing, and the skills for founding cities and performing religious rites. Berossos also recounted the story of the Flood with a man called Xisouthros as a version of Atrahasis, the Flood survivor (Dillery 2015: 74–84). As John Dillery (2015: 84) points out, through these culture heroes Berossos provides "a framework on which to mount the great narratives of Creation and the Flood," and by doing so, he managed to historicize these truly "timeless stories." Similarly, in Hellenistic Egypt, the priest and antiquarian Manetho painstakingly synthesized millennia of Egyptian records into a work in Greek (the *Egyptiaka*), also preserved only in fragments. This treatise was intended to inform and educate the new Macedonian rulers in local traditions. He posited the Great Flood as one of the points of convergence of Greek and Near Eastern deep "myth-history" and chronology, a topic that also preoccupied Greek historians (Moyer 2011: 111–13).

By Roman times, the *Theogony* and the Flood were part of the mythical world received from the Greeks, but the idea that the deluge was a universal event and the Eastern roots of the story were not totally forgotten. Roman writers from different areas of the empire represented the trope differently, however, as their narratives were informed by particular traditions. For the historian Diodoros of Sicily, writing in Greek in the first century BCE, the deluge was a primeval and historical event. In his account, if the Flood wiped out life completely, living things must have emerged again from the earth, and Egypt must have been where this happened, giving the combination of moisture and heat in the environment of the Nile (Diod., *Sic.* 1.9.10). He is somehow harmonizing Greek natural-historical views and creation myths in which water and mud appear prominently, such as in Egyptian, Mesopotamian, biblical, and Phoenician cosmogonies. In Syria, narratives that fed from both Greek and Near Eastern lore also circulated, though we have limited examples of this literature. For instance, the second-century CE author Lucian of Samosata provides one such testimony, when he transmits a version of the Flood at the beginning of his treatise about the Syrian Goddess. The account combines Greek and Mesopotamian traditions and identifies Deukalion with one Sisythes (or "the Scyth"), who cannot be other than the Flood hero Xisouthros in Berossos (Lucian, *De Dea Syria* 12–13; see Lightfoot 2003).

Another interesting witness in this story of cosmogonic reception is Philo of Alexandria, a Jewish intellectual writing in the first century BCE, who comments extensively on the Genesis account of creation and the Flood. His work prioritizes allegorical and philosophical interpretations of the Torah and teases out the intention of Moses as its author over the historicizing approach of other authors (Runia 2001; Lévy 2018). For instance, in his *Questions and Answers on Genesis* I, Philo centers his commentary on the second account of Genesis 2–3 (the Eden story), while he puzzles over the "six days account" of Genesis 1. He explains the repetition of the creation narrative not through textual criticism but offering a philosophical-theological solution with Platonic resonances, postulating that "perhaps those things which were created in the six days were incorporeal angels,... but now [in Genesis 2] they were produced in reality, being the copies of what had been created before, images perceptible to the outward senses of invisible models" (19).[4] In other of his commentaries he deals with the Flood. Philo puzzles over the mention of giants, whom he takes not as stemming from myths or fables, but as Moses's proof that there are different levels of earthly, heavenly, and divine origins among men (*On the Giants* 13.58).

Philo's work influenced the later writer Josephus (30–100 CE), who also navigated through the biblical traditions while subscribing to Greco-Roman genres. He provides a close account (in Greek) of the creation and the flood at the opening of his otherwise plainly historiographical work *Antiquities of the Jews* (chs. 1–3). As he expands and contracts the received narratives, Josephus adds nuances from the body of Jewish biblical commentary already circulating in his time, the Targumim and Midrashim. But cosmogony

---

[4] Translated in Yonge 1993.

and the figures of Adam and Eve also loomed large in the reworking of these stories in noncanonical Jewish and Christian writing, such as in Gnostic texts, Christian apocryphal texts, Jewish pseudepigrapha, the Kabbalah, or the Dead Sea Scrolls. At the same time, inasmuch as authors such as Philo and Josephus engaged with the Genesis tradition and Jewish history, they entered the "biblical tradition" themselves and were even seen as "proto-Christians." Paradoxically, it was because they became popular among Western Christian scribes and scholars that they had a better chance of preservation than other of their "pagan" counterparts (Mason 2008).

From gods to kings and back

The blurring of lines between myth and history had a political utility for statesmen and public figures. The Euergetes or "benefactor" that wanted his philanthropic deeds broadcasted and celebrated could play with self-representation as a real-life culture-bringer and progress-inducer, following in the footsteps of mythological heroes. And, indeed, Greek kings of this time, such as Dionysios I of Syracuse in the fourth century BCE or the Hellenistic kings, highlighted especial associations with the gods and flirted with the model of divine kingship that had been more at home in the Near East. In this they also followed the lead of Alexander, who already in life mythologized his own birth story, claiming Zeus as a father, and went on to represent himself as Zeus-Ammon while in Egypt (Whitmarsh 2015: 147–50).

Divine pretensions and associations must have inspired or reinforced a strand of mythical interpretation, which flipped the narrative around to propose that all gods had been originally human kings, only later worshipped and mythologized. The trend is known as Euhemerism after the first author whose work was famous for such an approach, one Euhemeros of Messene, probably from Sicily. He wrote a work called the *Sacred Inscription* or *Sacred History*,

Resilient Myths 173

around 300 BCE, of which only a few passages are preserved. As far as we can tell, the story takes place on the fantastic island of Panchaea, where the narrator encountered inscriptions and monuments that proved that the gods had been primeval kings and benefactors (Winiarczyk 2013). The traditional Greek theogony was thus transformed into a hypothetical history featuring "the deeds of Ouranos, Kronos, and Zeus." The inscriptions were set up on a gold stele "by Zeus himself at the time when he was king of the inhabited world and still dwelt among men."[5] In another part of the story, Zeus is said to have visited eponymous heroes or kings in Cilicia and in Syria. Their respective names, Kilix and Belos (Greek for Baal), respectively, tie them to the mythological realms of those areas of the Levant. Most importantly, Euhemeros's account portrays gods as people, as kings who were born and died and were buried. It is not unlikely that the tradition of gods who die and revive (in the guise of Canaanite Baal or Phoenician Melqart) had some influence in this sort of hyper-humanized narrative. If that is the case, it is possible that the mythologies Euhemeros was reinterpreting emerged in some place where Phoenicians and Greeks interacted for centuries, such as Sicily itself, where Euhemeros was most likely from, or Crete, where some Greek tradition placed the birth and even the burial of Zeus (López-Ruiz 2021).

Euhemerism constitutes its own type of rationalization of myth, in an atheistic vein (Whitmarsh 2015: 152–53). In that sense it follows the second broad path of interpretation mentioned in the previous section, in which I included philosophical and historicizing accounts. But the "gods-as-kings" trend had other, more immediate utilities. Euhemerism seamlessly tied together cosmogonic and historical narratives, and that is exactly what the author Philo of Byblos (not to be confused with Philo of Alexandria) does in his *Phoenician History*. This is another Greek-speaking, Near Eastern author writing

---

[5] Euhemeros, *FGrH/BNJ* 63, F2.5 = Eus., *P.E.* 2.2.57–59 = D.S. 6.1 and 5.46.1. Translated in Clay and Purvis 1999: 99–100, 105.

174 GREEK MYTHOLOGY

in the early second century CE, slightly before Josephus. Philo offered an updated reading of regional mythology, drawing on sources he claimed went back to the oldest Phoenician traditions, allegedly quoting an early, perhaps legendary Phoenician author known as Sanchouniathon (Baumgarten 1981). Instead of seeking hidden meanings behind the mythical parts of his materials, like allegory does, myths, in his view, preserved a collective memory of deep-past historical events and traditions misinterpreted and mystified with time into religion and myth. The only parts we have of his work are precisely the opening passages, his account of the creation and early civilization, which served as a preamble to his account of historical times. This is the familiar framework also used by Josephus and the Hebrew Bible redactors before him. But Philo "de-mythologizes" the cosmogony-theogony he is transmitting, by conveying it as the history of early kings and inventors.

The work of Philo of Byblos has reached us only in fragments quoted and paraphrased by Eusebius of Caesarea, the Christian scholar, who in the third and fourth centuries CE used these types of works to refute the pagan gods. Once more, what comes through of a pre-Christian mythology is both mangled and partially preserved thanks to Christian scholarship and polemics. Because of their theological implications, creation accounts such as these were of special interest for early Christian scholars, which explains why the opening passages are the only ones quoted from Philo's *Phoenician History*.

Philo's Euhemerized myth began with the first creative elements. This quotation illustrates how Philo's mythology connects to both Near Eastern and Greek cosmogonies and natural philosophy:

He (i.e., Philo) *posits as the source of all things a dark and windy air or a gust of dark air and a foul and nether chaos. These things were limitless and, for a long eon, had no boundary. He says, "But when the wind conceived an erotic desire for its own sources and a mixing together took place, that intertwining was called Desire. And this was the source for the creation of all things. It itself was not aware of its own creation. And from his entwining with the wind Mot came into being. Some say that this is mud, others the putrefaction of the liquid mixture. And from this mixture came all the sowing of creation and the birth of all things. There were animals with no sensation, from which came animals with intelligence. And they were called Zophasemin, which means observers of the heavens. And they had the shape of an egg. And Mot shone forth and the sun and the moon and the stars and the luminous bodies and the great stars."* (Eusebius of Caesarea, P.E. 1.10.1–2[6])

To highlight some aspects of this mythology, the idea of life coming out of mud or moist earth is not too far in principle from the Egyptian god Nun representing the primeval waters, and similar concepts in the Mesopotamian and biblical traditions; the primordial impulse of Eros or Pothos (Desire) goes back to Hesiod; and the theme of the egg appeared in Orphic cosmogony. This and other aspects that appear in Phoenician cosmogonies (air, Desire, Chousor "the opener," a Time deity or Aion), suggest earlier crossovers between Orphic and Phoenician creation myths, which were in turn heavily influenced by Egyptian cosmogony and religion, where the egg theme is attested (López-Ruiz 2010: 130–70; López-Ruiz 2018: 57–63).

Philo also reproduces a version of the succession myth, but one that combines Hesiodic and Canaanite/Phoenician features. He rehashes Kronos's conflict with Ouranos, only making the castration less central (mentioned only in a second conflict). But other details point to the survival of millenary tropes in his narrative. For instance, the Canaanite motif of the battle between the Storm god and the Sea is preserved as far back the Ugaritic *Baal Cycle*, and the name he records for the Storm god, Demaranu, is attested only in Ugaritic texts. Other Semitic characters and names are transliterated and lightly adapted into Greek (e.g., Adodos = Adad, Belos = Baal). Other times they are culturally "translated," in a process of interpretation

---

[6] Translated in Kaldellis and López-Ruiz 2019.

or equation (the Latin term *interpretatio* is used for this). We see this when Chousor is said to be Hephaistos (cf. Ugaritic Kothar-wa-Hasis), or Elos to be Kronos (cf. Ugaritic Ilu, Hebrew Elohim). Other gods mentioned, like Thoth, Melkathros (Melqart), Mouth ("Death"), and Dagon (a grain god) integrate Canaanite gods into a Greco-Roman version of the Phoenician past. Finally, the Zophasemin cited in the above passage are the first intelligent creatures to emerge. They are, literally, "heavenly observers" (cf. Hebrew *Zophe-shamayim*). This motif also appears associated with a theory of the beginnings of life in Egypt, transmitted by Greek writers, whereby first humans looked up at the cosmos and identified the moon and the sun with Isis and Osiris (Diod., *Sic.* 1.10.11).

Philo synthesized local mythology and presented it through the filters of a historicized myth (so-called Euhemerism) and through the lenses of cross-cultural interpretation (so-called *interpretatio*). These modes of engaging ancient lore were presumably apt for his educated peers, including local Roman Phoenicians like him, educated in a Greco-Roman way (López-Ruiz 2017; Delalonde 2021). At the same time, his cosmogony is an astonishing example of mythological resilience, a witness to millenary traditions that had otherwise gone under the radar of our limited preserved texts. His narrative also shows the capacity of myth to morph and adapt, to preserve by changing the frame. Not very differently, centuries after their religion was abandoned and substituted by Christianity, Norse writers recaptured and transmitted part of their mythological sagas through a historicizing, Euhemeristic account that could be palatable or tolerable to the Christian readership. These adaptations probably saved the little we have of this mythology that is otherwise marginalized and canceled as pagan (Lindow 2021: 103–32; cf. Roubekas 2017: 170–73).

The historicizing reading of myths had another flip side. If gods had been kings or human benefactors, then kings are potential god-material, by historical precedent, as it were. Euhemerism played with the god-king association and could be used to reinforce the idea that kings were chosen by gods or could be worshipped as gods (Lindow 2021: 103–32, 137). As mentioned previously, real-life leaders such as Alexander the Great and his Macedonian successors associated themselves with founding heroes and gods. Likewise, during the Second Punic War (218–201 BCE), the propaganda machine of both the Carthaginian leader Hannibal and his Roman rival Scipio drew associations between the generals and the god Herakles-Melqart. This syncretic figure merged the qualities of the divinized hero and son of Zeus for Greeks and Romans, while he contained a version of the Tyrian god Baal for the Carthaginians. Both divine figures were celebrated as founders of cities and culture-bringers, and the rival forces brandished the "Herculean" symbol while they competed to dominate the western Mediterranean and to appeal to Phoenician, Greek, Roman, and other local populations (Miles 2010: 248, 314).

The sustained and constantly evolving engagement with previous mythology, including ideological and literary revivals, allowed for a significant fraction of the Classical traditions to reach us, despite the inevitable destructions, selections, and omissions of Greek and Near Eastern texts and artwork. The philosophical and even mystical use of Greek myth provided another rescue boat for these traditions to weather even the sweeping wave of Christianity.

Philosophizing with myths

Back in Classical Athens, Hesiod's *Theogony* and the traditional view of the gods animated the plots of Greek tragedies and the monuments of the city. But already since the sixth century BCE, the pre-Socratic or natural philosophers had introduced new ideas about the origins of the physical world. The movement started, it seems, among Greeks from Ionia (i.e., the coast of Asia Minor, today's Turkey). Three figures represent this epistemological jump: Thales, Anaximander, and Anaximenes, all from Miletus. They postulated a different beginning of the cosmos, not from an enigmatic "Chaos" or from the reproduction of the gods that represented the different elements and realms; instead, they posited other physical or metaphysical elements as first principles, whether it was water, according to Thales, or the unlimited or indefinite (*apeiron*) for Anaximander, who also believed that human beings descended from other species. Anaximenes, meanwhile, set wind as the principle that transformed into other elements and was governed by the mind (*nous*). Many others followed, including Heraclitus "the Obscure," Pythagoras, Parmenides, and Democritus. They all partook in the search for a simplified view of the cosmos that stemmed from philosophical and scientific inquiry—at the time not considered separate forms of inquiry.

These thinkers did not so much express atheistic views as criticize the anthropomorphic representation of the gods in Greek tradition. Most famously, Xenophanes said that all people imagine their gods in their own physical semblance (blond, dark, etc.), and in the same way horses, cows, and other animals would represent their gods as horses and cows, or whatever their own form was, if they had the capacity to draw images (Whitmarsh 2015: 60). Behind this thinking was the search for explanations of the physical world independent from myths, while not excluding the existence of a divine realm, but rather its characterization. If a god or gods existed, this divinity would not be susceptible to colorful stories, but perhaps a more abstract, intelligent, and perfect entity animated the cosmos. Another branch of early philosophy concerned itself with the human world, especially with ethical and political questions and the use of language. Both strands of this early philosophical thinking about the world and human beings' place in it deeply influenced Socrates and his pupil Plato (Osborne 2004; Wright 2008; Stamatellos 2012).

Plato did not endorse the old myths either. Thinking of his contemporary Athenian community (ca. 424–348 BCE), he questioned what kind of example myths set for the malleable minds of children.

The glorified epic poems they learned by heart portrayed Kronos castrating his own father and Zeus battling and imprisoning enemies and committing incest and adultery, did they not? Thus, in Plato's *Republic*, Socrates imagines an ideal state governed by philosophers, where such false stories have no place (377d–78e). And yet myths, including creation myths, are not absent from Plato's dialogues. Storytelling proves to be a flexible tool of expression, example, and instruction, as it would continue to be until our days. If the traditional stories are not useful for Plato's purposes, his characters, including Socrates, deploy stories involving gods to exemplify various viewpoints in a way familiar to their audience. At the same time, stories were ideal vehicles to introduce innovative elements that would challenge those reprehensible aspects of the traditional myths (see, e.g., Edmonds 2004: 161–71). In regard to cosmogony and anthropogony, we can see this strategy in Plato's dialogues *Timaeus* and *Protagoras*.

In the *Timaeus*, the interlocutor (Timaeus) is an alleged philosopher from southern Italy, who presents a detailed account of the creation of the cosmos by a demiurge or craftsman deity. He details the motivations (to construct "the all" as "an intelligent whole," for "everything to be good"), the materials used (fire and earth mixed with water and air), and the shape and organization of this carefully crafted universe, which took the form of a perfect and self-sufficient sphere. Some of the themes in Timaeus's account draw on the idea of the first principles of the pre-Socratics, but they also innovate on earlier cosmogonic traditions—for instance, the idea of a demiurge god and the use of specific materials, such as earth and water, were shared with Near Eastern creation stories. The demiurge of the *Timaeus* moves beyond those creation narratives and is presented as an all-intelligent god who forms the universe as a material version of his own soul and mind. The expressly non-anthropomorphic nature of his god and his elements, and the alignment of cosmogony and geometry (the sphere as a perfect shape), are hallmarks of Platonic ontology.

180   GREEK MYTHOLOGY

Behind all of it lies the extremely influential idea that all that exists in the material world is a pale reflection of the most real, divine, and metaphysical world from which everything stemmed. The goal of the philosophical inquiry is to dissipate as much as possible the physical veils between human nature and that true reality, at least inasmuch as the soul can attain an approximation to that true reality through knowledge. The soul's disembodied experience while transmigrating from life to life is also its main path for learning, an idea that also appears scattered through other dialogues, especially in the *Phaedrus*, the "Myth of Er" in the *Republic*, and the *Meno*. These aspects of Platonic metaphysics are in dialogue with Pythagorean and Orphic ideas and Eleusinian Mysteries, all concerned with knowledge about the afterlife, while they also evoke the idea of divine epiphany that has long roots in Greek myth and religion, albeit deeply transformed (Nightingale 2021). The concept of the transmigration of the soul in the *Timaeus* also conveys the idea that the souls of women and animals had transferred over from previous men who failed to attain perfection—the gender hierarchy of Genesis 2 comes to mind here, where God created woman only after man and even after animals (see chapter 3). As in all of Plato's writings, however, it is impossible to completely disentangle which ideas represent Plato's thinking and which that of his dramatic characters.

The cosmological account in Plato's *Timaeus* became a crucial text for Roman philosophers. Perhaps most representative is the text known as the *Dream of Scipio*, by the famous Roman politician and writer Cicero (106 BCE–43 CE). He draws on Platonic ideas to elaborate a cosmological vision, in which Scipio the Elder (or the Great), the famous victor over Hannibal, appears to his grandson Scipio Aemilianus and shows him the universe in all its Platonic perfection, appropriately zooming in on the Earth and Rome's and Carthage's position in it and predicting Scipio's conquest of the latter (Cicero, *Republic*/*De re publica* 6, 9–26). Similarly, the Jewish author Philo of Alexandria tried to synthesize Genesis's cosmogony with that of the *Timaeus* (*On the Creation of the Cosmos According to Moses*). The thread continued through the Neoplatonists and Christian interpreters, who grafted the God of the Judeo-Christian tradition onto the Platonic Greek idea of an intelligent single deity behind the universe.

In another of Plato's dialogues, the *Protagoras*, the sophist of the same name narrates an anthropogony. The speaker uses the myth to illustrate how human beings all have, both by nature and by divine decree, the capacity to act justly as citizens of their community. But these qualities, he contends, need to be cultivated and polished in order to obtain political excellence, hence the need for the services of teachers of rhetoric and political skill, such as himself. The story begins with cosmogonic motifs, including the use of earth and fire, familiar from the *Timaeus*:

> *Once there was a time when gods existed, but mortal kinds did not exist. When the time ordained for their genesis arrived for them too, the gods formed them within the earth, compounding them from earth and fire and all those things mixed of earth and fire. And when they were about to bring them to light, they appointed Prometheus and Epimetheus to adorn them and to distribute to each of them the appropriate powers.*
> (Plato, *Protagoras* 320c[7])

Next, the gods commissioned Prometheus and Epimetheus to create living things and distribute qualities and defenses to each, balancing different types of characteristics: some animals thus are small but light and swift; others are slow but have natural armor; some have wings, others fur; some eat plants, others eat other animals; and so on (*Protagoras* 320c–324d). But Prometheus left his less thoughtful brother Epimetheus to do the work, only to realize in his final inspection that human beings had been left without defenses compared to their nonrational peers in the animal kingdom. As a last-minute resort, before all living things came into existence,

[7] Translated by M. Anderson in López-Ruiz 2018: 105.

Prometheus stole the wisdom of arts and crafts. He also stole fire, not from Zeus as in Hesiod but from Hephaistos and Athena, hence providing human beings with technical knowledge to compensate for their physical vulnerability, what Protagoras calls "wisdom concerning life." But, alas, they still lacked political wisdom (which only Zeus could grant) to guide them as they developed language and religion and formed societies for their own safety. As a result, they failed to prosper and nearly went extinct. Coming to the rescue, Hermes obtained permission from Zeus to bring to human beings "respect and justice," which was distributed to all. The takeaway is that justice and political wisdom are not like a learned technology that only experts know (as in the case of carpenters or other craftsmen) but are innate qualities that *everyone* is expected to possess, cultivate, and make good use of, since in fact people are held accountable if they do not do so.

The story also presents humans as the only among animals to believe in the gods, since they "received a share of the divine lot, and, in the first place, because of his kinship with god" (*Protagoras* 322). In other words, religion is a human quality, explained with obvious circularity through the unique bond between humans and gods. In this anthropogony, Plato is drawing on traditional themes, such as the involvement of Prometheus and Epimetheus, the use of clay, and the stealing of fire, while introducing new twists. For instance, not only woman (Pandora) is created and endowed with gifts, but so are all the living creatures; there is a comparison between nonrational and rational animals (human ones); and, especially, the idea that technology (fire, crafts) is not enough for humans to survive in their societies. Hence Plato deploys his own version of a mythological tale as an example, in order to provoke a debate about the relationship between human nature, education, and political life. The contrast between Prometheus ("Forethinking") and his brother Epimetheus ("Afterthinking"), who was "not at all very wise," is rather humorous but takes on its own consequences. In the background lies the story about Epimetheus bringing Pandora and marriage into the male universe, with all its woes, but here it is not her curiosity but his lack of wits and negligence that cost human beings eons of primitive living, until further divine intervention uplifts them into political existence.

Plato resorts to cosmogonic tropes in other parts of his work. Invariably, the frame of mythical storytelling provokes thinking outside the frame. Plato toys freely with Hesiod's myth of the metal Races at different times. In the *Republic*, Socrates uses the analogy to illustrate the innate qualities and aptitudes of citizens in the ideal state. In this story, God infused the soul of the rulers with gold, the most precious metal, then that of the auxiliaries or guardians with silver, and the farmers' and craftsmen's soul with iron and brass, although there is room for mixed offspring too; in this way, each citizen is marked from birth with an essential quality and assigned their appropriate role (*Republic* 3.414a–c). Socrates calls this a "noble lie" (also called a "Phoenician tale"); that is, it is a fictional story that nonetheless would have a constructive effect if taken as a truth or as a guiding example. Later in the same work, the degrading metals loosely represent the types of political regimes: aristocracy, timocracy, oligarchy, democracy, and tyranny, whereby the aristocratic and oligarchic class (gold-silver?) strives to restrain the populist tendencies (iron-brass?), and the mixture of metals (i.e., classes) produces unevenness and disorder and war (*Republic* 8.547a–c).

Finally, the idea of the human Races or Ages surfaces also in the *Statesman*, where the Eleatic Stranger draws a correspondence between two historical ages and two alternating directions of the rotating universe. This cycle is not marked by the metal metaphor but by the association of each age (and direction) with Kronos and Zeus. Echoing the dichotomy between the Gold and Iron Races, however, the first age is governed by Kronos and, in it, humans needed no laws or institutions, living in a more primitive state, while during the age of Zeus, the god is absent. This situation requires the human race to develop the skills for social organization, defense, and self-governance. Developing philosophy and wisdom thus become

184 GREEK MYTHOLOGY

necessary for survival in the absence of divine intervention (*Statesman* 269c–274e).

In the *Symposium*, we can see yet a bolder innovation in the story of the creation of human beings. This time the comedian Aristophanes volunteers a myth that makes all genders and sexualities equal from the start (*Symposium* 189c–193d). It goes something like this: Human beings descended from the planet-gods Sun, Earth, and Moon and were of one of three genders: male (from the Sun), female (Moon), and androgynous (Earth). Created in the planets' image, they were spherical in shape. With time, the semi-divine, round people became excessively powerful and arrogant, and Zeus punished them by cutting them in half. As a result, the severed halves are the lovers, forever driven to seek each other's "other half" in order to feel complete. Besides providing a wonderful tribute to the power of Love (the topic of the *Symposium*), there is an ironic twist to this image of origins: the Sun-children and Earth-children (all-male and all-female in their original form) represent the homoerotic lovers, who seek their other same-sex partners, while the originally androgynous Moon-children (male-female) represent lovers drawn to the opposite sex.

In this remarkably modern and egalitarian story, Plato's Aristophanes reverse-engineers a cosmogony from the observed dynamics of human love-attraction, thus subverting traditional gender stereotypes (the androgynous is the manliest gender and the "straight" proto-humans become homosexual lovers). Platonic ideas also shape the story, and the astral anthropogony brings to mind the spheres in the cosmogony of the *Timaeus*: the gods did not create the planets, but the planets (perfect spheres) are gods; if, instead of anthropomorphic gods, human beings were made like them, they would be comically round. In turn, the old trope of *hybris* surfaces when Zeus hampers down human ambition by splitting the first humans in half, while the myth poignantly explains the nature of love: we all are "tokens of a human being" and live in search for our other half: "For desire of the whole, therefore, and the pursuit of it, the name is Eros," says Aristophanes.[8]

Leaving aside other mythical narratives and references in Plato's works (see Partenie 2009; Collbert et al. 2012), his story of Atlantis provides a different and unparalleled iteration of the theme of the destruction of civilization by the gods, with overtones of the Flood mythology. As much as Atlantis has become most popular as a mystified lost city, Plato (the only source for the story) paints Atlantis as an overbearing, evil force that was rightfully crushed. In the story, the mythical, wealthy state tried to conquer the rest of the known world and was smitten by Zeus for its arrogance. In this sense, it is a tale of devolution. The Atlantians descended from Poseidon but were progressively corrupted by wealth and power, whence Zeus ordered Poseidon to sink them into the Ocean, much as Enlil ordered Adad and Enki/Ea to bring on the flood to humankind in the *Atrahasis* story. In the popular image of Atlantis, it is usually forgotten that it was Athens (a utopic Athens situated before historical times) that confronted and defeated Atlantis, to stop its aggression against "all of Europe."

In the end, the Atlantians and their god Poseidon represent an imaginary maritime civilization that became imperialistic and aggressive, pitched against a utopic and humbler Athenian society that maintained its values and its integrity. These "proto-Athenians" seem to encapsulate some traits of the Platonic ideal state (*Timaeus* 20d–25d, *Kritias* 108c–121c) and of the more austere Spartan society, and some authors think that Plato used Atlantis as a critique of the imperial Athens of Pericles, which dragged the Greek world into the long and bloody turmoil of the Peloponnesian Wars (431–404 BCE). The Athenian Parthenon celebrated the victory of Athena over Poseidon for the divine oversight of the city. But, just as the imagined Atlantis, fifth-century Athens became an imperial force in the

---

[8] *Symposium* 192, translated by M. Anderson in López-Ruiz 2018: 409.

186   GREEK MYTHOLOGY

Aegean and imposed its military and political power on other smaller states. Thus, Athens abandoned its traditional values attached to Athena and Hephaistos and gave in to the maritime power of Poseidon, sealing its own demise. The polis was "sunk" by the alliance led by Sparta, which in a sense remained closer to the values articulated in Plato's *Republic*, here projected onto the imagined "Proto-Athens" (Vidal-Naquet 1986: 263–84).

Greek Myths for Roman poets

Cosmogonies were not part of the traditional Roman repertoire. As far as we know, Roman mythology started with foundation stories, such as those of Aeneas and Romulus and Remus, which drew a continuous line between the state's origins and the ruling families of Republican and Imperial Rome. As Greek mythology became part of the Roman imagination, however, Latin poets adopted Greek creation themes and contributed their own versions in the young literary language that was Latin. In what is the richest Latin collection of Greek myths, Ovid (43 BCE–17 CE) masterfully interwove Greek stories in a long poem called the *Metamorphoses*, or "Transformations." He used as a thread the power of Love over mortal and immortal beings, and the transformations that its irresistible and sometimes violent impetus caused to those involved, a force that cuts across genders, species, and matter. His narrative is written in dactylic hexameters, the traditional epic verse of Homer and Hesiod, albeit in Latin. Ovid also winks at Hesiod's catalogue technique in his threading of characters and stories.

The *Metamorphoses* opens with a cosmogonic account. The moment of creation already set in motion the transformation of the universe that allowed all others to follow:

My mind is bent to tell of bodies changed into new forms. You gods, for you yourselves have wrought the changes, breathe on these my

*undertakings, and bring down my song in unbroken strains from the
world's very beginning even onto the present time.*

*Before the sea was, and the lands, and the sky that hangs over all,
the face of Nature showed alike in her whole round, which state have
men called Chaos.* (Ovid, *Metamorphoses* 1. 1–7[9])

As we can see, Ovid frames his cosmogony with a short preamble, in
yet another nod to the earlier poets. But he substitutes the traditional epic invocation to the Muses by one to the vaguer "you gods,"
showcasing from the beginning a more universal and non-
anthropomorphic idea of the divine that spoke to his contemporary
audience. Still, Ovid will slide into statements such as, "God—or
kindlier Nature—composed this strife...," or "When he, whoever of
the gods it was, had thus arranged...." Therefore, the god of Ovid's
creation story is also a demiurge or arranger who "molded the earth."
It is striking that he articulates the contours of the creation by mentioning what is *not there* yet, an image that lands close to the
Mesopotamian formulation of beginnings (remember the opening
of *Enuma elish*: "When the skies above were not yet named..."). But
the universe shaped by Ovid's God takes a life of its own, and here
the poet aligns with the thinking of the natural philosophers. Nature
follows its own path as Earth and its elements evolve from a state of
emptiness and disorder (a "chaotic mass") to one of complexity
accompanied by order and differentiation, culminating in the complex organisms that are animals and human beings. They are superior to other animals as intelligent creatures, made "of finer stuff,"
and it is they who "turned their eyes to heaven." These stargazers fit
into a trope that appears beyond Greek and Roman literature even
in the Phoenician and biblical traditions (see discussion of the *Noah*
movie in later section "A modern Noah and his Creator").

The idea of an initial material chaos carries Epicurean overtones.
This view had its roots in the writings of Democritus and also

---

[9] Translated in Miller 1916, modified.

188 GREEK MYTHOLOGY

Leucippus, who in the fifth century BCE posited that matter was made of changing and finite combinations of irreducible unchanging particles ("atoms," means "indivisible" in Greek). In following this trend, Ovid is not alone among Roman poets. A generation earlier than Ovid, the poet and philosopher Lucretius devoted an entire epic poem (*De rerum naturae/On the Nature of Things*) to exploring the poetic potential of the Epicurean atomist view of nature. Why not? Hexametric verse had been the traditional vehicle not only for epic but wisdom poetry and also of oracles and charms, and philosophers turn to Hesiod and Homer time and again as sources of hidden wisdom (see discussion on allegory in the section "Resilient cosmogonies"). As ideas about the true nature of the cosmos evolved, why not invest them with the same authoritative form of speech that immortalized the ancient representations of the gods and the world order?

Lucretius also pays homage to the force of love and desire. Fusing the old and the new, he begins his scientific-philosophical poem with an invocation to Venus (*De rerum naturae* 1.1–26; see López-Ruiz 2018: 411–12). Thus, Venus becomes Lucretius's Muse:

Since you alone govern the nature of things, nor without you
would any day rise into the regions of light
nor anything become capable of inspiring joy or love,
I seek you as an ally for these verses that I write
concerning the nature of things. (Lucretius, *De rerum natura*, 1.20–24[10])

Returning to Ovid, stirring a path between the traditional and the philosophical, his creation account stays away from the succession myth. There is no mating among the gods, no truncated births or castration, and no thunderbolt-throwing. Ovid leaves all that for his mythological representations of the gods in the stories that he chains together in the rest of the *Metamorphoses*. Still, some of Ovid's

---

[10] Translated by H. Eisenfeld in López-Ruiz 2018: 412.

cosmic elements (the Earth, the Sky, Chaos or "chaotic mass") have Archaic precedents. Especially, Eros appeared as a cosmic force in Hesiod and in the Orphic poems, and in the *Metamorphoses* it is love or passion, in its positive and negative aspects, that makes the world "go-round" in continuous transformation.

Also engaging with Hesiod, but this time with the didactic poetry of the *Works and Days*, Ovid provides his own account of the "Five Races." He returns to familiar tropes, such as the nostalgia for the primitive purity of the Golden Race or the violent turn of the Bronze Race. In between, the Silver Race represents the beginning of civilized life under Zeus, with the advent of seasons and agriculture, and with them also toil and social constraints. Ovid streamlines the story into four races (Gold, Silver, Bronze, and Iron), eliminating the awkwardly placed race of Heroes. Perhaps as another corrective to Hesiod, he integrates the Greek Flood story and the Races, making the cataclysm a direct punishment sent by Jove against the degraded Iron Race, who would thus be replaced by a better race. Indeed, the Roman account stressed the theme of theodicy. Ovid puts in the mouth of Zeus a story to exemplify the wickedness of the Iron Race that called for the Flood: the case of King Lykaon of Arcadia. Zeus tells the assembly of the gods how he visited Arcadia, disguised as a man, and Lykaon failed to believe he was a god, despite the signs that others did recognize. Lykaon in fact tried to kill Zeus to test his alleged immortality, and also tried to serve him cooked human flesh as a test of his omniscience (just as Tantalos did in another famous story). As a punishment, Lykaon was turned into an animal, becoming probably the first werewolf in preserved fiction.

Ovid then narrates the survival of Deukalion (Latin Deucalion) and Pyrrha after the Flood. He generally follows the Greek tradition (e.g., in Apollodoros's *Library*, cf. chapter 2), but in his version the Flood survivors receive no help from Prometheus, nor do they build an impressive floating vessel. Less heroically, they accidentally survive on a little raft, whereupon Jove takes pity on them and decides to let them live and reproduce. As in the Greek version, these human

190 GREEK MYTHOLOGY

forebears were wise enough to correctly interpret a prophecy given by Themis (divine justice), that they should sow the earth not with seeds but with the earth's "bones" (meaning stones), from which the new generation of women and men emerged, thus siring a truly autochthonous generation (see chapter 2). But Ovid again artfully combines the traditional motif of the Flood and anthropogony with a more "organic" view of natural processes: he imagines the rest of nature spontaneously returning to life thanks to the conditions after the flood (moist, light, heat), in another wink to Epicureanism and natural philosophy. Water becomes again a base for creation; or, rather, life brews in the sun-heated marshes, which, going back in a circle, recalls the role of mud and water in earlier Near Eastern cosmogonies (see chapters 1 and 3).

The mythical image of the Great Flood was popular enough in Rome that it could be used to magnify current events. That is what Horace (Ovid's contemporary) does when he compares the flooded Tiber River to "the time of Pyrrha," when fish were caught on treetops and helpless animals floated down the streams (*Odes* 1.2.5–12). In a shorter allusion, the other greatest poet of the Augustan era, Virgil (70–19 BCE) also evokes Deucalion, who threw those stones "into the empty world" (*Georgics* 1.61–62). He also resorts to the theme of the Races of humankind, but further reduces this story of human devolution to two stages, not identified with metals. The main change is the introduction of agriculture, fishing, and other labor needed for survival, all of which ruins the paradisiac state of bliss enjoyed by human beings "before Jove's day" (*Georgics* 1.121–46).

Virgil also toys with cosmogony in two other poems. In the so-called "Song of Silenus," the satyr-god is forced to entertain the nymphs and satyrs who are holding him hostage, and he resorts to myth-telling. He begins with a brief cosmogony, which evokes the vast void (again a form of Chaos). But in general, his short creation story aligns with the nature-based picture that Roman authors favored, in which "elements" emerged and mixed, until woods grew and living creatures walked on the mountains that "knew them not"

(Eclogues 6.31). Finally, Virgil embeds another "mini-cosmogony" at the end of Book 1 of the *Aeneid*. This time it is voiced by a Phoenician bard, who entertained Aeneas and his companions in the court of Queen Dido of Carthage. The poet is called Iopas, and his divine teacher is said to be Atlas, a figure mythologically situated in North Africa, where the Atlas Mountains take his name. This departure from Hesiod's and Homer's Muses is intentional and appropriate for the unexpected North African setting of this cosmogony singing. The Carthaginian's myth, in turn, focuses on natural and astrological elements, which makes it sound different from the standard Greek tradition. This is, in other words, an "alien" cosmogony, while still within a recognizable genre. Iopas the Carthaginian

> *Sings of the unpredictable moon, of the sun and its labors,*
> *Origins human and animal, causes of fire and of moisture,*
> *Stars: Lesser, Greater Bear, rainy Hyades, also Arcturus,*
> *Why in the winter the sun so hurries to dive in the Ocean,*
> *What slows winter's lingering nights, what blocks and delays them.*
> (Virgil, *Aeneid* 1.742–46[11])

Within the fiction of the *Aeneid*, this is a Phoenician-Carthaginian cosmogony, even if it does not particularly match up with what we know about Phoenician cosmogonies (discussed in relation to Philo of Byblos in the earlier section "From gods to kings and back"). If anything, Virgil's elaboration vaguely recalls the astral cosmogony put in Orpheus's mouth in Apollonius of Rhodes's *Argonautica* (*Argonautica* 1.493–515; see López-Ruiz 2018: 56–57, 66–67). We will never know if Virgil's intention was to challenge cultural stereotypes (the Carthaginians also sang epic songs and cosmogonies), or to signal that cosmogonies were an ancestral genre among Greeks and even "others," including Phoenicians, but not yet the "proto-Romans" whom Aeneas represents.

[11] Translated in Ahl, 2007 and López-Ruiz 2018: 67.

Resilient cosmogonies

Classical mythology survived even through the substantial political and religious changes of late antiquity and the Middle Ages, thanks to the continuous desire to read ancient texts for their literary and educational value. To the degree that the ancient gods remained a problem after pagan religions were officially buried, the effort never died to extract hidden wisdom about philosophical and theological matters in the ancient texts that justified the preservation of the pagan stories (Graf 2011; Ziolkowski 2013; Kaldellis 2021). The main strands of interpretation of mythical stories were firmly rooted in antiquity. They are Euhemerism and allegory. Euhemerism, which historicized the gods as ancient kings and benefactors, was repurposed from antiquity and became especially popular among early Christian authors (among others, Theophilos of Antioch, Clement of Alexandria, Lactantius, and very importantly Eusebios of Caesarea, through whom we have fragments from both Euhemeros and Philo of Byblos). Referring back to this tradition enabled them to dismiss the pagan gods as mere humans, and to engage with aspects of Greco-Roman myth while disassociating themselves from its theological dimensions (Roubekas 2017: 114–37; Kaldellis 2021: 169–70). Just as with allegory, Euhemerism also salvaged myths while demolishing their protagonists as viable objects of religious belief.

Allegory was a symbolic interpretation of myth already popular in Classical Greece. It sought deeper, hidden meanings behind the words of ancient authors. As Peter Struck (2004: 4) explains, "allegorical commentators tend to see a deep well of wisdom, which everywhere nearly vibrates with arcane observations on the structure of the world and the place of humans within it." The commentator of the cosmogony on the Derveni Papyrus, probably writing in the early fourth century BCE, already engaged with this mode of interpretation. For him, Orpheus said "great things in riddles" (Struck 2004: 31). The term used for "riddle" (*ainigma*) was also associated with didactic language/poetry and with oracles, and riddles and symbols (*symbola*) were tools of pre-Socratic philosophers. The Pythagoreans were especially notorious for passing down among "insiders" certain enigmatic phrases—for instance, that the sea is the tear of Kronos, or that the number five is justice. The semantic leap from a physical "token" (*symbolon*) used to recognize someone to a verbal password or shortcut that directs you to a different meaning can be tracked to this realm (Struck 2004: 78, 96–110). Allegorical or symbolic reading became more systematic and widespread, as it allowed readers of different cultural and religious backgrounds to continue to cultivate the Greek "classics," not only in the Hellenistic and Roman periods, but even later under Christianity.

Allegory was especially important for a branch of Platonism known as Neoplatonism. But the mechanism was eventually adopted by Christian writers, in a process that made it possible to continue studying and enjoying the otherwise theologically dissonant stories conveyed by the most revered Greek texts, especially Hesiod, Homer, and the tragedians, but also Virgil and Ovid. As Luc Brisson puts it, in quite a literal sense, allegory saved myths. Hesiod and Homer, foremost among other authors, came to be regarded as "proto-Christian" philosophers or theologians (Lamberton 1989, 1992; Brisson 2004; Graf 2011). Their antiquity, prestige, and literary quality made their well-known stories involving gods and heroes ideal to use as educative examples and allowed them to be the source of renewed interpretations. Attention usually concentrated on a number of key passages, in an inconsistent treatment often criticized by those who opposed the allegorical method. For instance, the Homeric image of the "cave of the nymphs" on Ithaca (*Odyssey* 13.102–12), with its two openings, inspired much allegorical interpretation. The Neoplatonist Porphyry likened it to Plato's allegory of the cave and wrote an entire treatise, *On the Cave of the Nymphs*, unveiling how the details of the image represented the entire material cosmos (Lamberton 1983; Akçay 2019).

Another favorite Homeric image for the allegorists was that of the golden chain of Zeus: In the *Iliad*, Zeus challenged all the gods to try to pull him down from Olympos with a golden chain, if they dared. That would show them how much stronger he was than all of them together, as he could easily pull them up with the chain and make them all dangle around in midair, together with the earth and the sea (*Iliad* 8.17–27). The passage has succession-myth overtones, inasmuch as Zeus betrays insecurity in his position, and perhaps overstates his power. From this and other mythological allusions to threats or attempts on the gods, we can surmise that the succession question was far from forever closed (López-Ruiz 2014a). But ancient philosophers were more interested in stretching the passage for cosmological wisdom beyond the surface of the story. Already in Plato's dialogues, Socrates proposes the Homeric image is about the movement of the sun and the heavens as something necessary for the existence of all things, human and divine. In the same way, he surmises, Homer mentions Ocean and Tethys as the origins of the gods (*Iliad* 14.201, 302), to signal that everything is in motion and originates in fluidity and motion (*Theaetetus* 152e).

These sorts of interpretations had a long run in Greco-Roman scholarship. They surface in the work of Byzantine scholars, to whom we owe much of the preservation of classical literature and the revival of its study in the European west during the Renaissance (Kaldellis 2021). Scholars such as Eustathius and Tzetzes (twelfth century), and philosophers such as Psellos (eleventh century) and Pletho (fourteenth–fifteenth century), revisited the "golden chain" episode to provide various insights into previous and their own readings of the myth. Some drew on Stoic views and tied the image to the four elements and the cyclical destruction of the universe, while Neoplatonic readings made the golden chain into the link between the metaphysical first cause of everything and the material, inferior realm, with Zeus as a key agent between them. Even in the highly complicated system of Neoplatonic metaphysics, the main concepts are still latched onto the figures of Ouranos-Kronos-Zeus and the succession myth. But far from a scheme of family succession in the divine throne, for the Neoplatonists these figures represented the different levels of reality and perfection in the universe: Ouranos represented "the One" (the cause of all); one level below Kronos was the pure intellect (the demiurge that generates the "world soul"); and, finally, Zeus, who gives birth to gods, angels, and heroes, holds the chain that links these superior realms to the ones below. A simple substitution of Christian names allowed them to maintain the value of the allegory of the golden chain for the connection between people, angels, and God (Brisson 2004: 114–25).

A special fascination (and interpretive challenge) surrounded the unnatural and violent acts enacted by Kronos, namely the castration of his father Ouranos and the devouring of his own children, the Olympian gods. One of the earliest examples can be found already in the Derveni Papyrus, where the quoted cosmogony is interpreted through natural allegory: the text presents an Orphic variation of the castration motif, in which it is Zeus who performs the act, and not with a sickle but by swallowing the genitals of Ouranos, the Sky, also called First Born king (Protogonos). The commentator says this is an "enigma" for Zeus's acquisition of the generative power of the Sun, which hides in the allegory in the image of the phallus (Bernabé 2004, fr. 3–18; cf. López-Ruiz 2018: 55–56). As an example of a later reading, Psellos followed the popular identification of Kronos with Chronos ("Time") and, drawing on Stoic concepts, inferred that the castration story meant that everything is contained in time and cannot escape time. But Zeus, whom Kronos/ Time failed to devour, is not only the source of the rest of creation but also the symbol of reason, hence only reason escapes the laws of time. Like other Neoplatonists, in his extensive treatises Psellos was determined to harmonize central aspects of the theologies of the Pythagoreans, Plato, the Orphic texts, and the *Chaldean Oracles* (a set of religious-philosophical texts compiled in Roman times and highly rated among Neoplatonists). Adding one more layer, Psellos made Christian theology part of the circle, tied through the figure of

Moses, whom, in his view, the ancient Greeks had plagiarized (Brisson 2004: 118–19).

While the Byzantines of the Roman East continued massaging the ancient myths following Classical Greek trends, the Christians in the medieval West were not so open to engaging with the ancient gods. But the Olympians survived, for instance, through their connection with the planets and the Zodiac signs, a form of natural allegory itself. Interest in astronomy and science eventually opened the door to translations of scientific Greek texts by Arab intellectuals, and other Greek and Roman works of literature slowly made their way into European thinking and education, via Arab and Byzantine scholarship. The reacquaintance with classical works in the West brought new efforts to reconcile Christian and pagan theology, returning once more to the common ground found in Mosaic scripture, with creation and the Flood narratives serving again as the key to show that Greek philosophy and cosmology/theology (Pythagorean, Platonic, Neoplatonic, Orphic) was in debt to the older wisdom laid out by Egyptians, Chaldeans, Babylonians, Hebrews, and Phoenicians, who were deemed precursors of Christianity and the oldest recipients of divine knowledge. Not only Aristotle and Plato, but Ovid and Virgil and other great Roman poets were also accepted, therefore, thanks to mythical interpretation, as heralds of Christian theology (Brisson 2004: 137–61; cf. Graf 2011; Ziolkowski 2013).

The Renaissance fostered new levels of love for and engagement with the Greek and Roman heritage in something closer to its own terms, as reflected not only in literature but also in the flourishing plastic arts of this period. Michelangelo's Sistine Chapel fresco somehow epitomizes the new union of classical aesthetic canons and the Abrahamic traditions, not without Platonic overtones (Michelangelo was both a stern Catholic and a student of the Florentine Neoplatonists): at the center of his composition, in the Chapel's most famous scene, God appears in the act of creating

FIGURE 4.2 Adam and Eve are expelled from the Garden of Eden, in a scene from the Sistine Chapel ceiling paintings by Michelangelo (1508–12). Source/Credit: Wikimedia Commons.

the first human being, their fingers not quite touching but establishing a connection between the metaphysical and material realm. Through Adam, the divine spirit infuses the rest of creation, which yearns for that perfection as it sinks into repeated downfalls, represented in the surrounding Eden and the Flood scenes (see Figure 4.2).

In adjacent panels, the prophets who accompany the Genesis characters share the space with Classical Sibyls. These are mythological wisdom-prophetic figures, one of whom (the Sibyl of Cumae) had guided Aeneas in the Underworld (Virgil, *Aeneid*, Book 6). But the Sibyls were also deemed predictors of the birth of Christ (Osborne and Brigstocke 2003). Michelangelo, therefore, brings to the visual arts a blend of Classicism, Platonism, Stoicism, and biblical traditions, a fusion already baked into the cosmogonic opening the Gospel of John that he surely knew: "In the beginning was the Word, and the Word was with God, and the Word was God" (John 1:1). The term *logos* resonated with both the Jewish tradition of Genesis (the creative word of God) and Greco-Roman philosophy, especially Stoicism, where the concepts of *logos* (word, reason) and *pneuma* (breath) became interchangeable first creative principles (Engberg-Pedersen 2018; Struck 2004: 126, 128, 191).

Quoting Brisson (2004: 161) again, allegorical interpretation "turned out to be a gigantic project for cultural integration. Yet its death warrant was not signed by the predominance of any philosophical system, ideological orientation, or even religion. Rather, its end came with the historical event of the great voyages of discovery." In other words, allegory was abandoned due to the eye-opening and horizon-broadening brought by exploration and exploitation of new continents, such as the Americas. The observation and study of the cosmologies and mythologies of other groups completely disconnected from the axis of Greco-Roman and Abrahamic traditions forced the search for more universal principles governing mythical thinking and religious beliefs. It was evidently no longer possible to postulate a historical revelation of the cosmic truth to only some ancient peoples, or to anchor it to specifically Western culture (via the Israelites and the Greeks, who drew it from the Egyptians and Moses). The study of completely new cultures and their narratives led early scholars of religion, such as E. B. Tylor or Max Müller, to also look for deeper universal truths behind them, only following what they saw as extant clues hidden in ritual actions of more "primitive" societies, instead of decoding Greco-Roman texts (see Pals 2015; Josephson-Storm 2017: 94–124). Still, social scientists such as James Frazer and others could not escape the inertia of heavily drawing on Classical myths to interpret faraway cultural systems and ritual worlds, going back in a circle to use ancient myth as some sort of key that hides deep universal human traits, even if they did so through modern anthropological lenses. Creation stories were often central to these interpretations of world religions, seen as clinchers for the relationship between ritual actions and social structures (see the Introduction). Even if the modern theories might have disfavored allegory as a heuristic tool to read or decode ancient texts, the same basic principle was at work: that myths acted, and continue to act, as symbols of deep significance.

Cosmogonies on the Modern Stage

We continue harnessing the familiar and alluring stories of classical myths to speak about the predicament of humanity in the twenty-first century, whether in our writing, our teaching, or in artistic adaptations. Here I focus only on cases of the visual arts and entertainment, where we can find aspects of the creation stories discussed in previous chapters recast in new ways. These offer just a glimpse of the currency and potential of these myths in contemporary popular culture.

Overall, cosmogonies are not a frequent topic in popular media. But recently, divine creation and destruction themes, largely drawn from the biblical world, have provided frames for popular shows. American TV series such as *Supernatural* (Eric Kripke, 2005–20) and *Lucifer* (Tom Kapinos, 2016–21) and the British *Good Omens* (Neil Gaiman, 2019, based on Terry Pratchett's 1990 novel) all chose as a backdrop the cosmic conflict between the forces of Heaven and Hell. This theme includes the mythology of Fallen Angels and the impending threat of the apocalypse in which these forces will come to the final battle of Armageddon, ending the world as we know it. The cosmology in these shows, overall, maps onto Judeo-Christian worldviews and characters. Nevertheless, the shows maintain Christian theology and dogmas at an arm's length by avoiding allusions to Jesus or his close retinue, probably to remain more universally appealing and preempt controversy. This strategy also allows them to move freely within a broader mythological world. For instance, in *Supernatural* the characters deal with all kinds of figures stemming from European folktale and fiction, such as vampires and werewolves, as well as pagan gods and demons; and in *Lucifer*, an otherwise unidentified mother goddess who has also been cast out of Heaven by God becomes a central character in the plot.

Stories about modern superheroes, such as those from the Marvel or DC Universes, tap mainly onto heroic narratives, but cosmogonic schemes are never far from sight (Kripal 2015). Modern superheroes themselves are mythically interesting and paradoxical. Much like the Olympian gods, they can be at once world saviors and hope givers and narcissistic and selfish; they battle chaos and restore order, while also causing cataclysmic destruction of cities (usually New York) or entire worlds. Some are intrinsically superhuman (Spiderman, Wonder Woman), others technologically or biologically enhanced (Iron Man, Batman, Captain America, Spiderman, Captain Marvel), and yet others are completely alien yet human-like (Superman). These twentieth-century superheroes created an entire post–World War II American mythology, partly out of new fantasy and partly creatively drawing on Old World myth; that is the case with the Norse god Thor and with Wonder Woman, an Amazon crossing into our world from an Atlantis-like utopic island.

But there is something titanic about these heroes too, and about the otherworldly enemies they face. Their clashes put at risk not only the human race but the universe as well. Cosmogonic tropes are more engrained in modern heroic stories than we might think, even when not explicitly alluding to ancient myth. This is especially true of certain types and plots, the so-called archetypes, especially exploited in science fiction after Joseph Campbell's books made them popular in the mid-twentieth century (see Campbell 2008). For instance, the theme of the "hero quest" is entangled with plots of primeval battles and clashes between chaos/evil and order/rightfulness, which in turn are intertwined with family conflict and psychological struggles (Salzman-Mitchell and Alvares 2018: 131–35). These themes provide the backbone of extremely popular book series for young adults, all featuring juvenile heroes, such as *Harry Potter*, *The Hunger Games*, and *Percy Jackson and the Olympians*, followed by numerous subsequent movies. Much closer to Hesiod are the graphic novels about the Greek gods by George O'Connor, collectively called *The Olympians*. The first one of the series, *Zeus: King of the Gods*, offers a snapshot of the *Theogony*, covering in a few brilliant strokes the birth of Zeus and his clash with Kronos, with particularly vivid depictions of the Titanomachy (see Figure 4.3). At the

Resilient Myths 201

FIGURE 4.3 Kronos fights with Zeus (small figure at the top, hurling his thunderbolt), from George O'Connor's graphic novel *Olympians*, Book 1, *Zeus: King of the Gods*. Source/Credit: @George O'Connor.

same time, O'Connor avoids the castration of Ouranos by his son Kronos and other motifs for the sake of the younger audience—a move Plato surely would have approved of.

Near Eastern creation mythology, on the other hand, is not nearly as represented in Western media, not least due to the narrow cultural scope of the average Western audience. To mention a few exceptions (and likely missing others) Gilgamesh has made it into some Heavy Metal themes and video games, and an animated Gilgamesh movie in Spanish is expected in 2024 (directed by J. M. Ferrucci and T. Lipgot). Perhaps the Flood story will be featured there. While Marduk and his cosmic victory are nowhere to be seen in popular media, the primeval water goddess of Babylon, Tiamat, became a five-headed dragon-like goddess, a Hydra of sorts, in the *Dungeons and Dragons* universe. Next, I discuss in more detail the cosmogonic undertones of some films and videogames, focusing on Underworld motifs, the Flood story, and heroic figures.

The Underworld frame

The Greek Underworld never fails to provide a great dramatic scenario. Already in Hesiod's *Theogony*, Tartaros was part of the initial cosmic structure (see chapter 1), and incursions in the realm of Hades are tied to famous adventures of a few heroes, such as Herakles, Orpheus, Theseus, Odysseus, and Aeneas. In American films, this type of adventure is freely attributed to other heroes. In *Wrath of the Titans* (2012), Perseus descends to Tartaros, where the gods Hades and Ares are holding his father Zeus prisoner. Zeus's brothers had not only defeated and taken away his weapon, the thunderbolt, but were threatening to revive or awaken the Titan Kronos, held in the depths of Tartaros. This is a twist on the *Theogony*, where it is Zeus who imprisons Kronos and the Titans in the Underworld. In this choice the modern mythmakers also depart from the ancient *katabasis* ("descent") motif, where the experience of accessing the Underworld and its inhabitants grants the heroes a unique knowledge and perspective onto the larger questions related to life and death and the will of the gods, whether by speaking to the survivor of the Flood or observing the destiny of the souls in the Beyond (sources in López-Ruiz 2018: 469–582).

One of the most prolific sources of inspiration for modern artists has been the myth of Orpheus. He tragically lost his newly wedded wife Eurydice to Hades after she was chased by a satyr and bitten by a snake while running away. We might recall that Orpheus was a mythical singer of cosmogonies too, who possessed such a supernatural musical and poetic skill that he could charm not only wild animals but even Hades and his dog Kerberos. Yet the poet could not bring his bride back successfully (see Figure 4.4). The 2001 musical film *Moulin Rouge* (Baz Luhrmann) brought the love story of Orpheus and Eurydice to a romantic Parisian scenario, and earlier famous makeovers include a surrealist film by Jean Cocteau (*Orphée*, 1950) and the tragic romance *Black Orpheus* (1959) of Marcel Camus, set in Rio de Janeiro's Carnaval (Cyrino 2010). More recently, the

FIGURE 4.4 John Roddam Spencer Stanhope, *Orpheus and Eurydice on the Banks of the Styx*, 1878. Source/Credit: ART Collection/Alamy Stock Photo.

musical *Hadestown* (Anaïs Mitchell, 2006) revisits Orpheus's failed attempt at rescuing Eurydice by making Hades into a soul-crushing factory and deploying the stories of Orpheus, Eurydice, and Persephone as vehicles for social critique.

Why is Orpheus such a compelling character? In antiquity, the singer was revered as the source of Orphic cosmogonic wisdom. In modern reception, Orpheus is mainly the hero who charmed his way in and out of the Underworld driven by love; but by doing so, he showed he could salvage the distance between the two worlds. Love, its power and its pain, is the spinal cord that connects all versions of the Orpheus story, reminding us also how Eros appeared as a cosmic force in other mythological accounts, from Hesiod's and Orphic cosmogonies to Ovid's *Metamorphoses*, where Love or Desire is the ultimate cause of all transformations.

Orphic themes also inspire the videogame *Hades* (Supergiant Games, 2018). Here the main character/player is Zagreus, a son of Hades who has to escape an Underworld full of traps, challenges,

204 GREEK MYTHOLOGY

and enemies. The choice is interesting as Zagreus is a name for Dionysos in Orphic texts, where he is invoked as the son of Zeus and Persephone and the potential successor in the divine throne. The repeated death and revival of the character in the game, which is part and parcel of videogame programming, takes on new meaning when attached to Zagreus/Dionysos, the "twice born" god of Orphic myth (see chapter 1).

A modern Noah and his Creator

"In the beginning... there was nothing."

In the darkness of the ark's haul, Noah pronounces these words for his family, while the deluge rages around them. This is a scene in the 2014 movie *Noah* (directed by Darren Aronofsky and cowritten with Ari Handel). The film stars Russell Crow as a rugged but devoted Noah, who struggles to decipher the designs of a distant Creator. More than a cataclysm-survival movie or a rehashing of the Sunday-school Noah story, the movie seems to be about human beings helplessly entangled in a cosmogonic struggle. "Nothing but the silence of the infinite darkness," he continues, whereupon the breath of the Creator brings light and day and night, and all the rest ("let there be light," as the Genesis six-day account has it). The scene overlays Noah's voice on a fast-paced montage representing the evolution of matter and life, from space rocks and gasses to the planet filled with water and the formation of simple organisms evolving into plants and amphibious beings and animals and, finally, *us*. The accelerated vision of creation ends poignantly with an image of two men coming to blows and shattering the creation: "Now it begins again... Paradise returns, but this time, this time there will be no men" (or so this zealous, Earth-saver wannabe Noah hoped for). Here Noah frames this cosmogony as an oral story passed down for generations, told around the fire from fathers to children—only this time it is told perhaps for the last time, as water, the primeval element of creation in Near Eastern myth, is destroying that same world.

There are many potential layers in this scene. For one thing, Noah's voice replaces that of Moses as the Genesis narrator—Moses is of course a much later figure than Noah in the Israelite story, and one who also survives or controls a water cataclysm, during the escape from Egypt. At the same time, with this scene Aronofsky and Handel's Flood narration engages with oral tradition, which perhaps justifies the deviance within the story-world of the movie. As we will see, they also resorted to noncanonical themes of the Israelite tradition. Thinking comparatively about cosmogonic texts, the enunciation that "in the beginning, there was nothing" aligns better with Hesiod's Chaos than with Genesis 1. At the same time, the images that accompany the creation narration convey a view from quantum physics and natural evolution, with a burst of light at the beginning that reminds us of the Big Bang.

Naturally, the makers of *Noah* did not please more literalist religious audiences and were criticized for their deviance from canonical scripture and for endorsing the evolutionary paradigm. Moreover, they represented a distant god only called "the Creator" (not God, the Lord, or Yahweh), whose main concern was the human exploitation and destruction of nature, and hence to save animals ("the innocents"), not Noah or human beings. This image of the Creator bolsters environmental concerns rather than piety, showing a more recent preoccupation with the climate emergency and environmental disasters now occurring all over the world (see Figure 4.5). Moreover, their more universal, abstract deity is much closer to Ovid's or Plato's God than to that of the Hebrew Bible. Seemingly, the writers merged and perhaps tried to reconcile two seemingly contradictory worldviews. Whatever the case, they modeled how scripture can come alive for readers and listeners of other times and can be interpreted by references to new realities or views not available to the ancient scripture's creators. In this, their work is not much

FIGURE 4.5 Flooding in Bangladesh, May 2018. Source/Credit: Rehman Asad, Alamy Stock Photo.

different than that of ancient playwrights, philosophers, and allegorical interpreters of Greek myth.

Besides other deviations from the Genesis narrative, the movie incorporates the character of the "Watchers" into its version of the Flood. This is only one of the points in which the filmmakers engage with a broader biblical tradition than that of Genesis concerning the Flood. These "Watchers" were "fallen angels," thrown down to Earth when they had tried to help the exiled Adam and Eve. In the movie, they take the form of rock giants, who find a new mission on Earth: helping Noah build his ark and defeat the evil local king Tubal-Cain (in Genesis 4:22 he is a descendant of Cain and the first blacksmith). The "Watchers" are drawn from the Jewish Midrash or biblical commentaries from late antiquity. They resemble the Giants or Nephilim from Genesis, who mated with mortal women before the Flood (Gen. 6:4), but the Watchers appear only in the much later apocryphal "Book of the Watchers," which is one of the books attributed to Enoch, the ancestor of Noah, composed in Aramaic in the second–first centuries BCE. The book is concerned with the realm of demons, Nephilim (giants), and fallen angels, and explores the divine justification of the Flood (Ben-Dov 2021). The Aramaic book of Daniel also mentions the figure of the "watcher, holy one" who came down from heaven to convey divine messages to king Nebuchadnezzar in a dream, which Daniel interpreted for him (Daniel 4:13, 17, 23).

In short, the movie *Noah* rewrites the biblical Flood story without the constrains of following a single canonical text, just as we know ancient writers did too. Myths in antiquity were already versatile and subject to fresh renderings that incorporated the old, the new, and the foreign. It is hard to disagree that, through its "purposeful ambiguities and allusions to dense scholarly texts," the movie "hints at untapped possibilities for mainstream cinema, demonstrating how rich and strange movies can be when they interact with older narrative traditions" (Sachs 2014).

Some heroic returns

Heroes draw us to their own earthly micro-cosmos and dazzle us with their extraordinary actions, but they are pawns trapped in the macro-cosmos dominated by the gods. Thus, in Hesiod's *Theogony*, heroes such as Perseus and Herakles are only mentioned in passing as monster-slayers, "fixers" of some mess or another on Earth stemming from the supernatural realm and affecting mortal communities (Salzman-Mitchell and Alvares 2018: 23–24). As we saw in also in the more anthropocentric "Five Races" and Flood myths, founding figures were also imagined as bridging primeval and historical eras as well as the divine-mortal divide (Bachvarova 2021). Herakles, Perseus, the Argonauts, Oedipus, Achilles, and other Homeric heroes represented the end of an epoch as well as a type of relationship with the gods. Modern remakes of their stories do not always dwell on the theological or cosmic level, and sometimes they dispense with the meddling of the gods altogether (as in the 2004 movie *Troy*). In other cases, the opposite happens: the writers amplify the cosmic dimension. This is precisely the take in *Clash of the Titans* (2010) and *Wrath of the Titans* (2012), both based on a classic 1981 film.

The writers of *Clash/Wrath* elaborate on the story of Perseus, a demigod son of Zeus and descendant of Herakles on his mortal side. He is most famous for killing one of the primeval Gorgons, Medousa, with the aid of Athena, whence he recovered his claim to the kingdom from his grandfather. In a familiar pattern, the ruler had tried to get rid of the infant hero to avoid fulfilling a prophecy that his grandchild would kill him and replace him, which of course is exactly what happens. This and other stories reenact in human scale the intergenerational divine struggle for kingship (Salzman-Mitchell and Alvares 2018: 25). They also build on the Hesiodic list of monsters that threatened cosmic order and that famous heroes slayed. In the movies, Perseus not only beheads the Medousa, as in the Classical myth, but the moviemakers take the license to borrow from other stories and add other monsters to the hero's feats, including the Chimaera and the Minotaur (who lives in a labyrinthic Tartarus), Cyclopes, and the "Kraken," a creature from Scandinavian mythology that substitutes for the classical Ketos of the Greek story. The movies take the mythically chaotic scenario of the heroic age (called *chaoskampf* in scholarship) to an entirely new level. They also frame Perseus as a pawn in a power game between Zeus and his rivals, including Kronos and Hades.

In a sense, the *Clash/Wrath* movies construct a second Titanomachy ("Titan war") around the foundational Greek hero Perseus, as does *Immortals* (2011) with the Athenian figure of Theseus. Instead of placing them in a legendary "Heroic Race/Age" that bridged mythical and historical time in the Greeks' minds, the entire mythical timeline is collapsed into one, such that the heroes take part in Zeus's defeat of Kronos. In turn, as Salzman-Mitchell and Alvares point out, the movies are animated by a modern (rather Wagnerian) view of humankind: When these demi-gods intervene,

FIGURE 4.6 Perseus leaves Zeus behind (Sam Worthington and Liam Neeson, respectively), in movie *Clash of the Titans* (2010). Source/Credit: Cinematic/Alamy Stock Photo.

they are not restoring order and consolidating Zeus's rule down the line, as they do in Greek myth; they instead bring down the corrupt and weakened Olympian gods, who ultimately will crumble down into dust (Poseidon, Zeus) or fade away and whither into mortal life (Hades). In other words, the heroes participate in the cosmic struggle, become the next step in cosmic rule, and inaugurate a new anthropocentric era (Salzman-Mitchell and Alvares 2018: 129–80) (see Figure 4.6).

In cosmogonic-theogonic terms, this plot is a modern resolution of the problem of the succession myth. We can think, for instance, of how Orphic cosmogony added the god Dionysos to the succession scheme, a move that harmonized the old theme of succession with the role of the god in Bacchic and Eleusinian mysteries (see chapter 1). Instead of adding slabs to the succession scheme, these modern cosmogonic movies do away with the gods all together. No substitute gods or new religion are suggested, and thus *Clash/Wrath* hails a human-centered, practically atheistic future. This seems a proper take for an anthropocentric, disenchanted modern West, even if this in itself is just a myopic Western perception of the world and a sort of myth itself (Josephson-Storm 2017). In any case, it is difficult to imagine this narrative built around any other than the "pagan" gods, to the extent that they are already long gone and replaced by other divine agents.

The depiction of the heroes overcoming the divine order and fostering a better age runs contrary to the "Races" mythological tradition. Whether in the renditions of Hesiod, Plato, or the Roman poets, there was generally agreement about the degradation of humankind as people draw chronologically and morally farther away from the mythical time when they enjoyed a more perfect union with the divine. But alternative ideas were not absent in ancient thinking either. As discussed in this chapter, the philosophers sought other paths to approach the metaphysical realm (sometimes articulated in mythological terms), and the Athenian playwrights toyed with the idea that the old Titan-Zeus rivalry would be settled thanks to the race of heroes, especially by Herakles, thus entertaining the possibility of attaining a better world order (Aeschylus's *Prometheus Bound*; see Salzman-Mitchell and Alvares 2018: 133–35). In other words, these heroes could bring hope for the human community. The *Clash/Wrath* movies explicitly play with that quintessential human feeling: hope. In Andromeda's words in *Clash*, "[W]e humans have hope when there is no hope and believe when to believe is idiotic. But sometimes, in spite of everything, we prevail" (Salzman-Mitchell and Alvares 2018: 147). If this speech sounds very American it is because individual and collective hope and endurance have become almost mythical American ideals. In contrast, in Hesiod's *Works and Days* (see chapter 2), it was not clear whether the human race was better or worse off because Hope was trapped in Pandora's jar, or what Hope even meant.

The enactment of cosmic fights is also central to renditions of Herakles's story. Leaving aside other Hollywood productions (the latest, in 2014, with a more-than-adequate Herakles played by Dwayne [the Rock] Johnson), I focus on the 1997 Disney *Hercules*. Besides ample liberties and sanitizing alterations to the basic story, the plot is structured around the clash between Zeus and his brother and rival Hades, who intends to overturn the world order. The antagonistic relation between Zeus and Hades is represented as a "good-evil" dichotomy stemming from modern fixations (also in *Clash/ Wrath*) and from Christian ideas of Heaven and Hell, which are fundamentally disconnected from the more neutral Greek idea of Hades and Tartarus, as a single destiny for all souls. In the movie, the focus on the conflict between the brothers Zeus and Hades serves another important function; namely, to avoid the topic of Hera's jealousy, which originally drives Herakles's myth, and with it other "R-rated" aspects of her relationship with Zeus, including adultery, incest, and domestic violence.

Moreover, in Disney's elaboration, divine-human relations are also flipped. Hercules is not so much a demigod (son of Zeus and a mortal woman, Alcmene) who needs to find his way to an Olympian apotheosis, but an "all-god." Again, avoiding the complications of his extramarital birth, he is simply the son of Hera and Zeus, put on Earth and forced to be mortal so as to hide from his nemesis, Hades. As a consequence, the success of this Hercules is *not* becoming a god but finding the value in human life, which resides in family and love, appealing values to the sensibilities of the modern Western audience. It is hard not to see Christianizing overtones in this Hercules, who shows humility, virtue, and self-sacrifice. But again, these associations had been rehearsed already by Stoic and Christian allegorists who made Herakles/Hercules into a symbol of moral and selfless endurance necessary to reach the divine. On the other hand, the clash of divine-cosmic forces in Disney's *Hercules* makes the story tighter and more appealing for modern audiences than his almost interminable series of labors and feats. Also seeking more appealing and relatable angles, at least for mature audiences, the Greek tragedians zoomed in on aspects of Herakles's suffering and madness, which is also the case of the troubled Herakles enacted by the Rock (Salzman-Mitchell and Alvares 2018: 103–18).

*

Perhaps we can finish with an image from the 2022 movie *Everything Everywhere All at Once* (dir. Daniel Kwan and Daniel Scheniert), and its twenty-first-century demiurgic figure: in a reality composed of infinite multiverses, it is a modern, gay teenager called Jobu Tupaki who acquires the power to manipulate matter (she is the "Alpha" version of Joy, the daughter of the protagonist couple). Humorously and tragically at once, this young female demiurge creates a black hole shaped like an "everything bagel," which threatens to destroy the entire universe. From the planets and Timaeus's universe to the cosmic egg and this "cosmic" bagel, circular shapes draw the imagination of the cosmogonist time and again. And in *Everything Everywhere*, as in so many of our creation stories, Love is once more the force that moves and saves the natural and human world from collapsing back into nothingness.

Conclusion

The Many Lives of Creation Stories

Cosmogonies provided a two-way road between the mythological past and lived experience. They framed the world inhabited by their audiences, while simultaneously projecting the questions and categories of the real world back onto the stories. For all our modern scientific savviness and advanced technology, we have no definitive answer to the ultimate question of how it all began, what the initial act of creation entailed (if there was one), and when and how the first of our human ancestors lived. As David Graeber and David Wengrow put it in their ambitious work *The Dawn of Everything*, "It is very tempting to make up stories about what might have happened: stories that necessarily reflect our own fears, desires, obsessions and concerns. As a result, such distant times can become a vast canvas for the working out of our collective fantasies" (Graeber and Wengrow 2021: 78).

The same gods of myth were the gods that people shared their food with, prayed to, and swore by, without cognitive dissonance (see the Introduction). At one end, creation stories were interwoven with ritual practices, whether through allusions to established rites and festivals or to religious landmarks. Prometheus had initiated animal sacrifice; the gods set up the social conventions that structured social life, such as marriage, work, and kingship; divine beings inhabited the mountain peaks, deep valleys, and rocky shores that existed in the background of the daily lives of countless generations;

214 GREEK MYTHOLOGY

and human-made temples served as houses for Zeus, Aphrodite, Baal, and other gods of cult. They were often covered in art that celebrated the events by which divine and cosmic order was established, contested, and reaffirmed. In other words, in the Near East as in Greece, myth permeated all aspects of society. Literary creations, such as the *Theogony*, the *Enuma elish*, or the book of Genesis, became pillars for entire cultures and their religious traditions, in some cases until modern times. On the other hand, primeval narratives often explained, reinforced, or critiqued established practices and ideas. The association between kings and gods and the supernatural representation of natural phenomena contained the seeds of new streams of interpretation and critique of ancient myths. Science and philosophy pushed the search for physical and theological answers outside the mythical frame, even as new thinkers and writers often returned to the familiar old myths in order to formulate new philosophies.

Some mythic motifs resurfaced across millennia and cultures, though always taking culture-specific forms, and have served as threads to run through these chapters. For example, in various creation stories, water often plays a primordial role, as do gods impersonating Earth and Sky. The motif of the struggle between different generations of gods, usually belonging to the same family, is also used in several mythologies to explain the origin of the "current" world order, usually with a Storm/Weather/Sky god at the helm. The older gods and various monsters fought and defeated by this god represent chaos and tyranny. Love and Desire, or Aphrodite/Venus, also gained a special position in Greco-Roman cosmogonies as a world-moving force, while Orphic theogonies positioned Dionysos, the god of wine and mind-alteration, as a possible successor to Zeus. As for human beings, their creation and demise were formulated in diverse ways. If one aspect sticks out, it is the idea of a demiurge god or gods, who created human beings as clay vessels (with earth and water as prime materials), although in all traditions there is a sense that mortals bear some divine component within them since their creation. Why they were created is not always made explicit, but sometimes it is to alleviate the gods' burden, or to manage the rest of nature. In the case of women, it is to keep the first man company, or to make men's lives insufferable. The idea that early people fell out of favor with the gods, more abruptly (as in Eden) or more gradually (as in Hesiod's "Five Races"), is also prevalent, as is the idea that at some point the gods wished to take their creation of humanity back, even if this obliteration is never complete. The Flood narrative is the most successful of these stories, where water, a cosmogonic first element in Mesopotamian tradition, becomes the utmost destructive weapon of the gods and the point of a cosmic restart.

Finally, I have already stressed the relationship of these myths to particular cities or regions or geographical landmarks such as mountains, rivers, or the sea, as well as to sites and objects of cult. Myths sometimes even remind us of the cosmogonic undertones of human actions, such as roasting meat, baking bread, giving birth, or working the land for the survival of the community. The list could go on. But perhaps the most surprising aspect of this story is how stubborn the ancient myths have proven to be. Despite changes in the entire system of knowledge as well as in their religious beliefs and cultural values over the centuries, authors and artists found ways to continue engaging with the traditional stories, instead of discarding them altogether, by recognizing their narrative power and the rich constellation of associations brought about by evocative names and tropes. The long reception of creation stories over millennia shows that ancient myths, especially when recast as wonderful literature, continued to engage readers and represent the human condition beyond political, linguistic, and religious divides and across the chasms of cultural change.

When some of these stories, in turn, attained "canonical" or "classical" status, they became much more likely to be preserved, and thus to become representatives of their culture and interwoven into the genealogy of its successors. This was in part how "Western culture" came into being. But here is the downside: the main advantage of texts, their durability, is also their shortcoming. The mouth-to-mouth transmission of stories was fleeting, but also much more malleable, adaptable to changing values, tastes, and sensibilities. Authoritative written works, by contrast, became less alterable, less alive. Plato already made this point in the *Phaedrus*. From this fixed status, however, there emerged a different creative effort. The effort to keep those mythical narratives relevant despite intellectual and religious change produced sophisticated interpretations, such as philosophical or allegorical ones, and inspired ever-evolving creative works. Connecting us with the symbolic and imaginary universe of our ancestors across the millennia, creation and heroic stories had, then as now, an inspiring and enlightening impact. I hope this book makes its own humble contribution to that path of learning about the myths from the ancient Mediterranean world.

A NOTE ON FURTHER READING
AND RESOURCES

Although I have quoted from the most relevant texts explored in this book, there is no better way to engage with ancient mythology than reading the full original versions, whether in the original language if that is available to the reader or in the translations available in English. Besides the many versions of the biblical account of Genesis, I recommend delving into the Mesopotamian creation and flood stories, for which Dalley (2000) is an excellent resource. Translations of the Ugaritic poems (*Baal Cycle* and others) can be found in Parker (1997). Among other great translations, Hesiod's *Theogony* and *Works and Days* can be read in Most (2006). For the Orphic cosmogonies, no publication that I know of contains all the fragments in English, but West (1983) is probably still the most useful overview of the primary sources, with translations of many fragments. A very handy translation also exists in Spanish in Bernabé (2003). Translations of many other Greek, Roman, and Near Eastern myths organized by themes are available in the sourcebook of López-Ruiz (2018). For general consultation, there is an ever-growing palette of online resources, but Gantz (1993) provides a most useful compendium of literary and artistic sources for early Greek myth, as do the entries of the *Oxford Classical Dictionary* (*OCD*) and the English version of the largest classical encyclopedia, the *New Pauly*. Essays expanding on various aspects of Greek mythology can be found in Woodard (2007), and I have cited secondary scholarship in the chapters, which contain further references to scholarship in the different areas.

BIBLIOGRAPHY

ABBREVIATIONS

LIMC *Lexicon Iconographicum Mythologiae Classicae* (Zürich, Munich, Düsseldorf: Artemis & Winkler Verlag 1981–1999, 2009). https://weblimc.org/page/home/Basel.

New Pauly H. Cancik, H. Schneider, and M. Landfester, eds., *Brill's New Pauly: Encyclopaedia of the Ancient World* (Leiden, 2002–2009).

OCD *Oxford Classical Dictionary*, 3rd ed. (Oxford and New York, 1996).

OF *Orphic Fragments* = Bernabé 2004.

WORKS CITED

Ahl, Frederick, trans. 2007. *Aeneid.* By Virgil. Oxford and New York: Oxford University Press.

Akçay, K. Nilüfer. 2019. *Porphyry's "On the Cave of the Nymphs" in Its Intellectual Context.* Leiden: Brill.

Alter, Robert. 1996. *Genesis: Translation and Commentary.* New York and London: Norton.

Alter, Robert. 2011. *The Art of Biblical Narrative.* 2nd ed. New York: Basic Books.

Bachvarova, Mary. 2021. "Of Gods and Men: Bridging the Gap between Cosmogony and the Heroic Age in Early Greek Legendary History." In *Narrating the Beginnings,* edited by Alberto Bernabé Pajares and Raquel Martín Hernández, 69–93. Wiesbaden, Germany: Springer.

Barber, Elizabeth Wayland, and Paul T. Barber. 2004. *When They Severed Earth from Sky: How the Human Mind Shapes Myth.* Princeton: Princeton University Press.

219

220   Bibliography

Barnett, R. D. 1945. "The Epic of Kumarbi and the Theogony of Hesiod." *Journal of Hellenic Studies* 65:100–101.

Bassi, Karen. 2005. "Things of the Past: Objects and Time in Greek Narrative." *Arethusa* 38, no. 1: 1–32.

Baumgarten, Albert I. 1981. *The Phoenician History of Philo of Byblos: A Commentary*. Leiden: Brill.

Beekes, Robert. 2010. *Etymological Dictionary of Greek*. 2 vols. Leiden: Brill.

Ben-Dov, Jonathan. 2021. "Neo-Babylonian Rock Reliefs and the Jewish Literary Imagination." In *Afterlives of Ancient Rock-Cut Monuments in the Near East: Carvings in and out of Time*, edited by J. Ben-Dov and F. Rojas, 345–79. Leiden: Brill.

Bernabé, Alberto. 2003. *Hieros Logos: Poesía órfica sobre lo dioses, el alma y el más allá*. Madrid: Akal.

Bernabé, Alberto. 2004. *Poetae Epici Graeci Testimonia et Fragmenta*. Pars 2, Fasc. 1, *Orphicorum et Orphicis similium testimonia*. Munich: De Gruyter.

Bernabé, Alberto, and Ana Isabel Jiménez San Cristóbal. 2008. *Instructions for the Netherworld: The Orphic Gold Tablets*. Boston and Leiden: Brill.

Bernal, Martin. 1987. *Black Athena: the Afroasiatic Roots of Classical Civilisation*. Vol. 1, *The Fabrication of Ancient Greece 1785–1985*. New Brunswick, NJ: Rutgers University Press.

Betegh, Gábor. 2006. *The Derveni Papyrus: Cosmology, Theology and Interpretation*. Cambridge: Cambridge University Press.

Bidmead, Julye. 2002. *The Akītu Festival: Religious Continuity and Royal Legitimation in Mesopotamia*. Piscataway, NJ: Gorgias Press.

Briant, Pierre. 2002. *From Cyrus to Alexander: A History of the Persian Empire 1*. Winona Lake, IN: Eisenbrauns.

Brisson, Luc. 2004. *How Philosophers Saved Myths: Allegorical Interpretation and Classical Mythology*. Chicago: University of Chicago Press. First published in German, 1996.

Bryce, Trevor. 2002. *Life and Society in the Hittite World*. Oxford: Oxford University Press.

Budin, Stephanie Lynn. 2003. *The Origin of Aphrodite*. Bethesda, MD: CDL Press.

Buonomano, Dean. 2017. *Your Brain Is a Time Machine: The Neuroscience and Physics of Time*. New York and London: Norton.

Burkert, Walter. 1979. *Structure and History in Greek Mythology and Ritual*. Berkeley: University of California Press.

Burkert, Walter. 1983. *Homo Necans: The Anthropology of Ancient Greek Sacrificial Ritual and Myth*. Berkeley: University of California Press.

Bibliography

Burkert, Walter. 1985. *Greek Religion*. Cambridge, MA: Harvard University Press.

Burkert, Walter. 1992. *The Orientalizing Revolution: Near Eastern Influence on Greek Culture in the Early Archaic Age*. Cambridge, MA: Harvard University Press.

Buxton, Richard. G. A. 1981. Review of *La cuisine du sacrifice en pays grec*. By M. Detienne and J.-P. Vernant. *Classical Review* 31, no. 1: 131.

Calame, Claude. 2009. *Greek Mythology: Poetics, Pragmatics, and Fiction*. Cambridge: Cambridge University Press. First published in French, 2000.

Calame, Claude. 2015. *Qu'est-ce que la mythologie grecque?* Paris: Gallimard.

Campbell, Joseph. 2008 (1949). *The Hero with a Thousand Faces*. Novato, CA: New World Library.

Carr, David M. 1996. *Reading the Fractures of Genesis: Historical and Literary Approaches*. Louisville, KY: Westminster John Knox Press.

Charpin, Dominique. 2010. *Reading and Writing in Babylon*. Cambridge, MA: Harvard University Press. First published in French, 2008.

Clay, Jenny Strauss. 1989. *The Politics of Olympus: Form and Meaning in the Major Homeric Hymns*. Princeton, NJ: Princeton University Press.

Clay, Jenny Strauss. 2003. *Hesiod's Cosmos*. Cambridge: Cambridge University Press.

Clay, Diskin, and Andrea Purvis. 1999. *Four Island Utopias: Plato's Atlantis, Euhemeros of Messene's Panchaia, Iamboulos' Island of the Sun, Sir Francis Bacon's New Atlantis*. Newburyport, MA: Focus.

Cline, Eric H. 2014. *1177 B.C.: The Year Civilization Collapsed*. Princeton: Princeton University Press.

Collbert, Catherine, Pierre Destrée, and Francisco J. Gonzalez, eds. 2012. *Plato and Myth: Studies on the Use and Status of Platonic Myths*. Leiden and Boston: Brill.

Connelly, Joan B. 2014. *The Parthenon Enigma: A New Understanding of the World's Most Iconic Building and the People Who Made It*. New York: Knopf.

Cross, Frank M. 1998. *From Epic to Canon: History and Literature in Ancient Israel*. Baltimore: Johns Hopkins University Press.

Cyrino, Monica Silveira. 2010. "To Love and Toulouse: The Orpheus and Eurydice Theme in Marcel Camus' *Black Orpheus* (1959) and Baz Luhrmann's *Moulin Rouge* (2001)." *Classical & Modern Literature* 28, no. 1: 129–48.

Dalley, Stephanie. 2000 (1989). *Myths from Mesopotamia: Creation, the Flood, Gilgamesh, and Others*. Oxford and New York: Oxford University Press.

Dalley, Stephanie. 2013. *The Mystery of the Hanging Gardens of Babylon*. Oxford: Oxford University Press.

Bibliography

Darshan, Guy. 2013. "The Biblical Account of the Post-Diluvian Generation (Gen. 9:20–10:32) in the Light of Greek Genealogical Literature." *Vetus Testamentum* 63:515–35.

Delalonde, Marc. 2021. *L'Histoire Phénicienne de Philon de Byblos su prisme du multiculralisme*. Rome: Edizioni Quasar.

Detienne, Marcel, and Jean-Pierre Vernant. 1989. *The Cuisine of Sacrifice among the Greeks*. Chicago: University of Chicago Press. First published in French, 1979.

Dillery, John. 2015. *Clio's Other Sons: Berossus and Manetho*. Ann Arbor: University of Michigan Press.

Doak, Brian R. 2012. *The Last of the Rephaim: Conquest and Cataclysm in the Heroic Ages of Ancient Israel*. Washington, DC: Ilex Foundation and Center for Hellenic Studies.

Edmonds, Radcliffe G., III. 2004. *Myths of the Underworld Journey in Plato, Aristophanes, and the "Orphic" Gold Tablets*. Cambridge and New York: Cambridge University Press.

Edmonds, Radcliffe G., III. 2013. *Redefining Ancient Orphism: A Study in Greek Religion*. Cambridge: Cambridge University Press.

Edmunds, Lowell. ed. 2014. *Approaches to Greek Myth*. 2nd ed. Baltimore: Johns Hopkins University Press.

Eisenfeld, Hanne. 2022. *Pindar and Greek Religion: Theologies of Mortality in the Victory Odes*. Cambridge: Cambridge University Press.

Eliade, Mircea. 2005 (1954). *The Myth of the Eternal Return: Cosmos and History*. Introduction by Jonathan Z. Smith. Princeton: Princeton University Press. First published in French, 1949.

Engberg-Pedersen, Troels. 2018. *John and Philosophy: A New Reading of the Fourth Gospel*. Oxford: Oxford University Press.

Errington, R. Malcolm. 2008. *A History of the Hellenistic World*. Malden, MA: Blackwell.

Fletcher, Angus. 2021. *Wonderworks: The 25 Most Powerful Inventions in the History of Literature*. New York: Simon & Schuster.

Foster, Benjamin. 1995. *From Distant Days: Myths, Tales, and Poetry of Ancient Mesopotamia*. Bethesda, MD: CDL Press.

Frazer, James G., ed. 1921. *The Library, Volume I: Books 1–3.9*. By Apollodorus. Loeb Classical Library 121. Cambridge, MA: Harvard University Press.

Fry, Stephen. 2018. *Heroes: The Greek Myths Reimagined*. San Francisco: Chronicle Books.

Gantz, Timothy. 1993. *Early Greek Myth: A Guide to Literary and Artistic Sources*. Baltimore: Johns Hopkins University Press.

Bibliography 223

George, Andrew. 2003. The "Epic of Gilgamesh": The Babylonian Epic Poem and Other Texts in Akkadian and Sumerian. 2nd ed. London and New York: Penguin.

Graeber, David, and David Wengrow. 2021. The Dawn of Everything: A New History of Humanity. New York: Farrar, Straus and Giroux.

Graf, Fritz. 1993. Greek Mythology: An Introduction. Baltimore: Johns Hopkins University Press. First published in German, 1987.

Graf, Fritz. 2011. "Myth in Christian Authors." In A Companion to Greek Mythology, edited by Ken Dowden and Niall Livingstone, 319–37. Malden, MA, and Oxford: Wiley-Blackwell.

Graf, Fritz, and Sarah I. Johnston. 2013. Ritual Texts for the Afterlife: Orpheus and the Bacchic Gold Tablets. 2nd rev. ed. London and New York: Routledge.

Graziosi, B. 2014. The Gods of Olympus: A History. New York: Metropolitan Books.

Graves, Robert. 1955. The Greek Myths. London: Penguin.

Güterbock, Hans G. 1948. "The Hittite Version of the Hurrian Kumarbi Myths: Oriental Forerunners of Hesiod." American Journal of Archaeology 52, no. 1: 123–34 (+ plate III).

Hall, Jonathan M. 1997. Ethnic Identity in Greek Antiquity. Cambridge: Cambridge University Press.

Hall, Jonathan M. 2002. Hellenicity: Between Ethnicity and Culture. Chicago: University of Chicago Press.

Hamilton, Edith. 1942. Mythology. Boston, MA: Little, Brown.

Hansen, William. 2020. Classical Mythology: A Guide to the Mythical World of the Greeks and Romans. Oxford and New York: Oxford University Press.

Heiden, Bruce. 2007. "The Muses' Uncanny Lies: Hesiod, Theogony 27 and Its Translators." American Journal of Philology 128, no. 2: 153–75.

Higgins, Charlotte. 2021. Greek Myths: A New Retelling. New York: Pantheon.

Johnston, Sarah I. 2018. The Story of Myth. Cambridge, MA: Harvard University Press.

Johnston, Sarah I. 2023. Gods and Mortals: Ancient Greek Myths for Modern Readers. Princeton: Princeton University Press.

Josephson-Storm, Jason A. 2017. The Myth of Disenchantment: Magic, Modernity, and the Birth of the Human Sciences. Chicago: University of Chicago Press.

Kaldellis, Anthony. 2021. "The Reception of Classical Literature and Ancient Myth." In The Oxford Handbook of Byzantine Literature, edited by Stratis Papaioannou, 162–79. Oxford and New York: Oxford University Press.

Bibliography

Kaldellis, Anthony, and Carolina López-Ruiz. 2019. "*FGrH* 790—'Philon of Byblos.'" In *Brill's New Jacoby Online*, edited by Ian Worthington. 2nd ed. Leiden: Brill.

Kirk, G. S. 1970. *Myth: Its Meaning and Functions in Ancient and Other Cultures.* Cambridge: Cambridge University Press.

Kitts, Margo. 1994. "Two Expressions for Human Mortality in the Epics of Homer." *History of Religions*, 34, no. 2: 132–51.

Kripal, Jeffrey, J. 2015. *Mutants and Mystics: Science Fiction, Superhero Comics, and the Paranormal.* Chicago: University of Chicago Press.

Lamberton, Robert. 1983. *On the Cave of the Nymphs.* Barrytown, NY: Station Hill Press.

Lamberton, Robert. 1989. *Homer the Theologian: Neoplatonist Allegorical Reading and the Growth of the Epic Tradition.* Berkeley: University of California Press.

Lamberton, Robert. 1992. *Homer's Ancient Readers: The Hermeneutics of Greek Epic's Earliest Exegetes.* Princeton: Princeton University Press.

Lane Fox, Robin. 2008. *Traveling Heroes: Greeks and Their Myths in the Epic Age of Homer.* London: Allen Lane.

Lattimore, Richmond, trans. 1961. *The "Iliad" of Homer.* Chicago: University of Chicago Press.

Lévy, Carlos. 2018. "Philo of Alexandria." In *The Stanford Encyclopedia of Philosophy*, edited by Edward N. Zalta. Stanford, CA: Stanford University. https://plato.stanford.edu/archives/spr2018/entries/philo/.

Lightfoot, J. L., ed. and trans. 2003. *On the Syrian Goddess.* Oxford: Oxford University Press.

Lindow, John. 2021. *Old Norse Mythology.* Oxford and New York: Oxford University Press.

Lincoln, Bruce. 1999. *Theorizing Myth: Narrative, Ideology, and Scholarship.* Chicago: University of Chicago Press.

López-Ruiz, Carolina. 2010. *When the Gods Were Born: Greek Cosmogonies and the Near East.* Cambridge, MA: Harvard University Press.

López-Ruiz, Carolina. 2012. "How to Start a Cosmogony: On the Poetics of Beginnings in Greece and the Near East." *Journal of Near Eastern Religions* 12:30–48.

López-Ruiz, Carolina. 2014a. "Greek and Canaanite Mythologies: Zeus, Baal, and Their Rivals." *The Religion Compass* 8, no. 1: 1–10.

López-Ruiz, Carolina. 2014b. "Greek and Near Eastern Mythology: A Story of Mediterranean Encounters." In *Approaches to Greek Mythology*, edited by

Lowell Edmunds, 154–99. 2nd. rev. ed. Baltimore: Johns Hopkins University Press.

López-Ruiz, Carolina. 2015. "Gods: Origins." In *Oxford Handbook of Greek Religion*, edited by Esther Eidinow and Julia Kindt, 369–82. Oxford and New York: Oxford University Press.

López-Ruiz, Carolina. 2017. "'Not That Which Can Be Found among the Greeks': Philo of Byblos and Phoenician Cultural Identity in the Roman East." *Religion in the Roman Empire* 3, no. 3: 366–92.

López-Ruiz, Carolina. 2018. *Gods, Heroes, and Monsters: A Sourcebook of Greek, Roman, and Near Eastern Myths in Translation*. 2nd ed. New York and Oxford: Oxford University Press.

López-Ruiz, Carolina. 2021. "Siting the Gods: Narrative, Cult, and Hybrid Communities in the Iron Age Mediterranean." In *Gods and Mortals in Early Greek and Near Eastern Mythology*, edited by A. Kelly and Ch. Metcalf, 37–57. Cambridge: Cambridge University Press.

López-Ruiz, Carolina. 2023. "From Kothar to Kythereia: Exploring the Northwest Semitic Past of Aphrodite." In *"Like 'Ilu Are You Wise": Studies in Northwest Semitic Languages and Literatures in Honor of Dennis G. Pardee*, edited by H. H. Hardy II, J. Lam, and E. D. Reymond, 353–73. Chicago: Oriental Institute.

Luhrmann, T. M. 2020. *How God Becomes Real: Kindling the Presence of Invisible Others*. Princeton: Princeton University Press.

Martin, Richard. 2003. *Myths of the Ancient Greeks*. London: New American Library.

Martin, Richard. 2016. *Classical Mythology: The Basics*. London and New York: Routledge.

Mason, Steve. 2008. *Josephus, Judea, and Christian Origins*. Peabody, MA: Baker Academic.

Meisner, Dwayne A. 2018. *Orphic Tradition and the Birth of the Gods*. Oxford: Oxford University Press.

Miles, Richard. 2010. *Carthage Must Be Destroyed: The Rise and Fall of an Ancient Civilization*. London: Penguin.

Miller, Frank Justus, ed. 1916. *Metamorphoses, Volume I: Books 1–8*. By Ovid. Revised by G. P. Goold. Loeb Classical Library 42. Cambridge, MA: Harvard University Press.

Mondi, Robert. 1990. "Greek Mythic Thought in the Light of the Near East." In *Approaches to Greek Myth*, edited by Lowell Edmunds, 141–98. Baltimore: Johns Hopkins University Press.

Montanari, Franco, Antonios Rengakos, and Christos Tsagalis, eds. 2009. *Brill's Companion to Hesiod*. Leiden: Brill.

Montanari, Franco, Antonios Rengakos, and Christos Tsagalis, eds. 2012. *Homeric Contexts: Neoanalysis and the Interpretation of Oral Poetry*. Berlin and Boston: De Gruyter.

Morales, Helen. 2007. *Classical Mythology: A Very Short Introduction*. Oxford and New York: Oxford University Press.

Morford, Mark, and Robert Lenardon. 2007. *Classical Mythology*. 8th ed. New York and Oxford: Oxford University Press.

Morris, Sarah P. 1992. *Daidalos and the Origins of Greek Art*. Princeton: Princeton University Press.

Most, Glenn. 1997. "The Myth of the Five (or Three or Four) Races." *Proceedings of the Cambridge Philological Society* 43:104–27.

Most, Glenn, ed. and trans. 2006. *Theogony, Works and Days, Testimonia*. By Hesiod. Cambridge, MA: Harvard University Press.

Moyer, Ian. 2011. *Egypt and the Limits of Hellenism*. Cambridge: Cambridge University Press.

Nagy, Gregory. 1990. *Greek Mythology and Poetics*. Ithaca, NY: Cornell University Press.

Nagy, Joseph Falaky. 2014. "Hierarchy, Heroes, and Heads: Indo-European Structures in Greek Myth." In *Approaches to Greek Myth*, edited by Lowell Edmunds, 202–44. 2nd ed. Baltimore: Johns Hopkins University Press.

Niditch, Susan. 1997. *Ancient Israelite Religion*. New York and Oxford: Oxford University Press.

Nightingale, Andrea. 2021. *Philosophy and Religion in Plato's Dialogues*. Cambridge: Cambridge University Press.

Nyord, Rune. 2021. "Ancient Egyptian Texts for the Afterlife?" *Ancient Near East Today* 9, no. 12. http://fundacion.ieae.es/wp-content/uploads/2024/07/2021_Ancient_Egyptian_Texts_for_the_Afte.pdf.

Osborne, Catherine. 2004. *Presocratic Philosophy: A Very Short Introduction*. Oxford: Oxford University Press.

Osborne, Harold, and Hugh Brigstocke. 2003. "Michelangelo Buonarroti." In *The Oxford Companion to Western Art*, edited by High Brigstocke. Oxford: Oxford University Press.

Osborne, Robin. 2009. *Greece in the Making: 1200–479 BC*. 2nd ed. London and New York: Routledge.

Pals, Daniel. 2015. *Nine Theories of Religion*. 3rd ed. New York and Oxford: Oxford University Press.

Pardee, Dennis. 2002. *Ritual and Cult at Ugarit*. Atlanta: Society of Biblical Literature.

Bibliography 227

Parker, Simon B., ed. 1997. *Ugaritic Narrative Poetry.* Atlanta: Scholars Press.
Parker, Robert. 2011. *On Greek Religion.* Ithaca, NY: Cornell University Press.
Parry, Milman. 1971. *The Making of Homeric Verse: The Collected Papers of Milman Parry.* Edited by Adam Parry. New York and Oxford: Oxford University Press.
Partenie, Catalin. 2009. *Plato: Selected Myths.* Oxford and New York: Oxford University Press.
Pedley, John. 2005. *Sanctuaries and the Sacred in the Ancient Greek World.* Cambridge: Cambridge University Press.
Penglase, Charles. 1994. *Greek Myths and Mesopotamia: Parallels and Influence in the Homeric Hymns and Hesiod.* London and New York: Routledge.
Pinch, Geraldine. 2002. *Egyptian Mythology: A Guide to the Gods, Goddesses, and Traditions of Ancient Egypt.* Oxford and New York: Oxford University Press.
Powell, Barry B. 1991. *Homer and the Origin of the Greek Alphabet.* Cambridge: Cambridge University Press.
Powell, Barry B. 2002. *A Short Introduction to Classical Myth.* Upper Saddle River, NJ: Pearson Education.
Powell, Barry B. 2021a. *Classical Myth.* 9th ed. New York and Oxford: Oxford University Press.
Powell, Barry B. 2021b. *Greek Poems to the Gods: Hymns from Homer to Proclus.* Oakland: University of California Press.
Raaflaub, Kurt. 1993. "Homer to Solon: The Rise of the Polis. The Written Sources." In *The Ancient Greek City State,* edited by Mogens H. Hansen, 41–105. Copenhagen: Royal Danish Academy of Sciences and Letters.
Roubekas, Nickolas P. 2017. *An Ancient Theory of Religion: Euhemerism from Antiquity to the Present.* London and New York: Routledge.
Rovelli, Carlo. 2018. *The Order of Time.* New York: Riverhead Books. First published in Italian, 2017.
Runia, David T., ed. and trans. 2001. *On the Creation of the Cosmos according to Moses: Introduction, Translation and Commentary.* Leiden: Brill.
Sachs, Ben. 2014. "Darren Aronofsky's Noah Tells the Story by the Book." *Chicago Reader.* https://chicagoreader.com/film/darren-aronofskys-noah-tells-the-story-by-the-book/.
Salzman-Mitchell, Patricia, and Jean Alvares. 2018. *Classical Myth and Film in the New Millennium.* New York and Oxford: Oxford University Press.
Santamaría, Marco Antonio. 2019. "The Orphic Poem of the Derveni Papyrus and Hesiod's *Theogony.*" In *The Derveni Papyrus: Unearthing Ancient Mysteries,* edited by Marco Antonio Santamaría, 47–64. Leiden: Brill.
Sasson, Jack. M. 2008. "Time and Mortality: Creation Narratives in Ancient Israel and Mesopotamia." In *Papers on Ancient Literatures: Greece, Rome,*

228 Bibliography

and the Near East, edited by Ettore Cingano and Lucio Milano, 489–509. Padova, Italy: S.A.R.G.O.N. Editrice e libraria.

Sasson, Jack M. 2022. "What Really Happened in the Garden of Eden." TheTorah.com. https://thetorah.com/article/what-really-happened-in-the-garden-of-eden.

Scodel, Ruth. 1982. "The Achaean Wall and the Myth of Destruction." *Harvard Studies in Classical Philology* 86:33–50.

Segal, Robert A. 2004. *Myth: A Very Short Introduction.* New York and Oxford: Oxford University Press.

Shaw, Ian. 2004. *Ancient Egypt: A Very Short Introduction.* Oxford: Oxford University Press.

Smith, Mark S. 2002. *The Early History of God: Yahweh and Other Deities of Ancient Israel.* 2nd rev. ed. Grand Rapids, MI: Eerdmans.

Smith, Mark S. 2014. *Poetic Heroes: Literary Commemorations of Warriors and Warrior Culture in the Early Biblical World.* Grand Rapids, MI: Eerdmans.

Smyth, Herbert Weir, ed. 1926. *Suppliant Maidens, Persians, Prometheus, Seven against Thebes.* By Aeschylus. Loeb Classical Library 145–46. Cambridge, MA: Harvard University Press.

Stamatellos, Giannis. 2012. *Introduction to Presocratics: A Thematic Approach to Early Greek Philosophy with Key Readings.* Malden, MA: Wiley Blackwell.

Struck, Peter. 2004. *Birth of the Symbol: Ancient Readers at the Limits of Their Texts.* Princeton: Princeton University Press.

Thompson, Tok, and Gregory Schrempp. 2020. *The Truth of Myth.* New York: Oxford University Press.

Trzaskoma, Stephen, R. Scott Smith, and Stephen Brunet, eds. 2016. *Anthology of Classical Myth: Primary Sources in Translation.* With an Appendix on Linear B Sources by Thomas G. Palaima. 2nd ed. Indianapolis: Hackett.

Tugendhaft, Aaron. 2018. *Baal and the Politics of Poetry.* London and New York: Routledge.

Vallejo, Irene. 2022. *Papyrus: The Invention of Books in the Ancient World.* New York: Alfred A. Knopf. First published in Spanish 2019.

Van de Mieroop, Marc. 2007. *A History of the Ancient Near East: ca. 3000–323 BC.* 2nd ed. Malden, MA: Blackwell.

Vernant, Jean-Pierre. 1980. *Myth and Society in Ancient Greece.* Brighton, UK: Harvester Press Limited. First published in French, 1974.

Vernant, Jean-Pierre. 1983. *Myth and Thought among the Greeks.* London and Boston: Routledge & Kegan Paul. First published in French, 1966.

Versnel. H. S. 2014. "What's Sauce for the Goose Is Sauce for the Gander: Myth and Ritual, Old and New." In *Approaches to Greek Myth,* edited by Lowell Edmunds, 202–44. Baltimore: Johns Hopkins University Press.

Bibliography 229

Veyne, Paul. 1983. *Did the Greeks Believe in their Myths: An Essay on the Constitutive Imagination.* Chicago: University of Chicago Press. First published in French, 1988.

Vidal-Naquet, Pierre. 1986. *The Black Hunter: Forms of Thought and Forms of Society in the Greek World.* Baltimore: Johns Hopkins University Press. First published in French, 1981.

Watkins, Calvert. 1995. *How to Kill a Dragon: Aspects of Indo-European Poetics.* Oxford: Oxford University Press.

Wasserman, Nathan. 2020. *The Flood: The Akkadian Sources; A New Edition, Commentary, and a Literary Discussion.* Leuven: Peeters.

West, Martin L., ed. 1966. *Theogony.* By Hesiod. Edited with Prolegomena and Commentary. Oxford: Oxford University Press.

West, Martin L. 1983. *The Orphic Poems.* Oxford: Oxford University Press.

West, Martin L. 1985. *The Hesiodic Catalogue of Women: Its Nature, Structure, and Origins.* Oxford: Oxford University Press.

West, Martin L. 1994. "*Ab Ovo*: Orpheus, Sanchuniathon, and the Origins of the Ionian World Model." *Classical Quarterly* 44, no. 2: 289–307.

West, Martin L. 1997. *The East Face of Helicon: West Asiatic Elements in Greek Poetry and Myth.* Oxford: Oxford University Press.

West, Martin L. 2000. "The Name of Aphrodite." *Glotta* 76:133–38.

West, Martin L. 2011. *The Making of the "Iliad": Disquisition and Analytical Commentary.* Oxford: Oxford University Press.

Whitmarsh, Tim. 2015. *Battling the Gods: Atheism in the Ancient World.* New York: Vintage.

Winiarczyk, Marek. 2013. *The "Sacred History" of Euhemerus of Messene.* Munich and Leipzig: De Gruyter.

Woodard, Roger D., ed. 2007. *The Cambridge Companion to Greek Mythology.* Cambridge: Cambridge University Press.

Wrangham, Richard. 2010. *Catching Fire: How Cooking Made Us Human.* New York: Basic Books.

Wright, Maureen R. 2008. "Presocratic Cosmologies." In *The Oxford Handbook of Presocratic Philosophy,* edited by Patricia Curd and Daniel W. Graham, 413–32. Oxford and New York: Oxford University Press.

Yonge, C. D. 1993. *The Works of Philo: Complete and Unabridged.* Peabody, MA: Hendrickson Publisher.

Zamora, José-Ángel. 2006. "L'ubriachezza a Ugarit: un'eredità discussa." *Mediterranea* 2:10–26.

Ziolkowski, Jan. 2013. "Medieval Latin Mythography as Death and Resurrection of Myth." In *Writing Down the Myths,* edited by Joseph Falaky Nagy, 87–106. Turnhout: Brepols.

INDEX

Note: Tables and figures are indicated by an italic "*t*" and "*f*", respectively, following the page number.

For the benefit of digital users, indexed terms that span two pages (e.g., 52–53) may, on occasion, appear on only one of those pages.

Abrahamic traditions, 196–8
Achaean wall, 89–90
Achilles, 25–6, 97, 103–4, 108, 110, 207–8
Aegean Sea, in Archaic-Classical period, 98*f*
Aeneid (Virgil), 4–5, 7–8, 97–9, 190–1
Aeschylus, 6
agriculture, 90–1, 105–6
Akitu festival, 152–3
Akkadians, 168–9
Akropolis, 93–7, 163–4
Alexander the Great, 167–70, 172, 176–7
Alexandria, 66
allegory, 173–4, 192–8.
　　See also *specific allegories*
Alma-Tadema, Lawrence, 18*f*
Alter, Robert, 116
alternative theogony, 52–60

Alvares, Jean, 208–9
amulets 67–70, 159–60
Anatolia, 112–13, 152–3.
　　See also Near East cultures
Anaximander, 97–9, 177–8
Anaximenes, 177–8
animals, 145–6
anthropocene, 208–9
anthropogony, 71–2, 93, 130–1, 145–52, 189–90
　　cosmogony and, 164–5, 178–9
　　from Dionysos, 101
　　Greek, 76–7, 94 n.5, 97, 97 n.6
　　Orphic, 32–3
　　Plato's, 178–9, 181–5
anthropology, 104
Aphrodite, 19–20, 77, 91, 127–8, 214–15
　　assumed daughter of Zeus, 38–9, 48, 57–8
　　birth of, 37–8, 61

231

Index

Apollo, 14–15, 89–90
  at Delphi, 43f, 61–2, 65, 91,
    94 n.5
  Homeric Hymn to Apollo, 27, 91
  Poseidon and, 89–90
  Temple of, 84f
  Zeus and, 48–9, 65
Apollodoros (Pseudo-Apollodoros),
    85–6, 167–8
Apollonius of Rhodes, 4–5, 66,
    167–8
Apuleius, 6–7
Arab world, 196
archaeology, 67
Ares, 48–9, 92–3, 202
Argonautica (Apollonius of Rhodes),
    4–5, 66
aristocracy, 87–8
Aristophanes, 6, 59
Aristotle, 162, 196
Aronofsky, Darren, 204–7
Artemis, 38–40, 48
Assyrians, 152–3, 158
astronomical observation, 33
Athena, 38–9, 46–8, 50–2, 55–6, 77,
    92–4, 96
  Athena Parthenos, 96
  Athena Polias, 94–5
  Athena Promachos, 163–4
  Hephaistos and, 181–2, 185–6
  Poseidon rivalry with, 97,
    185–6
Athens, 93–7, 168, 185
  birthplace of Athena, 48
  Classical, 6, 96, 177–8
  Kylonian pollution in, 160–1
  of Pericles, 185–6
Atlantis myth, 185–6
Atrahasis (creation myth), 51, 185
Augustus, 4–5
autochthony, 92–101

Baal (Canaanite god), 51–2, 132–7,
    136f, 142, 156, 172–3, 176–7,
    214–15
  Yam and, 134, 137, 155–6
Baal Cycle (epic), 51–2, 136f, 132–7,
    153–6, 175–6
Babylon, 85–6, 128t,
  Akkadians in, 168–9
  cosmogony in, 158–60
  creation myths/stories from, 120,
    153
  culture of, 110–11, 124, 152–3,
    158–60
  gods of, 130–1
  Greece and, 167
  muses of, 118–19
  myths and, 119–20
  old Babylonian texts, 139–45
  succession myth patterns, 131–2
  tradition of, 116
"Bacchic-Orphic" Gold Tablets, 68f,
    67–9, 101, 159–60
Basalt stele, 136f
beliefs, 14–15, 60–70
Bellum Punicum (Naevius), 4–5
Berossos, 169–71
The Birds (Aristophanes), 59
Black Orpheus (Camus), 202–3
brilliant gods, 50–60
Brisson, Luc, 193, 198
Bronze Age, 80–1, 90–1
  epics on, 89–90
  floods in, 88–9
  Late, 2–3, 114–15, 132
  Middle Age as, 83
Bronze race, 80–1, 83–4, 92,
    189
Byzantine empire, 196

Calchas, 24–5
Camus, Albert, 202–3

Index

Catalogue of Women (poem), 27, 62, 85–8, 95–6
Chaldean Oracles, 195–6
Chaos, 28–9,
concept of, 30–1
love and, 59, 115
time and, 54–5
in Western culture, 30
children, 150–1, 161
Christianity. See also Hebrew Bible
authors of, 192
Classical Greece and, 196
Greek myths in, 177
history of, 119–20, 174
Judaism and, 112–13
Judeo-Christian traditions, 180–1, 197–8
in Norway, 176
poetry and, 196
Stoicism and, 211
theology from, 195–6
Chronicle of the Single Monarchy, 125–6
Cicero, 180–1
Clash of the Titans (film), 209f, 207–11
Classical canon, 167–8, 215–16
Classical education, 7–8
classical mythology. See specific topics
Classical texts, 20
Classical traditions, 177
clay, 78f, 77, 141f
climate emergency, environmental disasters and, 206f, 205–6
The Clouds (Aristophanes), 59
Cocteau, Jean, 202–3
Coffin Texts, 120–1, 123
Connelly, Joan, 96
cremation rituals, 67

Crete, 41–2, 55–6, 61, 92, 160–1, 172–3
Crow, Russell, 204–5
cultural memory, 62
cyclic theogony, 51,
Cyclops/Cyclopes, 36, 42–4, 103–4, 134, 208
Cyprus, 37–8, 61, 78f, 167

The Dawn of Everything (Graeber and Wengrow), 213
Declaration of Independence, 163–4
Delphi, Greece, 13–14, 43f, 42, 92,
Apollo at, 43f, 61–2, 65, 91, 94 n.5
Pytho at, 94 n.5
rock vomited by Kronos, 43f, 41–2, 61
Demeter, 5–6, 40–1, 48, 70, 91
Homeric Hymn to Demeter, 51–2, 133–4
Democritus, 177–8, 187–8
Derveni Papyrus, 67, 159–60, 192–3
desire. See love
destruction myths, 139–45
didactic poetry, 189
dike, 83–4
Dillery, John, 169–70
Diodoros of Sicily, 170–1
Dionysios I of Syracuse, 172
Dionysos, 67–9, 100f, 99–101,
Homeric Hymn to Dionysos, 91
in Orphic myth, 56–9, 66–7, 70, 203–204, 209–10, 214–15
Zeus and, 55–6, 92–3
diplomacy, 42–3
Disney movies, 210–11
Divine (Theia) (Titan), 32–3, 39–40
divine councils, 156
divine-human relations, 91
divine leadership, 63–6

234 *Index*

divine order, 28
dowry, 106
Dream of Scipio (Cicero), 180–1
Dumézil, Georges, 12
Dungeons and Dragons (game), 201

Ea/Enki (Mesopotamian god),
    74–5, 118*f*, 129–30, 139, 142,
    159, 185, 128*t*
early humans, 85–90
Earth (Gaia), 28–9, 32, 35, 87
    Underworld and, 70, 115
The East Face of Helikon (West),
    112–13
Echidna, 31–2
Egypt, 66, 121*f*, 123, 175. *See also*
    Near East cultures
    Anatolia and, 152–3
    funerary texts from, 159–60
    gods from, 116–24
    Greece and, 138, 175–6
    Mesopotamia and, 51
    myths and, 137–8, 145
Egyptian Book of the Dead, 121*f*,
    120–2
elements, 20–1, 24–37
Empedokles, 161
Enuma elish (epic), 23–4, 116–20,
    124, 140–1, 155–6
    to Akkadians, 168–9
    comparisons to, 158–60
    gods in, 130–1
    Hebrew Bible compared
        to, 144
    influence of, 158–60, 128*t*
    legacy of, 187, 213–14
    Marduk in, 130–2, 140–2, 152–3
Epic of Gilgamesh, 8–10, 23–4,
    110–11, 139–45, 153–5

epics. *See also specific epics*
    on Bronze Age, 89–90
    cosmogony in, 51–2
    Epic Cycle, 4–5, 89
    epic poetry, 65, 81
        Greek, 27
    Greek myths and, 133–4
    history of, 60–1
    from Mesopotamia, 120–1, 187
    muses and, 52–3
    from Near East cultures, 139–45
    for Plato, 66–7
    preservation of, 92–3
    Ugaritic texts and, 51–2, 113–14
Epimenides of Crete, 160–1
Epimetheus, 102–3, 108
    Prometheus and, 35, 39–40,
        67–9, 77–9, 86, 105–6, 181–3
Erechtheion (temple), 95*f*, 93–7
Erechtheus (Euripides), 96
Eros. *See* Love
ethnic groups, 64
etymology, of gods, 38
Euhemerism, 172–7, 192
Euhemeros of Messene, 172–3
Euripides, 6, 96
Europe, 17–18, 67, 168–9, 196–7
Eusebius of Caesarea, 174
Eustathius, 194–5
Everything Everywhere All at Once
    (film), 211–12

Fabulae (Hyginus), 6–7, 167–8
family, 35–43
Five Races myth, 79–86, 88, 104,
    183–4, 207–8, 210
    Bronze race, 80–1, 83–4, 92, 189
    Gold race, 80–3, 189
    Heroes race, 80–6

Index

Iron race, 80–4, 86, 152, 189
Silver race, 80–5, 183, 189
floods
  culture and, 169–70, 207–8
  in Greece, 86–7
  in Hebrew Bible, 88–9, 145–52,
    171–2
  Panhellenic culture and, 95–6
  in resilient myths, 204–7
  in Roman empire, 170–1
Frazer, James, 11
Freud, Sigmund, 11–12
Fry, Stephen, 10
funerary texts, 159–60

Gaia. See Earth
Gaiman, Neil, 199
Genesis. See Hebrew Bible
giants, 44, 127–8. See also Cyclops/
    Cyclopes
  humans and, 36–7, 72, 151–2,
    171
  Hundred-Handers, 36
  rock, 206–7
goddesses, 19–20,
  in battle, 47f, 46–7
  in Greek culture, 37–9
  legacy of, 164–5
  limitations of, 48
  lineages of, 39–40
  ritual objects of, 154f, 153
  womb goddess, 140–1
gods. See *specific topics*
Golden Age, 84–5. See also *Gold race*
Golden Ass (Apuleius), 6–7
golden fleece, 93
Gold race, 80–3, 189
Gold Tablets, 68f, 67–70
Good Omens (TV show), 199

Goya, Francisco de, 41f
Graeber, David, 213
Graves, Robert, 10
Greco-Roman literature, 8–10, 164
Greco-Roman myths, 10–11
Greco-Roman philosophy, 197–8
Greco-Roman scholarship, 194–5
Greco-Roman tradition, 7–8
The Greek Myths (Graves), 10

Hades, 34–5, 40–1, 46, 51–2.
  See also *Underworld, Tartaros*
  Persephone and, 53, 55–6, 67–9
Hades (video game), 203–4
Hadestown (musical), 202–3
Hamilton, Edith, 10
Handel, Ari, 204–7
Hannibal, 176–7, 180–1
Harrison, Jane, 11
Hathor (Egyptian goddess), 38–9,
  144
Harry Potter (Rowling), 200–1
heaven, 124–39
Hebrew Bible, 7–8, 85–6, 106,
  112–13, 157–8, 204–7
  assimilation in, 135–7
  comparisons to, 139–45
  creation myths in, 114–17,
    146–51
  Enuma elish compared to, 144
  floods in, 88–9, 145–52, 171–2
  gods in, 102–3, 135–7
Hebrews, 51
Heliopolitan cosmology, 123
Hellenism, 168–70
Hephaistos, 181–2, 185–6
Hera, 48–9, 51, 55–7, 123, 211
Heraclitus, 177–8
Herakleidai, 87–8

Index

Herakles, 32, 53, 92–3, 104, 165, 210–11
    Perseus and, 32, 207–8
Herakles-Melqart, 176–7
Hercules (film), 210–11
Hermes, 5–6, 77–8, 90–1, 181–2
Herodotus, 6, 97, 127
heroes, 4–5, 34–5, 164–5, 207–12
Heroes race, 80–6
Hesiod, 19–20, 22 n.1, 111.
    See also *specific works*
    audiences of, 74–5
    clay for, 77
    cosmogony by, 22–50, 60–1
    creation myths/stories and, 66, 71, 73–4, 107–8
    culture and, 128t
    on deceit, 76–7
    elements to, 28–35
    on ethnic groups, 64
    on family, 35–43
    Heroes to, 86
    Homer and, 22–4, 64, 66–7, 110, 152, 167–8
    influence of, 162–5, 170–1, 177–8, 200–2, 207–8
    inspiration for, 82–3
    legacy of, 4–5, 7–8, 15–19
    on morality, 79–80
    muses and, 61, 101–2
    myths by, 24–8
    Orpheus and, 66, 131
    Perses and, 82
    Plato and, 79
    poetry from, 72
    on reality, 81
    on titanic rebellions, 43–50
    tradition of, 51
    on women, 106–7

Hestia, 38–41
Higgins, Charlotte, 10
Hittite epics, 113–14, 123, 125
    humans and, 155–6
    influence of, 125–30, 128t
    purulli festival, 153–5
Hittite Storm god, 136f
Homer, 4–8, 17–20. See also *specific works*
    Epic Cycles and, 89
    Greece and, 61, 93–4
    Greek myths and, 48
    Hesiod and, 22–4, 64, 66–7, 110, 152, 167–8
    Homeric universe, 51–2, 194
    on *hybris*, 89–90
    on immortality, 103–4
    influence of, 18f
    legacy of, 164–5, 186
    metaphors of, 108–9
    Orpheus and, 50–1
    philosophy from, 187–8
    Socrates and, 194
    underworld to, 133–4
Homeric Hymns, 5–6, 13–14, 18, 90–1
    goddesses in, 38–9
    interdependency in, 104–5
    legacy of, 22, 49
    themes of, 49
Homeric Hymn to Aphrodite, 5, 38–9, 161
Homeric Hymn to Apollo, 5, 27, 91
Homeric Hymn to Demeter, 5, 51–2, 133–4
Homeric Hymn to Dionysos, 91
hope, 101–11
Horace, 190
Hunger Games (Collins), 200–1
hybris, 75–6, 83–4, 89–90

Index

Hyginus, 6–7, 167–8
Hyperion (Titan), 32–3, 39–40

Iapetos (Titan), 32, 35, 39–40,
  67–9
Iliad (Homer), 4–6, 19–20, 164–5
  Achaean wall in, 89–90
  divine order in, 51–2
  goddesses in, 38–9
  influence of, 194
  success of, 61
  worldview in, 52
Ilu/El, 132–3, 155–6, 175–6
Immortals (film), 208–9
Inanna (Mesopotamian goddess),
  153
Indo-European studies, 12–13
Iron race, 80–4, 86, 152, 189
Isis (Egyptian goddess), 38–9,
  122–3, 138, 175–6
Isis and Osiris (Plutarch), 6–7, 138
Israel, 63
Italy, 67–9

Jebel al-'Aqra' (Mount Saphon),
  133–5
John, Ben, 21
Johnston, Sarah Iles, 10, 21
Josephus, 171–4
Judaism, 112–13, 180–1,
  197–8, 206–7. See also Hebrew
  Bible
Judeo-Christian traditions, 180–1,
  197–8
Jung, Carl, 11–12

Kapinos, Tom, 199
The Krater (Orpheus), 53–4
Kripke, Eric, 199

Kronos, 54–5, 178–9, 183–4.
  See also Five Races myth
  conflict with Ouranos, 175–6
  Delphi rock vomited by, 41–2,
    43f, 61
  Earth and Sky castration, 17, 20,
    36–8, 40–2, 45–7, 57–8, 127–8
  Hesiod on, 37–40, 42–3
  Kronids (children) of, 32–3,
    35–6, 52
  Ouranos-Kronos-Zeus, 48–155,
    172–3, 194–6
  in Pythagorean theology, 192–3
  succession of, 35–6, 42–3,
    46–7, 55–6, 84–5,
    128–9, 128t, 194–5
  Tartaros imprisionment of, 42,
    202
  Zeus clash with, 201f, 200–1, 208–9
Kumarbi (Hurro-Hittite god), 125–9
Kumarbi Cycle, 125–8, 155–6
Kwan, Daniel, 211–12
Kylon, 160–1

Lady Liberty statue, 163–4
"Lake of Memory," 67–9
Late Bronze Age, 2–3, 114–15, 132
Latin forms, 20
Leucippus, 187–8
Levant, 112–13. See also Near East
  cultures
Lévi-Strauss, Claude, 11–12
Linus, 53
Love (Eros), 28–9, 38–9, 59, 115
Lucian of Samosata, 170–1
Lucifer (TV show), 199
Lucretius, 187–8
Luhrmann, Baz, 202–3
The Lyre (Orpheus), 53–4

238   *Index*

Malinowski, Bronislaw, 11
Marduk (Mesopotamian god),
    23–4, 117–20, 132–3, 158, 201
    in Enuma elish, 130–2, 140–2,
    152–3
marriage, 76–8, 95–6, 101–11
Marvel, 199–200
memory, 25–6
    cultural, 62
    gods and, 26, 48
    "Lake of Memory," 67–9
    of oral tradition, 60–2
Menander, 6
Mesopotamia. *See also* Near East
    cultures
    culture of, 110
    Egypt and, 51
    epics from, 120–1, 187
    gods in, 118*f*, 125–7, 139–45
    Greece and, 123
    myths/stories and, 23–4, 144,
    149–50, 169–70
    Panhellenic culture and, 160–1
    Syria and, 167
    tradition in, 116, 152–3, 214–15
    weather to, 134
Metamorphoses (Ovid), 6–7, 53,
    186–90, 203
Michelangelo, 197*f*, 196–7
Middle Ages, 83, 192
Mitchell, Anaïs, 202–3
Mnemosyne (Memory) (Titan),
    25–6, 39–40, 48, 62. *See also*
    memory
monarchy
    aristocracy and, 87–8
    creation myths/stories for, 65–6
    in divine order, 28
    gods and, 57, 63–4, 172–7

in heaven, 124–39
    for humans, 156
    royal funerary game, 65
Mondi, Robert, 113
monsters, 31–2
Mopsos, 161
morality, 79–80, 89–90, 151–2
moral philosophy, 30–1
Mosaic scripture, 196
Moses, 25–6, 114–15, 171, 195–6,
    198, 205
mother Earth, 87. *See also* Earth
    (Gaia)
Moulin Rouge (film), 202–3
Mount Kasios, 134–5. *See also*
    Jebel al-'Aqra' (Mount Saphon)
Mount Olympos, 26–8, 32, 48, 61,
    63, 65, 127, 133, 135, 194
Mount Saphon, 133–5
Muses
    of Babylon, 118–19
    Calliope, 53
    in culture, 65–6
    epics and, 52–3
    gods and, 115
    Hesiod and, 61, 101–2
    history of, 15
    for mortal beings, 24, 28
    poetry and, 25–6, 62–3
mystical philosophy, 161
"Myth of Er" (Plato), 180
mythology. See *specific topics*
Mythology (Hamilton), 10

Naevius, 4–5
narration, 205
narratives. See *specific topics*
Native American culture, 15–16
nature, 11–12

Index

Near East cultures
  anthropogony of, 145–52
  cosmogony in, 152–60
  epics from, 139–45
  gods in, 139–52
  heaven in, 124–39
  myths/stories from, 112–14
  primeval elements in, 114–24
  scholarship on, 112 n.1
  traveling myths from, 160–1
Neoplatonism, 194–5
Nero, 163–4
The Net (Orpheus), 53–4
night, 50–60
Nintu. *See* womb goddess
Noah (film), 204–7
Norse culture, 15–16
Norway, 176

Ocean (Oceanids) (Titan), 32–3,
  48, 107
  Tethys and, 39–40, 46–7, 51, 194
O'Connor, George, 21, 201*f*, 200–1
Odyssey (Homer)
  elements in, 36
  goddesses in, 38–9
  nuances of, 76 n.1
  scholarship on, 4–8, 164–5
  success of, 61
Okeanos (Ocean) (Titan), 51
Olbia plaques, 69
Olympian gods, 24–6, 39–40, 59, 63,
  79, 164–5, 195–6, 199–200,
  208–9. *See also* Aphrodite;
  Apollo; Athena; Demeter;
  Dionysos; Hades; Poseidon;
  Zeus
  Ares, 48–9, 92–3, 202
  Artemis, 38–40, 48

Hephaistos, 181–2, 185–6
Hera, 48–9, 51, 55–7, 123, 211
Hermes, 5–6, 77–8, 90–1, 181–2
The Olympians (O'Connor), 201*f*,
  200–1
On the Cave of the Nymphs
  (Porphyry), 193
oral poetry, 22
oral tradition, 60–2
Orientalizing period, 23–4
Orpheus
  cosmogony from, 159–60
  cosmology from, 60
  Golden Age to, 84–5
  Hesiod and, 66, 131
  Homer and, 50–1
  influence of, 192–3
  legacy of, 203*f*, 202–4
  Orphic cosmogony, 175
  Orphic myth, 56–9, 66–7,
    70, 203–204, 209–10, 214–15
  Orphic Tablets, 68*f*, 67–70
  Orphic tales, 92–101
  Plato and, 59
  poetry and, 19, 52–60
  theogony by, 66–7, 99–100,
    214–15
  on underworld, 53–4
*Orpheus and Eurydice on the Banks of
  the Styx* (Stanhope), 203*f*,
  202–3
Ouranos (Sky), 41–2, 45–6, 128*t*.
  See also Hesiod
  castration, 57–8, 97–9, 127–8, 131,
    175–6, 195–6, 200–1
  Cyclopes (non-Titan) children of,
    44
  divine couple with Gaia (Earth)
    and, 36, 90

240 *Index*

Ouranos (Sky) (*Continued*)
  Kronos conflict with, 175–6
  Rhea and, 44
  Zeus descendent of, 35–6
Ouranos-Kronos-Zeus, 48, 55,
    57–8, 128–9, 153–5, 172–3,
    194–6
Ovid, 6–7, 53, 186–90, 193, 196,
    205–6. See also *specific works*

Panhellenic culture, 62, 95–6, 160–1
Panhellenic worldview, 60–2
Parallel Lives (Plutarch), 6–7
Parmenides, 177–8
Parthenon, 96–7
Peleus, 25–6
Peloponnesian Wars, 185–6
Percy Jackson and the Olympians
    (Riordan), 200–1
Persephone, 48, 55, 70, 202–4
  Hades and, 53, 55–6, 67–9
Perses, 73–4, 79–80, 82, 101, 109,
    111
Perseus, 27, 31–2, 37, 209*f*, 202,
    208–9
  Herakles and, 32, 207–8
Phaedo (Plato), 99–100
Phaedrus (Plato), 215–16
Pherekydes of Syros, 161
Philo of Alexandria, 171–2, 180–1
Philo of Byblos, 173–6
philosophy
  of divinity, 166
  Greco-Roman, 197–8
  history of, 59
  from Homer, 187–8
  of hope, 101–11
  moral, 30–1
  mystical, 161
  from Plato, 97–9, 180–6

  with resilient myths, 177–86
  of Socrates, 52–3, 59
  Western, 16–17
Phoenician History (Philo of Byblos),
    173–6
Phoenicians, 51, 60–1. See also
    specific topics
Pindar, 65
Plato. See also *specific works*
  Aristotle and, 196
  on children, 161
  education of, 178–9
  epics for, 66–7
  Hesiod and, 79
  influence of, 6, 99–100
  legacy of, 215–16
  Neoplatonism, 194–5
  Orpheus and, 59
  Ovid and, 205–6
  philosophy from, 97–9, 180–6
  Platonism, 193
  Socrates and, 99–100, 168
Plutarch, 6–7, 138. See also *specific*
    works
Porphyry, 193
Poseidon, 48, 51–2, 88, 94–5, 97,
    133–4, 185–6
  Apollo and, 89–90
  Athena rivalry with, 97, 185–6
  in *Odyssey*, 76 n.1
powers, of gods, 57–8, 132–52
Pratchett, Terry, 199
primeval elements, 114–24
primeval gods, 128*t*, 145
primeval narratives, 157
Prometheus, 79, 85–6, 88, 102,
    150–1, 162–3, 189–90, 213–14
  Epimetheus and, 35, 39–40, 67–9,
    77–9, 86, 105–6, 181–3
  Zeus and, 104–8, 148

Index 241

Prometheus-Pandora, 101, 147–8
Propp, Vladimir, 12
Protagoras (Plato), 79, 178–9, 181–3
psychoanalysis, 10–11
Punica (Silius Italicus), 4–5
Pyramid Texts, 120–1
Pythagoras, 66–7, 161, 177–8
Pythagorean theology, 180,
   192–3, 195–6
Pythian Apollo, 42. *See also* Apollo
Pytho, 13–15, 49, 94 n.5
"Pyxis of Painter C" 47*f*

race. *See* Five Races myth
Raglan (lord), 11–12
Rank, Otto, 12
A Reading from Homer (Alma-
   Tadema), 18*f*
Republic (Plato), 178–80, 183,
   185–6
Rhapsodies (Orpheus), 55, 57–8, 101
Rhea (Titan), 32, 39–42, 44
Riordan, Rick, 200–1
The Robe (Orpheus), 53–4
Rockefeller Center, 163*f*, 162–3
Roman authors, 4–5
Roman culture, 13–14, 18, 37
Roman empire, 168, 170–1, 196
Roman tradition, 19–20, 82–3
Rome, 6–7
Rowling, J. K., 200–1

Sacred Inscription/History
   (Euhemeros), 172–3
sacred narratives, 73
sacrifice, 75*f*, 103–11
Sagan, Carl, 1
Salzman-Mitchell, Patricia, 208–9
Sanctuary of Apollo at Delphi, 43*f*, 62
Sasson, Jack, 119–20

Saturn Devouring His Son (Goya), 41*f*
Scheniert, Daniel, 211–12
Scipio (the Elder), 176–7, 180–1
Scipio Aemilianus, 180–1
Seleucid kingdom, 169–70
Seneca, 6–7
Sibyls, 197–8
Silius Italicus, 4–5
Silver race, 80–5, 183, 189
Sistine Chapel (Michelangelo), 197*f*,
   196–7
Smith, William Robertson, 11
snakes, 94–5, 94 n.5
Socrates, 52–3, 59, 99–100, 168,
   178–9, 183, 194. See also
   specific works by Plato
"Song of Birth," (Hurro-Hittite),
   124–30
"Song of Hanna" (Hebrew Bible),
   102–3
"Song of Silenus" (Virgil), 190–1
Sophocles, 6
Stanhope, John Roddam Spencer,
   203*f*, 202–3
Statesman (Plato), 183–4
Stoicism, 194–5, 197–8, 211
strife, 105–11
Struck, Peter, 192–3
structuralism, 12
succession, 55
   of Kronos, 35–6, 42–3, 46–7,
      55–6, 84–5, 128–9, 128*t*,
      194–5
   of ruling gods, 128*t*
succession myths, 35–6, 84–5, 128*t*,
   128–9, 131–2
superheroes, 199–200
Supernatural (TV show), 199
Symposium (Plato), 184
Syria, 135*f*, 132, 134–5, 167, 170–1

242   Index

Tartaros (Underworld), 28–31,
    34–5, 59
    In Hesiod's *Theogony*, 131–2,
      128*t*, 202
    Kronos imprisioned in, 42, 202
    Typhon created by, 43–6
Tethys (Titan), Ocean and, 39–40,
    46–7, 51, 194
Thales, 51, 177–8
Theater of War Productions, 164–5
Thebaid (poem), 92–3
Theban myths, 92–3
Theia (Divine) (Titan), 32–3, 39–40
Theogony (Hesiod), 4–5, 7–8, 15–17,
    19–20, 43–50
    forerunners of, 125
    humanity in, 73–4, 105–6
    influence of, 50–1, 104, 129,
      213–14
    legacy of, 162–5, 170–1, 177–8,
      200–2, 207–8
    origins in, 71, 97–9
    sacrifice in, 75
    variants of, 51–2, 131
Theogony of Dunnu, 120
Thomson, Tok, 3
Thucydides, 6, 97 n.6
Tiamat (Mesopotamian goddess),
    51, 94 n.5, 117–19, 128*t*,
    130–2, 137, 141, 201
Timaeus (Plato), 71–2, 178–81,
    184–6, 211–12
time, 40–2, 50–60
Titan gods. See *specific Titan gods*
titanic rebellions, 43–50
Titanomachy, 34, 44, 200–1, 208–9
Torah. *See* Hebrew Bible
Trojan War, 2–5, 61, 83–4, 89
Turkey, 100*f*, 134–5, 135*f*
Typhon/Typhoeus, 15–17, 32

Zeus and, 16–17, 35–6, 43–6,
    48–9, 90, 131–2, 134–5, 138
Tzetzes, 194–5

Ugaritic texts, 51–2, 113–14, 132–7,
    175–6
Underworld (Tartaros), 28–9
    concept of, 29
    Earth and, 70, 115
    gods from, 138
    to Homer, 133–4
    Orpheus on, 53–4
    in poetry, 33
    in resilient myths, 202–4
    symbols from, 197–8
United States, 163*f*, 162–4,
    199–200, 202
Uruk, 154*f*

Vallejo, Irene, 168–9
"Venus in the Shell," 39*f*
Virgil, 4–5, 7–8, 97–9, 190–1, 193,
    196. See also *specific works*

Warka Vase, 154*f*
weapons, in Greek myths, 45*f*, 44–6
Wengrow, David, 213
West, Martin, 24, 112–13
Western culture, 30, 140, 215–16
Western education, 4, 12–13
Western philosophy, 16–17
womb goddess (Nintu), 140–1, 143
women
    in clay figures, 78*f*
    in creation myths/stories, 73–9
    dowry, 106
    in Greece, 84*f*
    in Hebrew Bible, 106
    Hesiod on, 106–7
    in marriage, 106*f*, 76–7, 105–6

Works and Days (Hesiod)
  deceit in, 75–6
  humans in, 210
  hybris in, 75–6
  influence of, 104
  muses in, 101–2
  myths/stories in, 79–85
  origin stories in, 72
  poetry in, 73–4, 189
  scholarship on, 4–5, 15–17, 27,
    62, 106–8
Wrath of the Titans (film), 202, 207–11

Xenophanes, 178
Xenophon, 6
Xisouthros, 169–71

Yam (Canaanite god), Baal and, 134,
  137, 155–6

Zeus. *See also* Kronos; *specific topics*
  Aphrodite, assumed daughter of,
    38–9, 48, 57–8
  Apollo and, 48–9, 65
  birth of Athena, 47*f*
  Dionysos and, 55–6, 92–3
  Perseus and, 209*f*
  Prometheus and, 104–8, 148
  Titanomachy, 34, 44, 200–1,
    208–9
  Typhon/Typhoeus and, 16–17,
    35–6, 43–6, 48–9, 90,
    131–2, 134–5, 138

The manufacturer's authorised representative in the EU for product safety is Oxford
University Press España S.A. of El Parque Empresarial San Fernando de Henares,
Avenida de Castilla, 2 – 28830 Madrid (www.oup.es/en or product.safety@oup.com).
OUP España S.A. also acts as importer into Spain of products made by the manufacturer.

Printed in the USA/Agawam, MA
April 4, 2025

885391.003